Marketing With Digital Video

How To Create A Winning Video for
Your Small Business or Non-Profit

Hal Landen

Second Edition
Completely Revised

Oak Tree Press, Bristol, Rhode Island

Marketing With Digital Video
How To Create A Winning Video for
Your Small Business or Non-Profit
By Hal Landen

Published by:
Oak Tree Press
9 King Philip Ave
Bristol, RI 02809
(401) 253 2800
http://VideoUniversity.com

ISBN, printed. 1-888093-09-9
ISBN, PDF ed. 1-888093-10-2
ISBN, LIT ed. 1-888093-11-0
First Printing 1996
Second Printing 1999
Third Printing 2000
Fourth Printing 2001
Sixth Printing 2003
Seventh Printing 2004
Eighth Printing 2005 Completely Revised
Printed in the United States of America

Publisher's Cataloging-in-Publication
(Provided by Quality Books, Inc.)
Landen, Hal M.
   Marketing with digital video : how to create a
winning video for your small business or non-profit / by
Hal Landen. — 2nd ed. completely rev.
   p. cm.
   Includes bibliographical references and index.
   LCCN 2005926033
   ISBN 1-888093-09-9 (print ed.)
   ISBN 1-888093-10-2 (PDF ed.)
   ISBN 1-888093-11-0 (LIT ed.)
   1. Video recordings—Production and direction.
2. Television in publicity. 3. Television advertising.
4. Video tape advertising. I. Title.
PN1992.94.L36 2005   791.45'0232'0688
                QBI05-200119

Contents

About the Author
Preface
Acknowledgments
Warning Disclaimer
Foreword

Chapter 11 - Cable TV and the Web 197

* Broadcast Quality * TV Advertising * Public Service Announcements * Telethons * Video News Release * Public Access *Leased Access * Infomercials * TV Trivia * Marketing With Video on the Web * Building a Business on the Web

Chapter 12 - Training, E-Learning, and More 221

* Training With Video * E-Learning * Simple Technique for Producing a Video * Orientation Video * Training Customers * In-house Video Studio * Buying Used Equipment * Marketing by CD ROM * Duplication and Replication * Family History on Video * Stay Tuned

About the Author

Hal Landen created VideoUniversity.com in 1997. Today, it is one of the most popular websites devoted to video production on the net. Before founding VU, Landen received extensive media experience beginning in 1975, when he accepted a job at ABC Sports, which was leading the way in innovative television. It was here working on ABC's *Wide World of Sports* and *The American Sportsman* that Landen learned from some of the best cameramen, editors and producers in the business.

His "education" at ABC led to a successful freelance career as a cameraman and producer. His award-winning work has taken him to such locations as the Philippines, the North Sea, Brazil, and El Salvador for clients such as Warner Brothers, AT&T and CBS's *60 Minutes*. His assignments have included a documentary in the Amazon jungle, television commercials, and interviews with Katharine Hepburn, Sean Connery, and Woody Allen.

Prior to this Hal Landen was graduated from Goddard College in 1971 with a major in English. Shortly thereafter he founded *The Country Journal*, a newspaper serving the people of north central Vermont. After successfully launching the paper, he moved to New York City to taste the creative possibilities of film and television.

He has produced hundreds of successful marketing and training films in a variety of industries and human service agencies. When asked to recommend books to help small businesses and non-profits use video, he found none that were suitable for business people. This prompted him to write *Marketing With Video: How To Create A Winning Video For Your Small Business or Non-Profit*, the precursor to this book. He has coached hundreds of successful first-time producers and pros.

Hal is the author and producer of books, special reports, DVDs and information products on the business of video production, including numerous articles and guides at VideoUniversity.com

He is an avid sailor. He has been restoring *The Satin Doll*, an ocean-going, 29-foot yawl which he sails often in Narragansett Bay and vicinity.

Preface

This is an amazing time to be producing videos for business or pleasure. Today's affordable digital technology no longer impedes the production of highly effective business videos. The delivery of business video is expanding in ways no one would have guessed just a few years ago.

Consider:

- A recent International Documentary Film Festival in Amsterdam included an entry called "Cell Stories," sponsored by Motorola, that was shot entirely with the video camera in the new Motorola cellphones.
- A PBS *Frontline* documentary series entitled *The Persuaders* showed a scene of political volunteers going door to door offering to show a short political video to potential voters on the volunteer's PDA. This kind of video marketing opens a whole new realm of possibilities for using video in one-on-one situations.
- Pocket-sized digital media centers with three inch screens can hold 5 or more complete feature films.
- Ad agencies are selling commercial air time for cell phone video.

Internet marketing and promotional videos are now commonplace. These powerful, amazing new technologies, however, cannot ensure that a business video will be effective. That's why I wrote this book–to help you produce highly effective business videos on a tight budget.

Hal Landen, Bristol, RI

Acknowledgments

I thank Jane Dawkins for her fine editorial work. Doug Graham, rocket scientist and VideoUniversity forum moderator, for his technical expertise and advice, Dianne Peters for her graphics expertise, Carol Lovelady for shaping the final digital files, Steve Yankee for his marketing expertise and friendship, Phil Goutel for his friendship and instruction in the art of mail order, Cherie Gingerich for her friendship, help, and wit, and to the many contributors to the VideoUniversity forums for sharing their wisdom and hard-won knowledge.

And to the many people who contributed to the earlier edition of this book, I thank Jodee Thompson for her astute editorial sense and tireless dedication, and Wyn Wade for his friendship and expertise in reshaping the early drafts of the manuscript. Special thanks to Annette Landen for her inspiration and encouragement and to Ted Trout-Landen, Ph.D. for his wit and grace.

For generously sharing their knowledge, I thank Gregg Johnstone, Roger Scott, Chris Hackenbrock, Linda Aumick, Elisha Birnbaum, Josephine Todaro, Gloria Smith, Lance Armstrong, Dr. Jeffrey Lant, Bob Wickhem, Justin Del Sesto, Steve Yankee, Charles De Arman of the National Archives, and George Ziener of the National Audiovisual Center.

For their wise counsel, I thank Terri Lonier, Kay Michelfeld, Chris Timmons, Jim Evers, Tony Vlamis, Matilda Gocek, Jim Detleff, Lorraine Staunch, Ernie Haim, Debbie Allen, Dan Poynter, John Kremer, Lonnie Gross and Jeff Malone of Metropolitan Pictures.

For their individual generosities, I am indebted to Barry Johnson, Terry Thomas, Al Randzin, Vittoria Violante, Julie Palinkas, Harriet Earnest, Phil Hamling, Richard Surving, Fred Najork, Carole Parker, John Knight, Robert Lobb, Curtis Menning, and Jay Conrad Levinson.

I am indebted to my many clients, whose contributions to this book are greater than they know. And to the memories of my friend, Dan Strickland, and my father, Ed Landen, who had one of the first TV sets on our block.

Warning-Disclaimer

Chapter 1

The Elements Of Video

Whether it's on TV, DVD, a videotape, CD ROM, the Internet, or devices like PDA's and cell phones, video is a powerful way to market products, services and ideas. From Fortune 500 Companies to kitchen table start-ups, they all use video to promote their businesses. Business video uses include plant tours, product demonstrations, fund raising, corporate image building, and many more. The printed brochures which often accompany these videos can't convey action, music and drama the way a video does. If you've ever requested a video and brochure from a company like Nordic Track, I'll bet you watched the video first. Video is an excellent marketing tool–and not just for business: United Way and many other non-profit agencies use video to show how they help people in need and how you can help, too.

Video is also a cost effective way to train people. Imagine training thousands of high school students in their first paying job at a fast food restaurant. How much management time would it take? How could you keep the training message consistent from year to year? It's easy with video.

Now the tools of production are available to all. Laptop computers can produce stunning broadcast-quality digital video. Digital video cameras can fit in the palm of your hand. They, too, produce broadcast-quality video and a surprising number of network news segments and documentaries are being shot with these tiny digital cameras.

Most of this book is devoted to marketing with video because there's no business like more business. Without marketing and sales, there is no business at all. After you learn how to produce an effective marketing video, you can use those same skills to produce other business videos. Along the way you'll learn about training videos, video news releases, video on the internet, and a host of others.

Corporate video is an $8 billion industry. Many corporate video departments actually produce more original programming than the TV networks. Is video profitable for them? You bet it is, but you probably don't need convincing. Perhaps you've already thought about how a video could help your business or non-profit agency until the costs, typically quoted at $1000 - $2000 per finished minute, stopped you in your tracks. Even a ten-minute no-frills video would cost at least $10,000.

Conventional wisdom says if you can't spend $10,000, don't even consider video as a promotional tool, but that same conventional wisdom said we wouldn't go the moon and that there would never be a market for personal computers. The experts are wrong again. This book will teach you how smart planning and technical advances can cut your budget to a fraction of the normal cost—sometimes as low as $1500 for the entire project—and even this is payable in installments.

Whether your budget is $1,500 or $115,000, money alone does not guarantee that the video will be effective. Just look at the thousands of expensive videos and even feature films which flop. A successful video does not require a big budget. This book can help you save thousands of dollars, but more importantly, it will help ensure that your video achieves a business goal.

But what about all the equipment and technology? Don't worry, many Hollywood producers are not technical people and very few of them own any camera or editing equipment. Many of these producers started with only a telephone and a typewriter. That's all they needed because they could hire professionals—artists and technicians with the right equipment and know-how. This book will teach you how to do the same thing as those Hollywood producers. In fact, you'll see why not owning the equipment is often the smartest approach to producing.

Why not just turn your entire video over to a video production company and let the experts worry about the details? That works very well for some people, but horror stories abound of budgets that hemorrhaged out of control and, worse, of videos that never achieved their goal.

This book will help you avoid those disasters. You'll learn how to hire a producer or production company and how to work with them to control costs and improve the quality of your video. You can choose to do as much or as little of this work as you like.

Most how-to books about video are directed either toward the home video user or the aspiring professional. This book assumes that you're neither, only that your business or non-profit agency has a product, service or idea to promote. A home video won't do the job, nor do you want to make a career of it.

You probably know more about filmmaking than you realize. You know when films work and when they don't. You may not know why. If you're like most of us, you've been watching television and movies for most of your life. That experience is more valuable than you think. You've already caught mistakes of professional filmmakers. Things like a microphone boom that accidentally dipped into the shot or a continuity mistake where an actress is wearing a ring on one finger in one shot, but on another finger in the next shot.

While these details are important, they pale in importance to the ultimate goal of any business video: creating a specific response among targeted viewers. This is the only reason to produce a business video. Long before the camera rolls and the director says "action," this goal must be precisely defined and thoroughly planned. Your experience as a viewer helps you see a video from your viewers' perspective, the first step in planning a successful video.

This book will guide you through the three interrelated steps of every video and film: pre-production, production and post-production. For now, think of them as: scripting, shooting and editing.

You will recognize the techniques of filmmaking, many of which haven't changed much since filmmaking began 100 years ago. The fast moving sequence like the car chase in the 1971 film *The French Connection*, with Gene Hackman, riveted viewers to the screen the same way a scene from a 1925 Russian film, *The Battleship Potemkin*, did. They both used close-ups, action shots and quick cutting to produce remarkable scenes. Even if you've never seen these films, you have seen this kind of scene in hundreds of movies.

What does this have to do with a marketing video? Everything. A marketing video must hold the viewer's attention or it's a waste of time. To keep that attention you can and should use every trick in the book—*this book*.

THE ELEMENTS OF VIDEO

All videos are created from elements like close-up shots, titles, music and narration. When skillfully combined, these visual and audio elements become a powerful tapestry much greater than the sum of its parts. Let's begin by identifying these elements.

TV commercials are an easy place to see all the elements of video. These commercials, representing some of the best filmmaking in the world, are actually short promotional films. Most are designed to get you to buy their products and services. Some are designed to get you to recognize a brand name or just feel good about a company or cause. Their goals are very likely the same goals you have for your marketing video. And the people who make these commercials are masters at it.

Granted, there are some differences between your marketing video and TV commercials. A marketing video will certainly be longer than a 30-second commercial. The budget for your marketing video might not even pay for the meals consumed by the cast and crew of a big budget commercial! Finally, the structure of a marketing video will undoubtedly be more complex than a 30-second spot.

Nevertheless, successful marketing videos have a lot in common with successful TV spots:
- Both are aimed at specific target audiences and have specific goals.
- Many tell concise, but complete stories.

- They go out of their way to try to hold your interest.

Studying commercials can teach you a lot about filmmaking and provide you with a rich source of ideas for your own video. Many of the styles and techniques used in expensive commercials can be duplicated quite simply and inexpensively in your video.

Of course, I'm not suggesting that you steal parts of these films. You'd be breaking the copyright laws which protect all the visuals, narration, music and everything else in the spots. However, the styles and techniques used in commercials are fair game. Filmmakers have copied and improved each other's styles since filmmaking began. As long as you don't use the *content* of other films, it's perfectly legal to copy *styles* and *techniques*. As you study commercials, you'll notice trends in the styles of filmmaking. You can use these styles just as other producers have.

One example, which became popular a few years ago, is a title screen consisting of simple white text on a black screen. A 30-second car commercial might have several of these text screens. After shots of a woman driving her small children on a dangerous wintry night, the commercial cuts to the word RELIABLE for a split second. The word is in white text on a black background. The next shot might be a young family smiling as they drive by a line at the gas station where the price of gas is high. Cut to the words 50 MILES TO THE GALLON. This technique has been used since filmmaking began 100 years ago. Think how the silent movies of Charlie Chaplin and others used title cards to convey dialogue and narration.

Some TV commercials today use this technique exclusively. There is no live action, simply a series of title screens with narration. Each screen has only a few words on the equivalent of a title card. It can be quite effective. You can easily and inexpensively adapt this technique for use in your marketing video.

<u>**VISUALS**</u> | <u>**AUDIO**</u>

RECONSTRUCTING THE VIDEO SCRIPT

The text screen just described is one of the basic elements of video. By taking a completed film, in this case a commercial, and describing its elements on paper, you will reconstruct its script and in doing so, learn about its elements. The script is a blueprint for creating an effective film of any kind. Study the blueprint of any successful project and you can learn how it was made and imitate that success.

To reconstruct scripts, you'll need a bunch of commercials on video. You can tape these on your home VCR, Tivo or DVD burner. I suggest the following guidelines in choosing which commercials to tape and study:

VISUALS	AUDIO
Shot #1 (5 seconds) WIDE SHOT OF GRANDMOTHER ON FRONT PORCH SWING. SHE IS READING A STORY TO A GRANDCHILD SITTING ON HER LAP.	
Shot #2 (3 seconds) CLOSE UP OF GRANDCHILD'S FACE LOOKING UP LOVINGLY TO GRANDMOTHER	
Shot #3 (1/2 second) Title Card: White text on black: ACME IS LOVE	

1. Study commercials that you like and that seem most effective. Since you'll be viewing these commercials a number of times, it's easier to study the ones you like.
2. Choose the types of commercials that you'd like to see produced for your company or non-profit. If there's a G.E. com-

mercial that you've always liked, could you substitute your company name for G.E.? If so, that's a good one to start with.

3.   Avoid, for now, commercials that consist entirely of computer-generated graphics and animations. They are technically more advanced and expensive to produce.

You can't tape or study too many commercials. For my money, the Sunday morning news shows have some of the classiest and most effective commercials on the tube. These are corporate image spots. Either way, tape and study commercials you like. You'll learn a lot by reconstructing their scripts.

When you have some interesting commercials on tape, you can begin to study them. First, turn the sound all the way down. This way you'll study just what's on the screen without being distracted by the sound track. The next step is to break the commercial into its separate parts, such as different shots, transitions and title cards. Take a sheet of paper and draw a line down the middle so you have two columns. At the top of the left column, write the heading VISUALS. On the top right, write AUDIO. Like so:

Many people are unaware that a single commercial is usually made up of a number of different shots. Each shot is made by turning the camera on and shooting a subject and then turning the camera off. These camera shots can be described by how much of the subject they show. For instance, a *wide* shot might show an entire house. A *medium* shot might show just the front porch. A *close-up* might show only the front door knob. These different shots are often edited together so skillfully that they seem to flow together. It can be hard to tell where one shot ends and the next shot begins. Watching without sound will help you see the edit point where one shot ends and the next begins. Watching it in slow motion can help you even more.

Now, with the sound off, play your commercial. Can you see where the first shot ends and the second one begins? The camera crew ended the first shot by stopping the camera. Then they either moved the camera closer or farther from the subject or photographed a new subject. Your job is to identify and describe these different shots and your goal here is a written description of every single shot or visual in the commercial. From these descriptions you can reconstruct the script that was a blueprint in the creation of this film. Here's an example:

The first two shots, a wide shot and a close-up, were made with a camera. The third, a text screen, was made with a computer. These are a few of the visual elements which make a film. Following is a complete inventory of all the visual building blocks used in filmmaking.

THE CAMERA SHOTS

Wide Shot

Also called the Establishing Shot. A wide shot that shows the subject(s) in their environment. In the script above, shot #1 shows the viewer most of the front porch with perhaps a bit of the neighborhood in the background.

Medium Shot

This shot is closer than the wide shot. When applied to people, it shows the subject(s) from waist to just above the head.

Close-up

A close-up of a person shows his or her head only. When the subject speaks directly to the camera, this is sometimes referred to as a "talking head."

You'll see these basic three camera shots over and over again. A few other camera shots are:

Dolly shot

The camera is placed on a moving platform (dolly) or vehicle to follow along with a moving subject so the camera moves over ground rather than panning from a fixed tripod.

Zoom shot

The camera lens zooms in or out—the most overused shot of home moviemakers.

Extreme Close-up

Eyeballs and mouth. Used often on *60 Minutes*. When applied to inanimate objects, such as a dime, the object may fill the frame.

Pan left/right

The camera moves horizontally to follow movement from the left or right. This shot may also be used to reveal all of a wide object like a train or the Grand Canyon.

Tilt up/down

The camera moves along a vertical path. Like the pan, this shot allows the viewer to follow movement like a rocket launch or to see all of a tall object like a skyscraper.

Aerial

A moving camera shot like a dolly shot except that it is made from a helicopter or airplane.

By indicating in the script each type of shot, the scriptwriter is telling the director and cameraman how to shoot the film the writer has envisioned. He's also telling the editor how to edit the film. *But more importantly, the script is a preview of the film on paper. It's a lot easier and cheaper to change a script on paper than it is to change a film or video.*

COMPUTER GENERATED TEXT & GRAPHICS

Text and graphics on television are created with computers rather than filmed with the camera. There are several basic types.

Text Screen

To Order your Ginsu Knife Set, call 1-800-CUT-FAST. Or send $19.95 to Box 777888999125 Radio City Station.

You've seen this kind of text screen thousands of times. This yellow text is on a blue computer-generated background. There's no movement on the screen unless the phone number flashes to make sure you see it.

Superimposed Text & Graphics

During a news show interview, we see a medium shot of the Secretary of Commerce for a Pacific rim country. Her name and title are superimposed over the lower third portion of the screen. This is called "a lower third."

You will also see arrows or hand-drawn lines superimposed over a video shot or still photo. A good example is the football play diagram. Hand-drawn lines are superimposed over a still shot of the football lineup. The lines are usually yellow and extend with arrows to show where the players will go. Similar lines may be drawn over a live shot or photo of a machine, a building or anytime a graphic explanation is useful.

Animation

The Simpsons, Walt Disney films, flying network logos, a spinning globe that opens a news show are all examples of animations. They're all created on computers. This painstaking work can cost thousands of dollars per second! Some animations are created in a photo-realistic style where you can't tell whether real objects were filmed with a camera or whether they were drawn by an artist like the series of *Jurassic Park* films. Animations can stand alone or they can be superimposed over the live video shots.

Go back to your commercial and identify all the visual elements—camera shots and computer graphics. This can take some practice and might be tedious. You may need to view the commercial in slow motion to be able to identify the beginning and ending of each shot.

Write each element in script form, leaving space between them so you can add details later. You don't need to be precise in listing the length of different shots. This would difficult to do unless you have a non-linear edit system on your computer. Many commercials you'll see are scripted down to fractions of seconds of screen time. Each second of video is actually made of 30 still pictures called *frames*. Each frame is on the screen for 1/30th of second. Some commercial scripts call for just one frame of a shot. This is called a "flash frame" and is so fast you can barely see it. This has been used for subliminal advertising. To study a commercial so precisely that you can count individual frames is not necessary. For our purposes, just note the approximate lengths of shots and a general description of each.

Some commercials will have over 100 different shots in all of 30 seconds. Each shot might last for only half a second or 15 frames. A classic example of this kind of fast cutting is the shower scene from Alfred Hitchcock's film *Psycho*. Some commercials use only one shot for the entire 30 seconds. However, it's more common to see five to twenty shots in a 30-second commercial. List these shots in order, describing the type of shot and duration.

TRANSITIONS

Another visual element to record in your script is the type of transition which joins shots together. Each shot has a beginning and an end. It is joined to the next shot at an exact point in one of four ways: *straight cut, fade, dissolve* or *wipe*.

The straight cut

Ninety-nine percent of these joints are made with the straight cut which simply butts the end of one shot with the beginning of the next. The order in which the shots are cut together and their length is one of the essential arts of filmmaking—editing.

The straight cut is used in a wide range of films from the simplest informational film to the most complex feature film. The artful use of straight cuts can turn a boring home movie into a compelling work of art. In scriptwriting all transitions from one shot to the next are assumed to be straight cuts unless otherwise noted.

Fade to and from Black

Most commercials actually begin with a black screen. The first shot fades up from this black screen. The duration of the fade varies from a fraction of a second to as long as two seconds. If you watched this process in slow motion, you'd see that the shot becomes progressively brighter until it is as bright as the shots that follow it.

"Fade up from black" is a visual clue to the viewer that something new is happening. It may be the beginning of the film or the beginning of a new section of the film. It can indicate to the viewer that a period of time has elapsed from the last section of the film. This lapse can be minutes or years.

"Fade to black" clues the viewer that a section of the film is ending. Most commercials end with a "fade to black." You'll often see these two transitions used together: Scene 1 fades to black. Scene 2 fades up from black. This often indicates that scene 2 is a different time or place. For example "Meanwhile, back in the drawing room, the butler was preparing his escape."

Dissolve

The dissolve is a transition that uses two fades. Shot #1 fades down. Shot #2 fades up. Only there's no black. As shot #1 is fading *down*, shot #2 is already fading *up*. The fading parts of these shots are superimposed over each other.

The dissolve often indicates to the viewer the same thing that fading to or from black does—we're now at a different time or place—but the effect of the dissolve is more sensual. Let's say the commercial is a series of 10 different still photographs without any movement at all. If the transitions between the photographs were dissolves rather than straight cuts, the photos would flow together, the way a good film does. This transition gives the photos a romantic feel.

Wipe

The last type of transition between shots is the wipe. There are many different types of wipes. A simple one is where the end of shot #1 moves off the screen to the left while the beginning of shot #2 moves in from the right until it fills the screen. Shot #2 appears to push the first shot off the screen.

Another is the circle wipe. The end of shot #1 develops a hole in the center that grows larger. Inside the hole in shot #1 is the beginning of shot #2. This circle finally fills the frame until shot #2 has completely replaced shot #1.

There are a number of other geometric patterns where shot #1 is replaced by shot #2. These include a vertical line, horizontal line, boxes, triangles, and more. Wipes, like fades to black and dissolves, may indicate a change in time or place. The style of using wipes as transitions was more common in comedies of the '40s than it is today.

Now that you know the possible transitions between shots, go back to your script and insert descriptions of transitions between the visuals in upper case, like DISSOLVE TO, FADE UP FROM BLACK, etc. Since most transitions are straight cuts, it's usually not necessary to note a straight cut.

VISUALS	AUDIO
	Wistful violin music fades up and continues throughout
Shot #1 (5 seconds) WIDE SHOT OF GRANDMOTHER ON FRONT PORCH SWING...	

Your reconstructed script is now one half complete. You have listed and described every visual that appears in the commercial. This process is a bit tedious, I know, but you begin to see just how much the filmmaker attempts to control the viewer. In a sense this control or manipulation is what filmmaking is all about. But you ain't seen nothing yet...

AUDIO

The sound track, which is often music and dialogue, helps shots flow smoothly into one entity. But even more significantly, the sound track often transcends the impact of the visual elements, leading the viewer to experience the commercial on an emotional level.

Now go through the commercial again and list all the audio elements in the right column in the order in which they appear. A virtue of the two-column script format is that we can see the timing relationship between audio and visual, i.e. exactly when an audio element occurs relative to the visuals. As you did on the visual side of the script, you'll want to describe the content and direction of each audio element.

There are four basic types of audio: *music, narration, synch sound and sound effects.*

Music

It's a pretty safe bet your commercial starts with music and that this music fades up. The same music may continue throughout, or it may cut or dissolve to another piece of music. Commercials use rock 'n roll, classical, country, opera and every other type of music. It may be purely instrumental or have sung lyrics.

Some scriptwriters specify exactly which song is to be used in their commercial. Others only describe a mood—upbeat, contemporary, happy—and let the editor find just the right music.

Different types of music, accompanying the same visuals, can dramatically change the mood and impact of a commercial. For instance, Vivaldi's "Four Seasons" will have a very different effect than Bluegrass music would over the same commercial, even though each may work quite well. Much of the music used in commercials has a lively beat to help drive the visuals and make the film more compelling.

Describe the music in your commercial on the audio side of the script. Note where the music starts and stops. In the following example, music begins before the visuals.

Narration

Narration is called voice over (V.O.) because it goes over the pictures. Usually you don't see the narrator, who may be male, female, young or old. Some of the great narrators are actors you know, like James Earl Jones, Martin Sheen and Gene Hackman. Others are sound-alikes who only seem to be familiar actors.

The script often describes the character of the voice, e.g. helpful young man, wise grandfather, the voice of authority. While most narrators are still male voices, I applaud the trend toward female narrators. Male or female, they all sound friendly and believable. Whether you know them or not, you'd probably talk to them on the phone if they called. Sometimes you do see the narrator on the screen. He's looking right at you and sincerely talking to you. He may be in an office setting or in front of a plain studio background. While he's talking, the camera may cut to other scenes he describes, but his voice continues over these other visuals. The scene may end by cutting back to him on camera as he continues talking to you. In scripts these options are referred to as an on-camera narrator and an off-camera narrator or Voice Over (V.O.). There may be more than one narrator. Sometimes a second or third narrator has a dialogue with the first.

Synch Sound

Synch sound is sound that seems to come from a visual. You see two people in the kitchen and hear them talking. Their dialogue is synch sound. It's called that because the sound is synchronized with

VISUALS	AUDIO
	Wistful violin music fades up and continues throughout
Shot #1 (5 seconds) WIDE SHOT OF GRANDMOTHER ON FRONT PORCH SWING...	Sound Effect: Robins singing in the background

the picture. Your camcorder records sound and picture simultaneously (in synch). Most bigger budget commercials are shot with a camera which records only the picture and a separate tape recorder which records sound. Before editing begins, these separate pieces of film, one with the pictures the other with the sound track, must be synchronized so that the actor's lips move exactly when you hear him speak. When they do, the picture and sound track are in synch.

Synch sound records every sound present when the camera is running. Whether any or all of these sounds are used is a decision that's made when the film is edited.

Sound Effects

Many sounds you hear in a film appear to be synch sound that one assumes was recorded when the pictures were filmed. In fact, a great many are sound effects that were recorded later in a special studio. Gun shots are a good example. Compare the sound of a gun shot in a feature film to the sound of a gun shot in a news show about street violence. Gun shots in the news sound like small "pops" and you rarely hear the bullet ricochet as it bounces off hard surfaces. Compare this to gun shots in feature films. They have a big, very full sound. A spilt second after the "big bang," you hear the bullet ricochet with a sound that sings for a second or two. These gun shots are created by sound effects people after the filming and during the editing.

Another common sound effect is footsteps. These enhanced footstep sounds are created by foley artists. According to Elisha Birnbaum, a foley artist in New York, the word *foley* comes from Jack Foley who pioneered this art in film. These sound effects had long been used in radio shows; however, in film these effects had to be exactly synchronized with the pictures. Other technicians found the name "synch sound effects" too unwieldy and so renamed the art "foley." Today foley artists recreate many of the sounds that the audience takes for granted, like punches and footsteps.

Not all sound effects are custom made. Some, like wind and lighting, are pulled from libraries of sound effects. One sound effect that might appear in the sample commercial we've been reconstructing is bird songs.

I'll bet you thought that these birds just happened to be in the background when the shot was filmed. Think about it. How did those bird sounds make you feel? Didn't they make you feel just a little happy or cheerful? Why, those manipulative filmmakers! They're playing with my feelings! Yes, they surely are. Welcome to the World of Filmmaking where nothing is as it appears.

SOUND TRANSITIONS

The same transitions that join visuals are used to join audio cuts. If you listen carefully, you may notice that music fades down slightly when the narrator's voice begins. The music may fade out at the end of the commercial. The bird chirp is probably a straight cut. Some sounds overlap just as a dissolve overlaps two shots.

The audio or sound track can have a remarkable effect on the visuals. Many sound tracks of commercials can stand alone without visuals. They could be complete radio commercials and, occasionally, you'll hear them used that way. The only visuals are those images that your mind creates as you listen to the story. The golden age of radio demonstrated how powerful this kind of storytelling could be. When a film's sound track is married to its visuals as in a commercial, the result is different and often greater than the sum of the two separate parts.

If you've managed to dissect a commercial into its various elements, you've learned some of the language of filmmaking. Now that you've been behind the scenes, I hope this will change the way you view, not only commercials, but all kinds of films. They're all created from the same basic elements which we will be discussing throughout this book. This is a great beginning toward making your own film.

The shots and sounds that you've painstakingly identified and described flow together in a sequence that tells a little story about one subject. Since commercials are so short, they may only have one such sequence, but longer films will have many more. They're called *scenes*. Each scene tells a small story that's part of a bigger story. Think of scenes as chapters in a book. They flow logically one from another, each building on the last.

Commercials consist of several types of scenes that are ideal to use in your marketing video. In fact, marketing videos are often described as long-form commercials. Next, we'll look at how these scenes might be used in your marketing video.

Chapter 2

Scenes From A Marketing Video

Just eight types of scenes can construct almost any marketing video:

Still Photographs
Testimonials
Re-enactment
Manufacturing Process
Product or Service in Action
Message from the President
Computer Scenes
"The People of Acme"

You'll recognize these scenes; they've appeared in successful TV commercials for decades. Your video could use just one or all of them. Here's a thumbnail script showing how they might be used in a promotional video for the Acme Sailboat Company.

Still Photographs

QUICK SHOTS OF THREE 100-YEAR-OLD PHOTOGRAPHS: THE ORIGINAL ACME FACTORY IN 1897 WITH HORSES TIED IN FRONT OF THE BUILDING; A SAILBOAT ON TOP OF A HORSE-DRAWN CARRIAGE; JOHN ACME AT THE HELM OF CRUISING SAILBOAT SURROUNDED BY OCEAN. Narrator: "The Acme Sailboat Company was founded in 1896 by world-famous sailor John Acme..."

Testimonial

AT A MODERN MARINA WE SEE LIVE SHOTS OF A STUNNING ACME SAILBOAT. A SALTY LOOKING MAN HOLDS A BABY IN ONE ARM AND LEANS AGAINST THE WHEEL OF THE BOAT. HE TURNS TO THE CAMERA AND SAYS, "My family and I just crossed the Southern Ocean in this boat. We hit a tropical storm. In any other boat, we would not be here to tell the story. This well-built boat saved our lives."

Re-enactment & Computer Scene

A BOAT DESIGNER AND A COUPLE ARE LOOKING AT HIS COMPUTER SCREEN OF THE INTERIOR OF THEIR BOAT. THE COUPLE LOOKS AT THE SCREEN AND EXPLAINS HOW THEY WOULD CHANGE THE BOAT'S GALLEY. THE DESIGNER WORKS ON HIS DRAWING TABLET AND SAYS, "You mean like this?" THE COUPLE EXCLAIMS, "Exactly!"

Manufacturing Process

IN THE HIGH-TECH ACME FACTORY FIVE SAILBOAT HULLS ARE IN VARIOUS STAGES OF COMPLETION BY WORKERS IN UNIFORMS. A WOMAN IN A RED HARDHAT ADJUSTS TEST EQUIPMENT ON A COMPLETED HULL. A CLOSE-UP OF THE TEST INSTRUMENT READS "100%." Narrator: "Every Acme hull undergoes a rigorous Quality Assurance Program..."

Product or Service in Action

A FAMILY OF FOUR ARE HAPPILY SAILING THEIR ACME BOAT IN THE EMERALD GREEN WATERS OF THE CARIBBEAN. THEIR BOAT IS PULLING AHEAD OF THREE OTHER SAILBOATS.

Message From President

PRESIDENT, JOHN ACME III AT HIS DESK. ON THE WALL BEHIND HIM ARE AWARDS FOR BOAT OF THE YEAR, 1ST PLACE IN A RACE, SAFETY AWARDS, ETC. JOHN SAYS TO CAMERA, "My family has operated this business since my grandfather started it. We take great pride in our boats and you have my personal guarantee that every boat..."

The People of Acme

MANY QUICK CLOSE-UP SHOTS OF ACME EMPLOYEES HARD AT WORK ON VARIOUS TASKS: SEWING SAILS, POLISHING BRONZE, WORKING ON COMPUTERS, SAILING A BOAT ON A BEAUTIFUL DAY, ETC. Music fades up. The narrator concludes, "Acme Sailboats, a name you can trust."

You could customize these scenes to write a script for just about any kind of marketing video. And that's just what we'll do in Chapter Five. Each of these scenes, as written, would run less than 20 seconds, but they could be any length and in any order you want. As we explore these eight scenes in more detail, you may want to make notes if you get a great idea for using one of the scenes in your video.

Still Photographs

Many big-budget commercials use still photographs. Historical photos, for instance, can help tell the story of a company's past. Photographs in a video can have superimposed text, graphics or animation. Some great films have been made almost entirely from photographs. One example is the "*Civil War Series*," the most popular series PBS has ever broadcast. Photographs can save money in your production. They are a cost-effective way to quickly show many clients, associates or products. When these photographs already exist, the savings are most dramatic. However, photographs can appear on the screen for only a short period of time. Think of how long you'll look at a photograph in a magazine—a few seconds at most, unless there are a lot of details that interest you. That is the one catch with using photographs. You'll need more photos for less screen time. A photo that's on the screen for 20 seconds can become pretty tiresome. It would be better to use five or six photos so each appears on the screen for only a few seconds.

Some photographs work better in video than others. Since Standard Definition television is a horizontal format, approximately four units wide by three tall, horizontal photographs fit the television screen best. To use all of a vertical photograph, you'd have to move back from the photo (which makes the picture smaller) or sacrifice some of the photo by cropping the top and bottom.

Clarity of photographs is essential in video. A photograph may look sharply focused in its original size, but when filmed for video, it is blown up to the size of a TV screen which may be 14" by 10" or larger. Every little defect will be magnified. The original photograph that looked clear and crisp may now look grainy and out of focus. If you're unsure about a photograph, inspect it under a magnifying glass. If it looks grainy there, it will look just as bad when you enlarge it to TV size.

The Testimonial

The testimonial has been used in TV and print commercials since time began because it is effective.

ROLLS ROYCE PULLS INTO FRAME. HANDSOME MAN IN BACK LOWERS WINDOW AND HOLDS UP BOOK *Marketing With Digital Video.* HE SAYS TO CAMERA, "My business was failing until I read this book. I owe my fortune to this book. If you're in business, get it."

You've seen many other testimonials in commercials. Many of them, as I'm sure you've guessed, are not real. They were performed by actors who were cast for the roles because they looked like "real people," not because they loved the product. If your business has helped your clients, you don't need actors. Let your clients tell the camera how your business helped them. One efficient way to get a lot of these testimonials might be to invite all those satisfied clients to a dinner party or an event at your office. In a separate, private room have a cameraman ready to film them one at a time. Interview each one of them about how they like your service and how it's helped them. It's a question of numbers: If you film 10 interviews for 20 minutes each, you might get only three really good ones, each with 10 to 20 seconds of great material.

While I've had the good fortune of filming only three testimonials and using some of each, this is unusual. Increase your odds by filming a lot more than you think you'll need. It's not unusual to film several hours of testimonials or interviews and use just a minute or so in your final video.

Smart photographers show only their best photographs. Their audience never sees the hundreds of mediocre shots they've made. A video is similar. It will be judged only by what you show your audience, not by how much you've shot. Most home movies are boring because they are too long. To make them interesting, hours of footage must be eliminated. No one but the person who filmed it would want to watch all of it. When filming testimonials, plan to eliminate 95% of what you shoot. Show your audience only the remaining 5%— those little gems that express the perfect thought.

Short statements by real people are called *sound bites*. This TV news term describes statements which concisely express an important message in just a few seconds. In a commercial or marketing video, a series of sound bites can have a more powerful impact than a narrator or spokesman saying essentially the same thing. Unpaid "real people" expressing their personal feelings about the virtues of Acme Corp. are also more believable than a narrator.

The best subjects for testimonials are people who are articulate and direct in normal conversation. They'll probably be the same way on video. People who tend to ramble on without getting to the point will also ramble on when you film them— and they'll cost more to shoot because in video production, time is money.

The visuals you see in a testimonial can help support your message, but it's the audio that "sells" the message. Good sound bites can often stand alone without pictures, perfect for a radio commercial.

It's easier to make a radio commercial from sound bites than it is to make a video. If the subject expresses a great thought in sentence form only once in a while, you can easily edit these great sentences together. The result is a complete thought that is both concise and compelling. In a radio commercial, no one would ever know that you had eliminated vast portions of the testimonial by cutting and pasting.

In video, however, those cuts are obvious. The picture changes with every cut and the scene looks choppy. Even though the sound bites might still flow naturally from one thought to the next, the viewer sees all the cutting and pasting and knows he's being manipulated. But, you can cover these visual cuts with other shots so the viewer isn't aware of the cutting you've done. We'll have some fun with these tricks later in the chapters on editing.

Longer sections of testimonials that can be used without editing give you the most options for making a believable testimonial. To be successful with testimonials, film a lot of people and then ruthlessly edit until you're left with only the best ones.

The Re-enactment

The following scene is from a video designed to promote a hospital's new division—a health service specifically for local businesses.

ACME HOSPITAL VIDEO

VISUALS	AUDIO
Scene #4	
MEDIUM SHOT **ADMINISTRATIVE OFFICE**	
WOMAN AT DESK PICKS UP **PHONE**	Hello, Health Services. May I help you?
	You'd like to send five employees over for OSHA tests now?
	Yes, we can take them now. Send them right over.

This 12-second scene is a re-enactment for the camera. It clearly demonstrates a benefit: this service saves time because businesses can use the service without prior appointments. The woman was not a professional actress. She was re-enacting for the camera what she did every day at her job. Commercials are full of re-enactments. This is probably the most prevalent type of commercial. They are produced as if they were scenes in a feature film. Slick vignettes are portrayed by professional actors who are cast to look like "real people." Although this kind of production is beyond the reach of most low budget producers, you can effectively use non-actors for these re-enactments if you:

- Film real people doing the things they do in real life;
- Avoid writing a lot of dialogue for these folks. Let them recreate dialogue in their own words; and
- Plan on filming these scenes several times until you get a take that is believable and to the point.

Think back to all the ways your business has helped your clients. Can you imagine a short vignette that illustrates this? Your vignette should clearly demonstrate a benefit. It could be generic without using specific details. This way you could combine several client situations into one short scene that demonstrates more than one benefit. Add a few lines to the scene above such as "Yes, the fee is still only $49.95 per person," and "We can show your employees how to avoid Repetitive Stress Syndrome at no extra charge." One short scene is now demonstrating several benefits.

Manufacturing Process

Manufacturing scenes are generally quite visual and can be fun to watch, even for viewers who may not be interested in manufacturing. Imagine that you've just filmed each step in a 1000-foot-long assembly line where lipstick is manufactured. This line begins with the pouring of red molten lipstick as it flows into molds and ends with the finished product in a gold case and blister pack. In reality, it takes one hour for lipstick to go from one end to the other.

Your own mother wouldn't watch this film for an hour. To avoid boring the audience, show them only the most interesting steps with close-ups. Instead of an hour, show the entire process in 40 seconds.

Cut out all the factory sounds and replace the sound track with up-beat fast-moving music. You've just transformed a tedious industrial operation into a montage of lipstick machines in motion.

This 40-second scene will hold a viewer's interest because it's *entertaining* and *informative*. Even the viewer who doesn't care how lipstick is made exclaims, "So that's how they do it!" Holding your viewer's interest is crucial in any marketing video. With 109 TV channels and the ubiquitous remote, viewers won't watch anything that bores them for even a second. Lose their attention and your video may be a waste of time and money. While we're entertaining, let's also show how *well* we manufacture lipstick. Most of the process is controlled by computers so we'll show quick shots of computer screens rapidly counting and monitoring lipstick production.

To demonstrate that we take *quality control* seriously, we'll show white-uniformed inspectors wearing "Quality Control" name tags. These people carefully inspect each lipstick. Some of the lipsticks are tossed in a small bin labeled "Rejects."

In a mere 40 seconds we've entertained and informed our viewer while selling him or her on our company. This was no accident. Each shot the viewer saw was carefully planned and scripted. Most were close-ups. On television, close-ups are more effective than wide shots because the TV screen is smaller and more intimate than the movie screen unless you have a $100,000 home theater. If your video might appear on a PDA or cell phone screen, close-ups will work much better than wide shots. Television excels as a close-up medium.

Close-ups can make your company look better than wide shots. Good looking close-ups are also easier to film than wide shots because it's much easier to clean and polish the small area in a close-up than it is to make a large room look presentable. The close-ups our viewer saw were spotlessly clean. The large room that contained our 1000-foot assembly line needed painting and was cluttered with junk. The viewer, however, wasn't aware of these defects. We showed the entire room, but only for a couple seconds. One quick shot near the beginning oriented the viewer. In that wide shot, the viewer's eye was drawn to a fast moving red lipstick in the foreground. He didn't have time to study the room. From that shot we cut immediately to close-up motion shots of lipstick assembly. The viewer's attention stayed with the motion. Some commercials are made entirely of close-ups. Even some television shows, like CBS's long-running *60 Minutes*, consist mostly of close-ups.

Product or Service in Action

Would you believe I made a marketing video about garbage trucks? These weren't ordinary garbage trucks. They were the new kind designed for recycling. Older style trucks normally require two men—one to drive and one to pick up garbage cans. This truck only required one man. The most important scene in the video showed him and his truck in action on an actual route.

The driver was a satisfied customer who had purchased the garbage truck. Ideally, we would have staged a garbage route where the driver stopped and started his work just for the camera. But he agreed to let us film him only if we didn't interfere with his schedule. I spent most of the afternoon chasing him on foot with camera rolling. He met his schedule and I almost died. But, I did get what I wanted—footage that showed how easy it was for one man, rather than two, to collect and separate garbage under real conditions.

While demonstrating this main benefit to potential customers, I also showed how several features made this one-man operation possible: Step-up doors on both sides of the cab and dual steering wheels with dual controls enabled the driver/collector to get out on one side of the cab and re-enter through the other side. We showed these features as benefits which increased efficiency.

All these important benefits were described in the script, but when it came time to film, I was amazed at how quickly the driver actually did his job. When you film under "battle" conditions like these, expect the unexpected. After filming his pick-up route, we followed the truck to the various recycling centers where tin cans, glass and newspapers were recycled. When edited, the entire scene lasted only about two minutes, yet it clearly demonstrated the truck's superiority.

At the end of our run, I asked the owner/driver how the truck saved his company money. He answered that "it saves money because it enables one man to do the job of two." Then I asked him about service, reliability and other issues our audience would want to know. That interview yielded a solid 20-second testimonial.

The product/service demonstration can be used in many different businesses. Whether it's computers, mining equipment, or non-profit agencies, showing the product or service in operation can effectively demonstrate benefits to the viewer. How does your company or non-profit help your customers or clients? Don't just *tell* your viewer the answer, *show* them features and especially the benefits you offer.

Message from the President

The message from the president is a question mark in most of the business videos I produce. My advice is usually not to include it. You've seen exceptions in commercials by famous CEO's of large companies. However, unless you or your president are experienced public speakers or actors, think very carefully beforehand.

It's one thing to speak well in front of a group. It's quite another to have that same presence and confidence when the lights, camera and microphone are pointed at you. Most people tend to freeze in this situation. It looks a lot easier on TV than it actually is. Often the message that you wish to express is best handled by a professional narrator, on-camera actor or a good testimonial.

If, however, you insist on being on camera, here are some tips that may help: prepare your remarks in advance; write your message in a clear conversational manner; memorize the main points and fill them in with some detail while you're speaking. Then ask a friend to videotape you with an ordinary camcorder. Show the tape to a few disinterested parties. If they honestly like what you show them, you may be able to duplicate your performance in front of the real camera. You can always decide later in the editing room whether this scene helps or hurts the video.

The worst that will happen is that you may decide six months from now that your personal message does not help the video. Cutting your scene will mean re-editing. You may also have to re-do the narration and music to make the new version flow naturally. And you'll need new copies.

If you're not the president, it may be politically difficult to avoid this scene. In this case try to keep the president's message short, 15 seconds or less.

Incidentally, if you want to improve your communication and public speaking skills, an excellent way to start is to look for a local branch of Toastmasters International *http://www.toastmasters.org*

Computer Scenes

If your company uses computers to serve your customers, these scenes can add visual interest as well as contribute to the overall impression that your company is efficient and up-to-date. CADCAM screens, for example, are useful for demonstrating your design and manufacturing process. Other businesses may find that an order-taking program, database, or virtual tour program best illustrates a benefit. While graphics screens are more interesting than text screens, the important question is *what is the benefit to the viewer?* A brief view of a text screen from a word processing program might be useful if you were promoting secretarial or writing services.

In one video, we wanted to show how easily a company could custom design and manufacture parts to customer specifications. The scene began with a close-up of a hand sketching a part on a cocktail napkin. (Many of the design requests came in just this way.) Then we showed that same design being rendered on a CADCAM computer screen. From here we cut to a computer plotter outputting the design as a blueprint. Finally, we cut to a computer-driven milling machine producing the part.

In just 15 seconds we demonstrated a complete custom design and manufacturing process. Every shot was a close-up and although the scene did have a short narration, it might easily have stood without narration. The scene was short, interesting to watch and made the point: Acme will custom design and manufacture your part.

Some situations may warrant filming a CADCAM or other application outside your company in the offices of your suppliers or customers who have these programs. If you imply that you use technology to help your customers, I hope it's true. Honesty is good business, but this is not a lecture on business ethics. Advertising has always had its own approach to the truth.

In any case, most computer scenes last only a few seconds. Yet in those few seconds, you can convey the idea that your company uses the sophisticated tools to help your customers.

The People of Acme

This is a short scene of quick cuts, called a *montage*, consisting of many close-ups of the hard-working people of your company. Each of these people shots is quick, in some cases, a second or less. The scene may be narrated or just have uplifting music. The "People of Acme" scene sends an important message to your customers because no matter what business you're in, you are in the service business and service is people. Your business may be judged entirely by the quality of service you provide. Rather than *telling* how great your service is, *show* the faces of service—your people. They are dedicated and hard working. They care. But wait, you say, our people aren't like that. Our people are late for work, lazy and surly to our customers. (You don't need a marketing video, you need a better Personnel Director.)

Video magic to the rescue. Like the testimonials we filmed earlier, the key to making this scene work is a high shooting ratio. To make a 20-second scene with perhaps 10 or 15 faces convey your message, you may need to film 30 or 40 people. If you film this many shots, you'll undoubtedly get 20 good seconds of the Acme people. Like the testimonials, it's not what you shoot but what you show.

To emphasize their humanity, most shots will be close-ups of faces. We see a variety of people: on the assembly line, in corporate offices on the phone with customers, and at high-tech stations. They are smiling, concentrating, caring, all working together to make a better world. If G.E. can use that idea, you can too.

And just to make sure this message gets through, put music under these faces. Music that inspires. It might be anything from Mozart to "We Are The World" to convey a sense of the human spirit striving for excellence. And to make absolutely sure our message works, we can write a little narration that goes something like this, "The people of Acme are always there for you. It's their teamwork and dedication to quality that makes Acme the world leader in customer service."

Get the idea? Here's another example of narration for your people scene, "All the sophisticated technology that Acme possesses means nothing without our best asset—our people. Acme is people helping people."

You'll see this scene used again and again, especially in the Sunday morning, corporate image commercials. It is a powerful message. An added bonus is that you'll put more of your employees in the video. This in itself is a morale builder. People like to see themselves on TV, especially when you show them at their best.

These eight scenes—Still Photos, Testimonials, Re-enactments, Manufacturing Process, Product or Service in Action, Message from The President, Computers and The People of Acme—are the building blocks of every marketing video. You've probably already begun to imagine how some of them might work in your video. In the following chapter you'll learn how to write a script using these eight scenes.

The lengths of the scenes can be tailored to suit your needs, from 20 seconds to several minutes. Scenes can be used in any order and each scene could be divided into several parts. For instance, your video might begin with a short testimonial, then cut to several other scenes and end with another part of that same testimonial, "I would recommend Acme to anyone."

Studying television commercials is an easy way to learn about filmmaking and marketing. Now it's time to turn our attention to full-fledged marketing videos. Chances are you already have one or more of these videos around the office, perhaps from a suppliers or a competitor. They're not hard to find. Request videos from ads you see —but do be considerate and only request videos for products or services you might actually buy. *The Marketing Video Magazine* DVD in the Appendix contains a number of examples from marketing videos you may want to study.

As you watch marketing videos look for the eight scenes we've just discussed. Put yourself in the shoes of their intended audience—the prospect. How did the video make you feel about this company? Is the presentation slick, amateurish, fast-moving, boring, too long? By studying marketing videos, you can emulate the most effective ones and learn from the rest.

Chapter 3

Script Preliminaries

IMPORTANCE OF THE SCRIPT

Great movies, television and videos all begin with great scripts. More than any other single factor, the script determines a video's success. Look at some of the fare that comes out of Hollywood: despite spending millions of dollars, many of these films are neither entertaining nor profitable. Throw money at a mediocre script and you get an expensive— but still mediocre—movie.

Alfred Hitchcock felt that when his script was completed, his film was essentially in the can: shooting and editing the film were anticlimactic. The real work had already been completed in the script. Many of his films are considered classics. Not only were they box office hits when they were released, but they withstand the test of time. They'll continue to be entertaining and profitable 50 years from now. Great films are made from great scripts.

Whether you're going to write a script yourself, hire a scriptwriter, or simply hire a video production company to do it all for you, it is very much in your financial interest to learn what makes a good script. Here's why. The script is a blueprint for both the shooting and editing of a video. These two phases, production and post production, are where most of your budget will be spent. Just as a blueprint allows you to get competitive bids for the construction of a house, the script allows the producer to get several bids for the production and post-production of a video. The same script can be produced on different budgets.

The script brings order to a complex process full of details. From it you can separate and list the various elements you'll need for shooting, like props, actors and sets. You can also develop a schedule for acquiring and filming these elements in the most cost-effective manner. The script becomes the master plan for your video.

A script can be written with the most basic word processor — the pencil—or with a program like Script Werx (see the Appendix). While writing and rewriting allow you to experiment with script ideas without spending a dime, the most important thing to remember is that the time to rewrite is *before* you begin production, not after! Changing the script after the video has been photographed and edited will often require reshooting and reediting. These expenses can be avoided.

SEVEN QUESTIONS TO ANSWER BEFORE WRITING THE SCRIPT

The following seven questions should be answered before any scripting begins. These answers are the first page of any business video script. They will be quite useful throughout the process of producing your video.

1. Who will watch this video? For how long?
2. In what setting will they watch it?
3. What is the goal of this video?
4. Will printed materials accompany the video?
5. How will the video be distributed?
6. Will the video be shown in other countries?
7. Will the video need to be regularly updated because of changing technology or products?

Let's look at these questions one by one.

1. Audience

The audience is everything. They are your reason for making this business video. Their reaction to the video determines whether it's successful. If you make the video to please only yourself, at best you are making an art film, at worst a home movie. Neither will succeed in marketing your business.

One of the most important jobs you have as the producer is to think like your audience. What kind of people are they? What do they care about? The more completely you answer these questions, the better prepared you are to direct the video toward this audience and their concerns. One of the marketing rules of thumb is to ask your customers what they want, and then to give it to them. Sounds obvious, doesn't it? Yes, but it's amazing how often producers forget this simple rule.

Large corporations spend millions to learn who their customers are, what they like and dislike and what motivates them to buy. Answering these questions about customers has become an industry in itself called market research. Although you and I don't have the time or money to do such extensive market research, a little common sense can help determine what your audience wants.

Put yourself in the shoes of a viewer. Let's say you've just requested videos from two competing companies. You suspect that the product or service they provide may save your business money. You pop the first DVD in your DVD player, noting that the box label says it is 3 minutes 45 seconds. This video begins by explaining how this company will save you money. It then demonstrates a couple of the more common ways the product/service helps people in your business. Then you see three short testimonials by people in your business. One of these is from a Fortune 500 company. The video closes by inviting you to call an 800 number for more information.

You're just about to reach for the phone; but wait, what's this other video? The case says it runs 16 minutes. You pop it in. It begins with the president speaking in a monotone about how his company was started by his grandfather in 1943. You listen for a few seconds and then reach for the "Fast Forward." A minute later the president is still talking. You can't hear what he's saying, but you guess it's not that interesting. The video is still fast forwarding as you start to go through your mail, but then you remember that first video. You dial their 800 number.

No matter who the audience is or what they want, *short marketing videos are more effective than long marketing videos*. Making long marketing videos is the most common mistake of first-time producers. Think like your audience. Would you watch a long marketing video from another company? Probably not. Remember this is not entertainment like a sitcom, feature film or talk show. The attention span in the Internet age is very short. Your audience simply won't tolerate a long video.

TV commercials are called *short form* marketing videos. Consider all they can do in just 30 seconds. They make you feel that G.E. really is bringing good things to your life. They bring a tear to your eye over the reuniting of family members thanks to AT&T. They get you to pick up the phone and buy Ginsu knives. What's that? You never buy what they're selling? Well, someone is or they wouldn't keep spending all that money for advertising.

The marketing video has an advantage over commercials—the audience actively chooses to watch this video. They are motivated or they wouldn't have asked to see your video. They will give you a bit of their time IF you get to the point—show them how you can help them or address other concerns they have. But don't overstay your welcome. If you learn nothing else from this book, remember this—*short marketing videos are more effective than long ones*.

Training videos are another story. Their audiences are motivated to watch a much longer video. The issue gets confused when you are demonstrating a product or training potential customers. How much training detail should you include? Should you promote benefits? One way to deal with these questions is to imagine you're producing two different videos—one for training and one for marketing. Looking at it this way can help you decide how to approach each video. In Chapter 12 you'll learn how to produce several kinds of training videos.

For now, let's agree that marketing videos and training videos are very different. The audience of your marketing video won't sit still for a long, drawn-out video. What do they want? To answer that you'll first need to know who they are.

If they're materials design engineers, they will have specific concerns and questions; if they're elementary school art teachers, they'll have very different concerns. So, occupation is a prime characteristic of the audience; others are age, gender and education. If you've been in business for awhile, you already have a very good idea who your prospects and customers are.

Not all videos will have a specific audience; some are intended for a general audience. But the more clearly you identify your audience, the more accurately you can target your video message to them. Write a description of your audience with as much detail as possible, including occupation, age, sex, education, how they like their coffee or any other information that will help you sell to them.

2. The Viewing Setting

How your video will be viewed also determines the kind of script you write. For instance, a video that is intended primarily for use at a trade show booth will probably be shorter than other marketing videos. It may be just two or three minutes long and run as an "endless loop." The trade show video must be short because most attendees won't stand still long enough to watch a 10-minute video. A video for a trade show display would be much shorter than a video you would mail to prospective clients.

Trade show videos are most effective without a lot of narration. Music and a few text headlines on the screen are better than wall-to-wall narration. If you've ever manned a trade show booth, you know that it's a grueling job for all the exhibitors. After you've played your video a few hundred times, your neighbors in adjoining booths are likely to ask you to turn the volume down or off!

Consider a second scenario where the viewer's environment affects the script. A salesman is meeting with a prospect in her office. They both want to talk about how the salesman's company manufacturing capabilities can help her business. She asks to see the plant's assembly line. He presses "play" on his portable DVD player and now they're both watching that assembly line. The conversation is going well and he begins building his case, but just then the video's narration begins and their conversation ends. To keep their conversation going, he must turn the volume down. By turning the volume down, he loses the narration, music and all the other sound elements that worked so well in the video.

This doesn't mean a marketing video shouldn't have narration. It just means that you might want *two* different versions of the video: one with narration to mail to clients, and a second one without narration and perhaps a few additional text screens for the situation we've just discussed. This is a simple editing job.

If your video will be used in two distinct viewing settings, e.g. one for trade shows and another to be sent to prospective customers, it is best to produce two separate videos, each with its own purpose and style. The easy way to do this is to first write and produce the longer video—the one you'd send. From that video, write a second, much shorter script with little or no narration, and more titles to emphasize the main ideas.

Produce the second video by re-editing the first. Although you may have to add a few titles and perhaps find a new music track, you won't have to film any additional material. You'll get two videos for little more than the cost of one.

Another way to save money when you need two videos for different settings is to write two scripts. Shoot all the material for both scripts, but edit only the one you need first. You can edit the second video when time and money permit.

Most marketing videos will be used in a variety of settings, including presentations to groups or individuals, as well as continuous use at trade shows and on the Internet. Identifying as many of these settings as possible will help you write and produce different versions of the video with different goals.

3. The Goal

Consider the goals of these four marketing videos:
1. To increase enrollment at Acme Prep School.
2. To turn around a public relations disaster for Acme Chemical Company.
3. To solicit donations and volunteer workers for Acme Hospital.
4. To have prospective customers call 800-BIG-TRUK and learn more about Acme's $200,000 drilling truck.

A business video must have a clearly defined goal. Without one, it is little more than a home movie. The goal may be for people to pick up the phone and place an order, but it's more likely that the video will set the stage for a later sale by a salesperson. The goal might be to demonstrate how your new product will help your clients save money. The goal might be to make viewers feel you are the expert in your field and that they can call you for answers. The goal might be to promote your manufacturing plant as the most cost-effective way to produce their product. There are as many possible goals for videos as there are businesses. In fact, many more, but keep your video focused on one clear goal. Then list three to five of the most important messages that will help achieve this goal.

4. Will Additional Support Materials Accompany The Video?

Some information is more appropriate in print than it is in a video. Price lists and technical specs, for example, may be more useful in print. Printed literature can be randomly accessed in the same way as computer data. In a book it's easy to turn to chapter three and find specific information quickly. VHS videos, on the other hand, are not random access; they are linear. So to find something in the middle of the tape, you must fast forward and guess where your information is. CD ROMS and DVDs are random access and can include pdf documents or other documents, as we'll explore later.

Although your company's phone number may appear at the end of your video, don't count on the viewer's willingness to search for it. This important phone number should also appear on an accompanying business card or literature, as well as on the video's case and label. If you want your prospects to call, make it very easy for them to find your number.

To decide whether material should be in video or print, look at the advantages of each. Video is very effective at making a visceral appeal, like those TV commercials that are aimed at the heart. They're designed to elicit an emotional response. Video is also good at projecting a corporate image. The Sunday morning TV commercials are largely corporate image spots.

Video excels at physical demonstrations. It's easy to show how a product works in a video, just like a live demonstration. Even when working parts are hidden, a simple animation can graphically explain inner workings.

Compared to a printed direct mail piece, much of which is thrown away unopened, a video is harder to resist. People want to see what's inside. They may not open your direct mail or take your phone calls, but most of them will watch your video out of curiosity. Like the Trojan Horse, a video can carry your message into their home or office with the least resistance.

First, consider all the information that would interest your audience. Then divide this material into a print stack and a video stack. It won't all be clear cut. A testimonial that you've filmed for the video might also work in print. These media may refer to each other. The video may refer to the printed material e.g., "See the price list (fact sheet or technical data) that accompanied this video." Print ads or literature may say "See our new video for a demonstration of this product."

Let print and video each do what they do best. Generally, short videos with a few simple messages make the most sense. Other information is sometimes best handled with literature, a phone call or in a personal meeting. Consider print and video separately so you can plan an effective marketing campaign where each element has a clear and separate task. Each element of the campaign should support and reinforce the other elements.

All marketing elements should convey a consistent corporate image and style. Just as business cards and stationary use the same logo and colors, keep your video consistent with your corporate identity.

5. How Will The Video Be Distributed?

When this book was first published, VHS tapes were the primary format of distribution. Today we have DVDS, CD ROMS, the Internet and other ways to distribute videos. Consider them all, even VHS, because it will be around for some time to come. While the question of distribution may not directly affect your scriptwriting, it's better to consider it now rather than after the video is completed. Too many videos are produced that never achieve their goals because no one thought to make and execute a distribution plan. This plan can be simple: for instance, you might send copies of the video or CD with a cover letter to the most recent subscribers of *Sailmaking Today*. If this magazine existed, you could rent its mailing list from a list broker. You might also tag future advertisements with the line, "Send for free video."

We'll discuss budgeting in greater detail later, but here's an example of what it might cost to implement a simple distribution plan:

100 DVD ROMs including an eight-minute video and pdf files of product literature, including duplication, color label and jewel case	$400.00
100 Priority Mail Flat Rate Large Envelopes with postage	$385.00
100 names and addresses of targeted prospects printed on mailing labels	$ 32.00
TOTAL VIDEO DISTRIBUTION COSTS	**$817.00**

This is just an example. Don't use these prices for budgeting just yet. There are a lot of other variables to consider. First, sending just 100 is unlikely to make any sales unless they are highly qualified prospects. You may want to start by putting the video on your web site. The Internet may seem like the perfect way to distribute your video (and in some ways it is) but the catch is that many people still do not have fast Internet connections. Watching a video on a slow dial-up connection can be like watching a random slide show which keeps stopping for no apparent reason. So don't bet that everyone on the Internet will see your video the way it was intended. You will probably also want to offer your video in VHS, CD or DVD.

For those with fast cable modem or DSL connections, the Internet may be the perfect distribution method if you can afford it. The price of bandwidth is declining, but if five thousand people watch your five megabyte video in one month, the cost can run you from $150.00 to $750.00. The quality of service you get is usually related to the cost. To give you an idea - five MB of video full-frame high- quality video runs at 3.6 MB/sec, so 1 hour of digital video(DV) takes up 13 gigabytes (GB). At this point, no one is providing full-frame video on the Internet. Typically, you see a small window of compressed video, but even that takes significant bandwidth.

By the time you read this, the cost of bandwidth will undoubtedly be lower than the prices I quoted above. Just don't forget that hundreds of companies went belly-up by betting on showing lots of video to viewers with fast Internet connections.

It's tempting to think of distributing your video solely through the Internet, but what about those potential customers who'd prefer to watch it on their DVD player? This media is not quite universal. It will be, but the question is when.

In any case, now is the time to begin planning distribution. It's not enough just to produce a great video. That video must reach its target audience.

6. Will The Video Be Shown In Other Countries?

Unfortunately, you can't simply send your finished VHS or DVD video to a viewer in France and expect him to watch it on his home VCR. If it's a DVD, he or she MAY be able to view it but it's dangerous to assume. The reason is because different countries have different video standards. The three primary standards in the world of video are NTSC, SECAM and PAL. The U.S., Japan, Kuwait, Sweden and about 35 others use the NTSC standard. A VHS tape or a DVD produced in America in the NTSC standard cannot be viewed on the most common VCRs and DVD players in France because France uses the SECAM standard which is not compatible with NTSC or PAL, a standard used in the rest of Europe and most of the world.

It isn't very expensive to transfer your video from one standard to another. If you have prospective customers in other countries, it's wise to plan ahead for this conversion. It would also be wise to ask people in those countries if multistandard DVD players or VCRs are common there. Many European DVD players are multistandard, allowing viewers to watch videos from other countries. A list of countries and their standards is included in the Appendix and is also available at our VideoUniversity web site.

Unlike VHS videos which are analog, the video files on a DVD are encoded in what's called MPEG video. But this has nothing to do with whether the video is in either the PAL or NTSC standards. DVD discs are still either PAL or NTSC standard. Most DVD players do not convert video standards. However, the good news is that multistandard DVD players are becoming more common. The bottom line is, if your video is likely to go to another country you will want to investigate these issues *before* you write the script.

Aside from the technical issues, there's a more important reason to consider this issue before writing your script—*language*. It's not a big deal to translate English narration to French, Japanese or any other language. Translating and rerecording narration into a second language is fairly straightforward and inexpensive. It can be as simple as calling a language instructor at a local college and having the instructor read his or her written translation for the new language version of the narration. And if you do a second language version of your video, you can put this on a DVD, just as feature films commonly offer different language versions on their DVDs.

The real scripting problem comes from what's on the screen. For instance, in a scene where actors or "real people" speak on camera, it can be quite a project to rerecord their voices in another language and then match each word and syllable to the movements of the actors mouths. This is called *dubbing*. You've probably seen foreign films that were dubbed. These films were originally recorded in one language, then, through an expensive and tedious process, the voices were rerecorded in a second language, and then synchronized so that the actors appear to be speaking the second language. This is called lip synching. (Some low budget films make little effort to synchronize the sounds with the actors' lips. Others are very well done. Just rent a DVD with different languages to see this in action.)

If your video is going to France but your on-screen actors speak in English, you'll have to go through this process. If, on the other hand, your actors don't have on-screen lines, you'll only need to rerecord the narration in French. Planning ahead for foreign distribution can save you a bundle. Knowing that you'll eventually need a

French version, you might write a script with no on-camera dialogue. The video would be narrated by an off-camera narrator. However, if you need a French version but had not planned for it, you might need an expensive foreign language dubbing session or need to reshoot scenes with actors who speak French. Both expenses can be avoided by planning ahead.

7. Video Needs Regular Updating

Business videos are often considered capital expenditures so you'll want to design the video to last as long as possible. Most marketing videos can be used for several years before they need to be updated.

Updating a video can be as easy as reshooting one scene of an outdated product or a new chairman of the board and then replacing that scene, rewriting the narration and possibly changing some on-screen text. If, on the other hand, this outdated product or chairman were referenced throughout the video, you might be forced to reshoot and re-edit most of the video. If you know you'll eventually be replacing a scene or two, write a script that easily allows for it.

Examples of the 7 Questions in Various Videos

Answering these seven questions will help you produce the most effective video with the smallest possible budget. In video production, planning makes all the difference. The following examples show what this first page of a script might look like.

ACME PREP SCHOOL

1. **Audience**: Primary - 7th grade boys from upper middle class families. Secondary - their parents.
2. **Setting**: Primary - School Open House (will require large screen TV). Secondary - homes and schools.
3. **Goal**: To increase enrollment at Acme Prep.
4. **Printed Materials**: School catalog.
5. **Distribution**: 100 copies mailed on request and available on the web site.
6. **Countries**: USA only.
7. **Updates**: Change music in two years. Change content

in three years.

ACME CHEMICAL

1. **Audience**: Local environmentalists and plant neighbors.
2. **Setting**: Shown to local civic groups in travelling show.
3. **Goal**: To show benefits to society of the chemicals we produce. To stop rumors of plant hazards by demonstrating our safety procedures.
4. **Printed Materials**: Free samples of our ACME aspirin & booklet *How Acme Aspirin Fights Childhood Diseases.*
5. **Distribution**: Shown only to groups by Acme PR people.
6. **Countries**: USA only.
7. **Updates**: To be determined from audience feedback.

ACME HOSPITAL

1. **Audience**: Primary - Wealthy Donors. Secondary - Civic-minded volunteers.
2. **Setting**: One-on-one personal presentations to wealthy donors. Group presentations to civic groups.
3. **Goal**: To raise $2 million by April 1 as integral part of capital campaign. To enlist volunteers.
4. **Printed Materials**: Booklet *Wellness Programs at ACME Hospital.*
5. **Distribution**: Shown by Board Members & PR Dept. And available on the web site until April 1.
6. **Countries**: USA only.
7. **Updates:** None.

ACME MINING EQUIPMENT

1. **Audience**: Purchasing agents & engineers of international mining companies.
2. **Setting**: At trade shows. In their offices.
3. **Goal**: To inexpensively demonstrate our truck throughout the world. To have perspective buyers call our office for more information.
4. **Printed Materials**: Technical specification brochure.

5. **Distribution**: To qualified leads from trade magazine
ads. Approx. 200 in first year and available on the web site.
6. **Countries**: USA & Canada in first year. Mexico, South
Africa, Brazil in second year.
7. **Updates**: New video in three years when improved
truck is available.

Begin each script by answering these questions and you will
control costs, define your video, and ensure its success. These answers stay with you throughout the entire production process.

Take a moment now and write your own answers. As you begin
writing your script and planning production, this one page introduction will help you stay on track. It's easy to go off on a tangent during
scripting.

You've just written the first page of your script. Now, let's have
some fun!

Chapter 4

Writing The Script

Writing an effective video script is hard work, but it can also be fun. By writing it yourself, you're not only saving hundreds or thousands of dollars, you are also creating a marketing tool to help grow your business. Even if you pay someone else to write your script, you still have to approve and revise that script. After all, who knows your business as well as you do? And who cares about its success as much as you?

We'll begin the script by brainstorming a few good scenes. Next we'll play with the structure and order of these scenes so they tell a logical story. Then we'll illustrate the story and add some narration. After we have a good basic story we can polish it till it shines.

BRAINSTORM A FEW GOOD SCENES

Put on your creative cap. Pull out all the stops and let your imagination run wild. No matter what you do here, you won't end up in jail or broke! The only rule is that there are no rules. If you can imagine it, write it. Don't make any assumptions yet about whether your ideas are practical to produce on a low budget. To start, look again at the list of marketing scenes:

Still Photographs
The Testimonial
Manufacturing Process
Product/Service in Action
Message from the President
The Re-enactment
Computer Scenes
The People of Acme

Which of these jumps out at you? It's probably one that best addresses your main goal. Start with that one and write two or three sentences describing this scene and how it will promote your business. You don't need a lot of detail, just the essence of the scene. Write the first thing that comes to mind and don't censor your thoughts, say "Satisfied Customer tells how much he likes our service, how fast we deliver, and how much we helped his business."

Set that scene aside. Starting now you have ten minutes to write ten more of these. Put this book down, grab paper and pencil and check the clock...

How'd you do? Surprised at how much you wrote? You've made a good start. Keep going with it. And remember, anything is fair game at this point. If you get a great idea, don't worry about what it might cost to produce. Write it down anyway. Later I'll show you some great tricks for producing expensive looking scenes on a shoestring. Keep that little devil, your internal censor, away! It's not time for him yet. Keep this process going over the next few days and you'll probably find you've invented quite a few interesting scenes. Keep pencil and paper close because you never know when a scene will pop into your head – driving to work, perhaps first thing in the morning, or even in the middle of the night.

Some of your scene ideas will be purely visual. That's good. You'll need a lot of visuals. Don't worry about the narration right now. Describe the visual—what your viewers see. Draw a sketch if you like.

SCRIPT FORMATS

A sketch can be invaluable when a visual is difficult to describe with words. If it is vital for a viewer to understand a physical detail, a sketch can make this detail clear. Put together enough sketches and you have a storyboard.

While a storyboard can map out all the visuals of a video, there are some problems with this method. One is that a sketch, like a photograph, doesn't show motion. It is one frozen moment. A moving subject or a camera move, like a pan or a zoom, must be described with words. All the sounds—whether music, dialogue or narration—also require written descriptions. Using an occasional sketch can clarify a scene but for most videos, drawing an entire script with storyboards is too much work, especially since these scenes will have to be described in your script anyway.

Storyboards and the two-column format we examined earlier each have their advantages, but the easiest format to use in this early stage of scripting is a single-column format.

Scene #1

MEDIUM-WIDE SHOT GRANDMOTHER ON FRONT PORCH SWING. SHE READS STORYBOOK TO GRANDCHILD SITTING ON HER LAP. Wistful violin music fades up and continues throughout. Sound Effect of robins singing in the background. Narrator: "The love of family is..."

Note that the visuals are upper case and the audio is lower case. With this format you can describe both audio and video in as much detail as the two-column format. However, the two-column format offers a number of advantages: the timing relationship of audio to video is more precise; the separation of the audio and video elements makes it clearer for the cameraman, actors and others.

While it is *possible* to create a two-column format in a word processor, trying to keep the columns in synch can cause extreme mental fatigue, hardly conducive to great scriptwriting. I recommend that you either stick with the single-column format, or purchase a script formatting program such as ScriptWerx, available in the Appendix or from www.VideoUniversity.com. In any case, don't let computer issues get in the way of your scriptwriting. Remember, *Gone With The Wind* was written with a typewriter.

Below is a list of standard script terms and abbreviations, but please don't overuse them. In many video scripts there will be no need to use any of these abbreviations. Never use them in a screenplay for a feature film until you completely understand screenplay formatting rules.

LS	Long Shot or Wide Shot
MS	Medium Shot
MCU	Medium Close Up
CU	Close Up
XCU	Extreme Close Up
Two Shot or Three Shot	indicates two or three people in a shot
Subjective Shot	indicates the camera will see what the character sees. See the 1946 film *Lady In the Lake*
EXT and INT	used to indicate exterior and interior settings.

SOT	Sound On Tape indicates that the voice, music, or background sounds will be from the audio track of a videotape.
SOF	Sound On Film same thing for film.
VO	Voice Over is the narration over a scene.
OSV	Off Screen Voice is a voice we hear from a person who is not visible in the scene.
MIC	Microphone.
POV	Point Of View. In feature film scripts may indicate that a shot will be seen from the point of view of a particular character.
OS	Over The Shoulder shot shows part of the back of a person's head and possibly some shoulder as that person is typically looking at or talking another person.
ANNCR	Announcer.
SFX or F/X	Special Effects. (Audio FX) or video special effects created in post production which appear to alter reality.

LOOK FOR SCENES THAT SAY IT ALL

Sometimes one particular scene can express your message in a nutshell. I produced a marketing video for a company that sells and installs video surveillance equipment. The video shows how they design custom security systems from blueprints and surveys of buildings. It shows their full inventory of surveillance equipment, indicating that customers can always get immediate replacement parts. It demonstrates how they conceal cameras and it includes testimonials from high-profile customers. But one scene, in particular, pretty much says it all.

The scene begins by showing an intruder hiding on the property. Cut to a bank of video monitors each showing a different camera view of the building. As the intruder moves to the front entrance, he is seen by multiple cameras. Every move he makes is on at least two monitors. The monitors have a motion detector that superimposes a yellow box on the intruder. The scene ends by printing a polaroid of the intruder's face.

This first scene lasts only 20 seconds, but in those 20 seconds the viewer fully understands the system's value. There's no narration over this scene, only music from the old *Mission Impossible* TV series. In 20 seconds we've shown the essential message; everything else in the video builds on it.

Another example of a scene that says it all is the closing scene from a video promoting a shelter for battered women. It begins with three short testimonials from women of obviously very different backgrounds. Each woman explains in emotional terms how the shelter protected her and her children from an abusive spouse. More importantly, they explain how far they've come in building independent lives. One was on welfare, but now has a job and is attending college.

The target audience for this video was mostly white middle class male executives. These politically and socially conservative people hold the corporate purse strings for community donations. They probably wouldn't be receptive to "women's libbers" preaching about the evils of men, but they might respond to the idea that domestic violence costs the business community, both in lost productivity and higher taxes.

The closing scene is of a policeman patrolling in his squad car. As he talks about it he is obviously sympathetic to the plight of battered women, but when he analyzes the costs to taxpayers of answering domestic violence complaints, he directly addresses the concerns of the target audience. This one scene summarizes the message of the video: supporting the shelter not only helps victims of domestic violence, but also saves tax dollars.

Look for testimonials that build your case. Think about customers who've complimented your business. What good things did they say about your business? Go ahead and put words in their mouths. They won't mind. At this point, they're just a figment of your imagination.

2nd PASS - THE REWRITE
Rewriting is the key to good scriptwriting. Keep thinking like your audience. Put yourself in their shoes. What do they want to see?

They won't be interested in everything you might want to say about your business. What's in it for them? Write scenes for your audience.

By now, you've got a stack of possible scenes. Give each the acid test—is your viewer interested? If not, move that scene to the reject pile. As you review your stack of selected scenes, add some details. Perhaps the background shows an important prop like a computer screen your audience would want to see. For a testimonial, superimpose a name, title and company that all your clients would recognize. Make notes about things you might want to explain with narration. You'll write a complete narration later, but the notes will give you a head start. Remember, narration cannot be used over a testimonial or other scene where someone's talking. When you have a handful of promising scenes, you'll need to bring some structure and sense to this disorderly collection.

Structure The Script

The script should tell a story. No matter how long or short it is, a good story feels complete. It has a beginning, a middle and an end. Each of these three elements has a purpose and a feel. The beginning may state a theme: Acme solves problems. You may see several brief examples of how Acme solves problems. The middle of the story develops the theme in more detail: Acme solves problems with a flexible formula of customer service. This middle section, or second act, is where many plays and business scripts get into trouble –it is often too long and convoluted. Try to keep it short and give your viewer what he or she wants to know.

Act III, the end, is where you tie it all together. You might restate your theme and bring the story full circle, back to where it started. If your story began with three short testimonials, you might end with different parts of the same three testimonials. These concluding testimonials should make a stronger impact than the first three. Viewers will recognize this as the end. Music swells and your logo, address and phone number fly in. Fade to black.

Even feature films usually have three acts. If you look for it, you'll be able to see where Act II ends and III begins. It's a turning point in the story. You'll know it when you see it even though there's no curtain to signal the act change.

Good stories flow naturally from one chapter or scene to the next. One way to accomplish this is to end a scene with an implied question. Begin the next scene by answering that question. In good films and music, you often know what's coming next. You've been led to expect something. When you've led the viewer to expect something, don't be coy— give it to him. "The unique design of the ACME 2000's retaining arm keeps the paper from jamming." How? *Show him* exactly how it does this. Don't save this detail for another time. Put it right there where it belongs.

Another way to structure your script is to think of it as an electronic brochure done with moving pictures and sound. Think about printed brochures you've seen. The ones you liked were probably very appealing graphically. For our purposes their editorial content is more important. They presented just a few simple ideas that were slanted to your needs and they were easy to digest (meaning they were short). Structure your video in the same way. Present a few simple ideas and briefly illustrate them.

Another print format to consider is the magazine story versus the newspaper story. The magazine story often starts in the middle of the action. It sucks you in and once you're hooked, it then explains how the story got to that point. The ending, like our three-act play, concludes with a bang, a thump, a climax.

Newspaper stories, on the other hand, are written in a top-down style. You get the most important information at the beginning. Every paragraph that follows is in order of descending importance. This style evolved so that the editor could chop off the last few paragraphs if that space were needed for something else. The reader wouldn't notice because those missing paragraphs didn't significantly change the story. The newspaper style is *not* appropriate for a marketing video. You want the big close of a magazine story. So the viewers will stand up and shout "I want my Acme Widget"!

Start moving your index cards or computer scenes around. Play with the order. What would make an attention-grabbing beginning? Is there a theme in that opening? Develop that theme in the middle section and restate it for a dramatic close. Tell a story.

Narration

After you've ordered the scenes so they tell a rough story, write narration that supports this story. The narration connects the visual ideas in a logical progression so each scene flows easily to the next. Some people prefer to write the narration first. If that seems easier, do it. Think of it as writing the narration for a story on audio cassette. Later you can plug in visuals to illustrate this oral story. Keep the narration short and directed to your audience.

You can also write narration one scene at a time. If the narration doesn't quite fit one scene, try moving it to another scene. Narration can help connect a scene to a theme of the video. Narration doesn't have to be the obvious description of what's on the screen: "Now you are seeing the door of the car." The viewer doesn't need that much help. Think about the commercials you studied. How did their narration relate to what was on the screen? Sometimes you'll hear the narrator talking about benefits that aren't directly related to the visuals on the screen, but the narration works anyway.

Write narration as if you were speaking to just one person, rather than how you think narration should be written. Write short simple sentences. Avoid run-on sentences which are continually modified by additional clauses. Read it aloud. Is it easy to read? If it's hard for you to read, it will be even harder for your narrator to read and harder yet for your audience to understand. Write narration that's easy to read and natural sounding. Just don't write too much of it! Let your visuals tell the story as much as possible.

THE THIRD PASS

Rewrite, rewrite, rewrite. By now you have a script. Chances are it's far too long. That's all right. Let's simplify and shorten it. If the viewer is not likely to be interested in a particular scene, eliminate it. You have to be ruthless. Yes, you say, but I really want to tell him about our XYZ process. Sorry, but that isn't good enough. Unless the process is interesting and has some benefit for the viewer, it doesn't belong in your video. If your audience will only sit still for a three-minute video, your video had better be only three minutes long.

Time yourself reading the narration and any testimonials or other speaking parts. Read it aloud at a comfortable easy pace. Let's say your script takes nine minutes to read. Add about 10% to this figure and you'll have the approximate running time for the video. One reason to add that 10% is to allow some extra space around the narration. Wall-to-wall narration which fills every second of the video is not especially pleasant or effective. We're not selling Ginsu knives like a late night screaming infomercial. Don't risk losing your audience.

Some scenes play well without any narration. Take a guess at how long these scenes will run and add that to the running time.

Revising the script is how you turn a mediocre script into a great one—one that accomplishes your goal. The time to stop revising is when you believe the script accomplishes that goal and is as good as you can make it.

SCRIPT MISCELLANY

All scripts go through revisions. To avoid confusion, put a date and version number on each new draft. You might label different versions with decimals to indicate that version 3.1, for instance, had only minor changes from 3.0, whereas version 4.0 had major changes.

Add scene numbers to your script so cameraman, actors, and editors can easily refer to different scenes. These scene numbers appear only in the script, not in the completed video. It can also be helpful to add a few important camera directions. For instance, indicate a close-up of an important detail, or a wide shot of a large area. Any more than this is not worth your time right now.

What about a title for your video? Many marketing videos don't need titles for the same reason that commercials don't need them. No one but the scriptwriter cares. However, a title that makes the viewer want to see your video may be worthwhile. It should be short, sweet and to the point.

Here are some examples of titles from actual marketing videos:
Smith Mining Equipment Presents: The Triple H Ground Drill
Zircar, The Solution People
Voices—A Vision of Pre-Parenting Education
New Horizon Resources—A Tradition Of Caring.

You may not even need a title. Many business videos use a title only on the CD ROM face or on the box. Others begin with an opening title sequence using only the company name. Here's an example:

Scene 1

Title Sequence (8 seconds): Fade up to LIVE SHOT OF THE PLANET EARTH. ACME LOGO SPINS OUT TO FILL THE SCREEN. Fade to black. Sound Effect: Sounds of swirling wind.

Stock Footage

This dramatic space footage is available for use in your video. It's called stock footage and it can do a lot for your video. It can fill a hole in your script and can make your company appear more important. It can save you the expense of filming a scene that's remote or difficult to do.

Since this NASA footage was bought and paid for by your tax dollars, NASA can't very well copyright it. You can purchase this shot and a lot of other great footage from NASA at very low cost. In fact, almost everything the U.S. Government has ever filmed can legally be used in your video for the modest price of the copy. You just have to know where to go. You'll find all of this information in the Appendix. See why I wanted your imagination to run wild?

In addition to low-cost government sources, commercial stock footage houses can provide almost any footage you can imagine. The three TV networks each have stock footage libraries which are also listed in the Appendix. Most anything you've ever seen on television news can probably be purchased for use in your video. But before you turn to the Appendix, there's some bad news.

Hang on to your hat because this footage often costs $20 a second! That's not a misprint. Ten seconds of stock footage will cost $200. Five minutes of stock footage costs $6000. PLUS you must pay to search the stock library, which in itself can be a considerable expense. Think about the thousands of hours of television that have been produced. And even when you find the right footage, you can't use the original footage. You must pay to have the footage copied.

Contrary to popular opinion, films and television that are produced entirely from stock footage are more expensive than those which don't use any. There is, however, an alternative to paying a stock footage house. Your business associates may have produced videos with footage you could use. For instance, does your company belong to an industry association? Is your agency a United Way agency? Some of your suppliers or customers may have their own videos.

Make a list of organizations that might have footage you're seeking. Locate their headquarters and ask to speak to the PR department. Tell them what you're doing—producing a promotional video. You're looking for a scene that depicts a certain subject and you wonder if they might have any video like that. Ask if you might use a short part of their video. They may ask you how long a shot or scene you need. Tell them 30 seconds at most. Of course, you won't be using their narration or music—you have your own. Tell them you'd be glad to pay for any duplicating expense. (Many times they won't even charge you for this, but expect to pay about $30.)

The PR person you speak to may need to check with his or her boss, but you will often get permission you seek. You might want to offer them a "Special Thanks" credit at the end of your video. In the case of NASA footage, consider a "Special Thanks to NASA," unless you'd rather not leave the impression that NASA does business with your company.

In the conversation with your new PR friend, make it clear that you will not state or imply that their company approves of your company. And don't. You may want their help again. It's a nice gesture to send them a copy of your video when it's completed.

If they don't have video or film footage, they may have photographs you could use. In any case, they'll probably ask for a letter on your stationery formally requesting one-time use of their footage, explaining the purpose of the video, and possibly absolving them from any liability. They may ask to see your script. Send it to them, but be clear that this script is still an early draft. Let your new friend tell you what to write in the letter.

Depending on how large the organization is, your next step may be to speak to their video librarian. Assuming you have a preliminary go-ahead from PR, describe to the librarian exactly what footage you're seeking. You've got to know what you're looking for. You can't expect them to randomly browse through their footage until you find something that might work in your video.

When the librarian suggests a few possible scenes or shots that may suit your needs, ask to see a copy on VHS or whatever format is easiest for them to make. If the copy they send works for the scene you have in mind, you will want to request that this same footage be copied to another format with higher resolution. Exactly which format you'll need is a topic for the next chapter. If you don't find video footage you can use, you may have to cut or revise the scene in question.

End Credits

The purpose of end credits is to acknowledge and thank people who have worked on a film. Many business videos, however, don't have credits at the end for the same reasons that commercials don't have credits. They would take too long and the viewer doesn't care.

Some end credits are appropriate. A "Special Thanks" credit to an organization that provided footage is a nice gesture. If that provider was a big name your viewers know and respect, that name may help your cause. One credit that should appear is your company name, address and phone. If you have a list of credits, you can roll them up the screen like you've seen in feature films, then simply fade to black.

Chapter 5

Producing The Script

A producer has ultimate authority and responsibility for making a successful film or video. The project begins and ends with the producer who acquires a script by hiring a scriptwriter, buying the rights to an existing script, or writing it. The producer then hires a director, actors, and technicians to film the story. The producer rents the camera equipment, locations and props to film all the scenes in the script. Most people and equipment are hired by the hour, day or week, so when they are on the clock, the producer is paying for their time. This on-the-clock time for people and equipment is the lion's share of the budget. When the producer is satisfied with what has been filmed, this army of people and trucks of rented equipment are sent home and taken off the clock.

Now, editing, the second phase of producing the script, begins. In larger productions the director is the one person who stays on the payroll through both phases. This director hires an editor and a roomful of editing equipment. The editor catalogs the thousands of different shots in the raw footage. Each shot is sorted into its respective scene number from the script.

This collection of shots and sound takes is then edited until it conveys the information and impact the script intended. Completed scenes are placed in order by scene number. Any additional elements—such as sound effects, music, narration, titles and special effects—are produced and then edited into the film.

The producer oversees and pays for each step of the process. If the producer is not satisfied with the results, he or she may decide to pay to rewrite, re-edit or reshoot any scenes that are weak. When satisfied with the results, the producer sends the director and editor home. The producer arranges for the distribution of the film in theaters, home video, the internet, and television and contracts for both American and international distribution. The producer accounts for all the money spent and, hopefully, for any profits made. These profits pay off any loans or partnerships which financed the film.

PRODUCING ON A LOW BUDGET

The total budget for your business video may be only a few thousand dollars rather than the millions needed for even a low budget feature film. Even so, you still need to follow most of the same steps of a feature film. You'll just have to do more of the work yourself.

We'll start by eliminating most of the technicians and artists. Instead of hiring people to find the props, cast actors, and scout locations, you can do most of these jobs yourself. The two people you must hire are a cameraman and an editor, both with equipment. Before you hire them, you'll need to become more familiar with video technology. If you're the non-technical sort, don't worry. I'll make this easy for you.

FORMATS

One of the producer's jobs is to decide which video format to use for filming and editing. This is an important choice that affects the budget and technical quality of your video. There are at least 25 different formats in use today. They can be broadly divided into two categories — film and video. The following are some of the more common formats listed roughly in order of quality and cost. Thanks go to Adam Wilt who has rated the video formats on a scale of 1 to 10.

FILM
35 millimeter
16 millimeter

VIDEOTAPE
D-5 (10-bit uncompressed digital) 10
D-1 (8-bit uncompressed digital) 9.9
Digital Betacam, Ampex DCT 9.7
D-9 (Digital-S), DVCPRO50 9.6
DV, DVCAM, DVCPRO (D-7) 9.2
MII, Betacam SP 9.1
D-3, D-2 (composite digital) 9
1" Type C 8.9
3/4" SP 6.5
3/4", Hi8, SVHS 5
Video 8, Betamax 4
VHS 3
EIAJ Type 1, Fisher-Price Pixelvision 1
Confused? Don't worry I'll simplify it all in a moment, really.
But first let me put this format alphabet soup into perspective for
you.

An Overview of the Film and Tape Formats.

35 mm film was, for decades, the format used to produce the feature films you see in movie theaters. It was and is also used for many
TV shows and commercials. Producing a script in 35 mm costs at
least $3000 per minute. **16mm** is a smaller size film that, at one time,
was the standard format for shooting TV magazine shows like *60
Minutes*, low budget features and most documentaries. This format
is quickly losing ground to video.

While the 16mm film format was declining in the 1980s, a video
format called **Betacam** (not to be confused with Betamax, the obsolete home format) was becoming the standard. It cost less than 16mm
film and was used to produce TV magazine shows, high-end corporate videos and many other . The Betacam cameras, when new, cost
approximately $30,000. The editing equipment is even more

expensive. The rule of thumb for producing in Betacam is that it should cost about $1000 per finished minute. If your video is intended for television, you'll want to see the discussion of "broadcast quality" in Chapter 11.

There are a few other formats you need to be aware of. They're not mentioned in the list above because they are not production formats, i.e. you cannot shoot in these formats. You can, however, distribute your videos in these formats. The first is VCD or Video Compact Disk. This is simply a CD with moving pictures and sound. A VCD can hold up to 80 minutes of full-motion video and stereo sound. At 352 by 240 pixels it's about the same resolution as VHS, but a lot less than either DV or DVD. They are both 720 x 480 pixels in NTSC which is the video standard used in America. A VCD can hold 650 to 700 MB. You can play a VCD on any computer CD ROM or DVD drive or on a stand-alone DVD player.

DVD is, of course, the format that is replacing VHS videotape. The DVD is an evolution which, like CDs and CD ROMS, provides interactive high capacity multimedia data storage on a disk. A DVD can accommodate a full-length movie at twice the resolution of VHS tape. For more information see the article entitled *DVD Primer* at *www.VideoUniversity.com/dvdprimr.htm*

Some more technical stuff you might want to know about:

Video Compression Schemes

Uncompressed video provides the highest quality, but is not commonly used because uncompressed video takes an inordinate amount of storage space and is too unwieldy for most computers. The DV format, which has become so popular throughout the industry, is compressed by a five to one ratio. This is a fixed rather than a variable compression rate.

Then there's MPEG-1 and MPEG-2. MPEG1 is compressed A LOT but it is good enough for CD ROMs and VCDs. MPEG2 is the high quality compression which is used for broadcast or DVDs. And now there's MPEG-4 which is the latest generation, intended for internet as well as digital devices like cell phones and PDAs.

High Definition and HDV

If you want to work in video or television, you must know that the FCC is requiring TV broadcasters to begin broadcasting digital TV. The larger markets are broadcasting digital TV right now. Many of them are also offering High Definition TV (HDTV) programming. Other American stations will be broadcasting HDTV soon. Digital television, whether it is Standard Definition (SDTV), Enhanced Definition (EDTV), or one of the HDTV formats looks a lot better than current analog television. The HDTV screen is a different shape as well. Standard televisions are 4 units wide by 3 units high, but HDTV is 16 units wide by 9 units high. This is a much w-i-d-e-r format, ideal for grand vistas like the Grand Canyon. Some people call it HDTV or even High Definition TV, but others just say High Def.

A new format has emerged called HDV which is a combination of "HD" and "DV". This format is a very clever way to get HD video onto DV tape. This may well be the format which replaces DV. You can learn more about this format at *www.videouniversity.com/hdv.com*

THE PRODUCING PROCESS

To better understand how these formats work, let's take a closer look at the producing process . All business videos will be released on one or more of the following home formats:VHS, Video Compact Disk, DVD; or one or more of the internet formats such as Windows Media, Real Player or Quick Time.

This final distribution format (the one your audience will watch) is not the same format you use to *produce* the video. Not long ago, choosing a format required a major tradeoff between cost and quality. Today, there are many good choices that provide high technical quality, and are cost-effective.

As Adam Wilt says "You won't find a better videotape format in terms of price/performance for standard-definition television than **DV** or its related formats **DVCAM** and **DVCPRO** and **Digital8**. Also, DV is the first broadcast-quality tape format that is small enough to accidentally fall into a cup of tea. Trust me on this; no need to try it yourself."

For an excellent article on understanding the DV formats, see Adam Wilt's article at *www.VideoUniversity.com/dvformat.htm*

These DV formats have revolutionized the industry and are found everywhere.

You can choose other formats such as Betacam SP or Digital Betacam. These fine formats may still be required by some clients and may be necessary in some situations, but the differences between these and the lower cost formats has shrunk dramatically. Betacam equipment is no longer being manufactured. It's a brave new world!

Before digital video became widespread, the biggest problem in video was generation loss. Take VHS as an example. You may remember, or even have, an old VHS camcorder. Some great things have been shot with VHS camcorders and these tapes can look just fine, but there's just one catch: If you edit that tape on a tape-to-tape editing system, you are copying parts of the *first* tape to a *second* tape. And when this editing is complete, you copy the *edited* tape to *another* tape which you can give away or sell in any quantity you like. The catch is that each time you copy a VHS tape, either in editing or in duplication, you introduce generation loss.

This generation loss can make your video look terrible. It's as if you took a Fax copy and made a copy of it and then made another copy from that copy. It starts to look pretty bad. The reason is that Fax technology is not digital. In video, the lower formats like VHS suffer significant degradation from this generation loss, while higher formats suffer very little, and the digital formats not at all.

That's why the affordable DV formats have created such a revolution in the video field. Generation loss can be largely avoided with the use of inexpensive digital cameras and editing systems. A professional-looking video does not have to cost as much as a car. Now, rather than worrying about how to afford a professional format, we can concentrate on the other elements like storytelling, casting, shooting, lighting and editing to make a professional-looking video.

While some people still use the "medium grade" formats like ¾ SP, Hi-8 and SVHS, there's no longer any reason to buy this equipment or use these formats unless your brother-in-law has a whole SVHS studio and will let you use it for free! The digital revolution has pretty much made those formats obsolete.

This is most of what you need to know about formats. To know more, just jump on our website at *www.VideoUniversity.com* You'll find many experts to guide you through this ever-changing technology.

THE VIDEO PRODUCTION BUSINESS

Before you start searching for a cameraman, take a quick look at how the video production business is organized. Producers can hire either a production company or individual freelancers. Freelance cameramen and editors often own equipment which they rent as a package deal along with their services. Production companies, on the other hand, can put together an entire production from script to screen, or just provide equipment and services la carte. Some production companies have producers and technicians on staff. Others hire freelancers when needed.

Now that inexpensive digital camcorders and home computers can produce broadcast quality video, there are lots of new producers and production companies. Every year the equipment gets better and cheaper. Today you can own all the equipment for a lot less than the cost of a new car. In the old days (and still true in Hollywood) producers did not own equipment. All they needed was a telephone and a typewriter. Today, it's a cell phone and a laptop, but the concept is still the same. The producer's job was to hire camera people, editors and equipment as needed.

There are good reasons for using this same approach today:

1. You don't have to make the investment in buying and maintaining equipment that might well become obsolete before it is fully amortized.

2. You can hire people on a per job basis who are more skilled in the individual crafts of shooting and editing video.

3. You can focus on the business of finding new clients, selling services to them and keeping them happy.

Producing a business video yourself does not necessarily mean you will do all the scriptwriting, shooting or editing, only that you will ensure that these tasks are completed on a specific schedule and budget. Some people can do it all themselves. Others hire freelancers to perform specific jobs.

Wherever you fit on the do-it-yourself scale from doing it all to hiring it all, you will need a minimum of a camera person or Director of Photography who has camera, tripod, batteries, microphones, headphones, a mixer, a monitor or small tv, lights with stands, extension cords, tape stock and lots of little things too numerous to mention. Some situations will require only minimal equipment. Sometimes available light and the onboard microphone may be just right, but it's rare when you can shoot an entire video without any lights or additional audio equipment.

After the shooting's done, you will need to edit that raw footage, add titles, music, narration. Today, this work is done entirely on a computer using a Nonlinear Edit program such as Final Cut Pro, Sony Vegas, or Adobe Premiere Pro .

To produce a low budget business video, most people will need to hire some outside help and/or rent additional equipment. You may find a production company that can supply it all or you might hire these people and rent equipment separately.

The freelancers who do this work may go by various titles like producer, cameraman/director, filmmaker, videographer, or production company. The person you hire may use any or all of these titles; the title is not as important as the skills he or she possesses.

HIRING A PROFESSIONAL CAMERAPERSON

Before you run out and buy that that nifty camcorder you've been eyeing, stop and think for a moment. You've probably seen business videos that look like home movies – they were probably filmed by amateurs. Your camera skills may very well be appropriate for an in-house training video. Potential customers will not see these videos so there's little risk of harming your corporate image.

To produce a professional-looking promotional video, you need a professional cameraman, one who makes a living filming other people's videos!

If you're disappointed that you won't be shooting your video, take heart. You will be learning a lot about about the entire process when you hire and direct a professional. Unlike a feature film producer, you won't be hiring a separate director. The cameraman and you will share that job. The person you hire must be able to offer you three things:

1. **Experience** in shooting and directing promotional videos. You will, of course, want to see some of these other promotional videos.

2. **Equipment.** Ideally, the cameraman will own the right kind of camera, lights, tripod and microphones to shoot your script. Some freelancers rent this equipment as needed.

3. **Attitude.** You need to hire someone whose professional attitude is dedicated to helping you produce an effective video on a budget.

Choosing the right Director of Photography or cameraman is important. Unlike the feature film producer, you're on a very tight budget. You can't afford the luxury of re-shooting scenes; the production of your video must typically be completed in one or two shooting days.

How well your cameraman films a particular scene will determine not only how appealing the images of that scene will be, but also how expensive and successful the editing will be.

When filming a scene, a professional takes a variety of different shots to give the editor several editing options. Two of these are shots called *cutaways* and *inserts*. With these the editor can, for example, cut the scene to run longer or shorter. Without these special shots, the editor may have only one option for editing a scene instead of several. A professional *always* shoots cutaways and inserts. We'll fully explore cutaways and inserts in the chapters on shooting and editing.

If your cameraman doesn't notice an accidental microphone in the shot or a defect in a prop, you may be stuck with using that mistake in the final version of your video. If the lighting or composition are off, the final scene may not be as powerful and polished as you envisioned. His or her skills, or lack of skills, with hundreds of details can spell the difference between a video that looks like a home movie and one that looks like a big time commercial. With a good script and good footage, almost any editor can make a good video. Without both, it's more difficult (and usually more expensive).

Hiring a good freelance cameraman is something like buying a good house. Smart shoppers look at a lot of houses before they buy. The search is an education in itself. The more houses you see, the more you understand the market and the relative value of different houses. You learn more about the business of buying and are more likely to make a good deal that will stand the test of time.

In this video age where many home computers come ready to edit video, you'll find hundreds of hobbyists and semi-pros who would love to produce your script for little or no money. Your wisest option is to choose from the hundreds of cameramen, directors and editors who make their living producing corporate video, network television, documentaries and more. Within this pool of talent you'll find men and women with a wide variety of skills, prices and personalities. With so many to choose from, you are in a buyer's market. There's no reason to hire the first person who seems qualified. Take your time and interview carefully until you have at least two good candidates.

WHERE TO FIND FREELANCERS

You can find a cameraman with the right experience, equipment and attitude in five primary sources:

1. The Sunday newspapers
2. Local corporations with video departments
3. Local TV stations
4. The Yellow Pages, Chambers of Commerce or local internet listings
5. Word of mouth.

The Sunday newspapers

The Sunday newspapers have an advertising section devoted to wedding services where you'll find wedding photographers, many offering video as a sideline. Others specialize only in wedding videos. Many of these people own all the digital camera and editing gear needed to produce a complete video. Their package prices start as low as a few hundred dollars.

There is, however, a catch. While today's wedding videos are very artistic, they still follow the somewhat predictable events of a wedding. These event videos are not scripted and typically run for an hour or so. The audience will watch such a long video because they like to see themselves, family and friends at what is, hopefully, a once in a lifetime event.

This is quite different from your business video which must convey a few simple ideas or feelings to an audience that is not nearly as receptive. Producing long videos by formula doesn't necessarily eliminate these producers from contention, but their skills may not match your needs. You may find some wedding videographers who do weddings only as a sideline. Their primary business is corporate videos, freelance camera work for TV, or other areas of video production. People with these backgrounds can be ideal candidates.

Even if you don't find people with the right experience from this group, local wedding videographers can be a valuable resource for renting equipment or editing time.

Corporate Video Departments

Business video is becoming so widespread that many corporations have audio/visual departments complete with video personnel and equipment. The larger ones have separate video departments. Some of these corporate studios rival TV networks in the quantity and quality of original programming they produce.

Many of these corporate video departments sell their services to outside clients. You may also find individuals who moonlight. One caution in working with corporate moonlighters is to make sure the individual is using the facility and equipment with his or her employer's approval. A call to your local Chamber of Commerce is a good starting point to find these corporations.

TV Stations

Local cable or small TV stations may actively seek your business. While their primary productions are commercials, local sports and news shows, and talk shows, many of these stations offer production services to outside producers. Watching their shows and commercials will give you a sense of the overall quality of their productions. Don't be misled by the subject or content of a show; look instead at the underlying quality of production.

Since your video will probably be shot on location at your place of business, you'll want to look at other productions the station filmed on location. Those produced entirely in their studio—whether they are computer graphics or talk shows—will not help you evaluate what a director or camera person can do for you on location.

If you see a commercial or show that is particularly well made, call the station and ask who produced it. Ask if the station provides production services to outside producers and if they produce business videos. The staff may also include producers who freelance their services outside the station.

The Yellow Pages

Directories of local businesses such as the Yellow Pages, Chamber of Commerce listing or internet listings may be another good source of freelance cameramen or producers. Look under the classification, "Video Production Services." The number of companies listed in this category grows every year. This is good news for your production, but you still must be discriminating. Remember, you're looking for a skilled person, as opposed to a company that merely rents camera equipment or editing facilities. Don't hire a company that dazzles you with their impressive equipment and editing rooms. Your most important task at this point is to hire the right *person*. The equipment is still secondary.

Word of Mouth

Ask for recommendations from other businesses or non-profits which have produced marketing videos. Take a look at their videos and tactfully ask about their budgets. Ask if the person or company they hired was helpful and easy to work with. Ask what they would do differently the next time.

One source of talent you may be inclined to pursue is ad agencies. There are two reasons not to do so. The first is that producing your video through an ad agency will cost more because they will markup the budget. The second is that small ad agencies are generally more experienced with print media than they are with video. Although they may show you videos they've "produced," in most cases they subcontracted a producer to do the actual production work. You may, however, find talented script writers within ad agencies. If you consider using one to help with your script, make sure the writer has written more than just narration scripts which, as you've seen, are only half of a video script.

Let's review for a moment the ideal candidate for the professional partner in your production. He or she is a cameraman/director who owns their own camera equipment, has a helpful attitude and has filmed several effective marketing videos. Some of the individuals you interview may be multi-skilled: scriptwriter, shooter, and editor who owns editing equipment. These additional skills and equipment are all to your benefit, but they are not essential.

VISIT YOUR CANDIDATES IN THEIR BUSINESS

It's wise to visit prospective cameraman/directors in their offices rather than yours. You will learn more about them. Although you may be eager to show them your business and talk about how it could be filmed, that is premature. The important thing right now is to hire the right person.

Some may operate out of offices in their homes; others will have separate business locations. When visiting any production company, there's a natural tendency to be overly impressed with the equipment. A giant Hi Def Flat Screen TV and lot of video gear can be dazzling, no question about it. This is one reason to visit several production companies. Don't hire the first company you meet just because you see an impressive looking editing system.

Remember you're hiring a *person*; equipment and office are secondary. Collect résumés from several potential candidates and be sure to ask for references. An ideal reference would be a small business like yours that hired this person to produce their first corporate video on a small budget. These references can help you make a smart choice, but it's surprising how many people don't contact references. Perhaps they assume that a reference wouldn't be offered unless it were a glowing testimonial. That's no excuse for not checking them.

THE SAMPLE REEL

Another tool to help you choose the right person is called the sample reel. This is like an artist's portfolio; the difference is it's on video. A sample reel is a marketing tool designed to impress you. Typically, it will contain excerpts from several different productions. Viewing several sample reels will help you select the right candidate.

One of the most important questions to ask is exactly what role the person played in each production. Although most freelancers are honest, a few unscrupulous ones may show you videos they've "produced" when, in fact, they have misrepresented or exaggerated their role in the production.

Ideally, you'll see videos that were produced, directed, shot and edited by your candidate. You may see sample reels with excerpts from network TV or even feature films. Be a bit wary here. Your candidate's role in these productions is the question. If he was a production assistant on a major feature film, that could mean that he managed crowd control by keeping onlookers out of the shot. That's a perfectly honorable role. Many great directors and technicians began their careers as production assistants. But such a person is probably not yet ready to help produce your video.

Two other things to evaluate in viewing sample reels are *photography* and *editing*. There is a saying among freelance cameramen, also called shooters, that reputations are made by handheld shooting, but these same reputations are kept by shooting on a tripod. Most home movies are made by handholding the camera which usually results in shots that are shaky and difficult to watch. Shots made on a steady tripod are easier on the eye and less likely to cause seasickness among viewers.

Professionals know how to minimize the shakiness of handheld camera shots. They also know when a handheld camera will help a production and when it will detract. The vast majority of shots are better made with the camera on a tripod. Professionals forego the fun of handholding the camera for the sake of a better looking film.

You can often tell if a shot was made on a tripod or handheld by carefully watching the edge of the frame. Irregular movement at the edges of the frame is usually a sign of a handheld shot. Marketing videos should display little, if any, handheld shooting. Shaky handholding distracts the viewer from the message of the video. You'll learn more about handholding the camera in the chapter on shooting.

Lighting is another element of photography to watch for in sample reels. This is more difficult to evaluate unless you have some experience with lighting for photography. A film that is made without lighting equipment is said to be made with available light. This is the light that already exists in the room or setting where the scene is filmed.

One simple way to tell if lights were used in filming is to look at the close-up shots of people. Lights cast shadows and if you look closely at a close-up of a face that's been lit, you will probably seen a soft shadow from the nose or the chin. One side of the face may be slightly brighter than the other side. The subject's hair may have a glow around the outline. And finally, if you look closely at the eyes, you may notice a tiny highlight in the eyeball which is a reflection of the light itself. If you see none of these clues, the shot was probably not lit with anything more than the available light in the room. It's easier to study lighting by turning off the sound.

Good lighting can make an uninteresting scene look dramatic. In photography, lighting is one of the telltale skills that separates talent from mediocrity. Some shooters excel in using only the existing or available light to make pleasing pictures. But it is rare that an effective marketing film will use no lights at all. Lighting, like the other components of photography, either contributes to the effectiveness of the video, or it detracts. If it makes the viewer feel good about the product, service or company, it works.

The editing of a sample video is also difficult to evaluate without previous experience in editing. But I'll make it easy for you. *Good editing should be invisible to the viewer.* If it stands out so that you're aware of the editing, it is probably not good editing. If you notice your attention wandering during any part of the film, you're probably watching a scene that's too long. Producers and editors try very hard to keep the viewer glued to the screen.

A sponsored production is one where someone besides the producer paid the bills. These productions are a partnership between the producer and the sponsor. Like all partnerships, sponsored videos involve compromises. The producer was not free to make the video he or she wanted. The objective was to satisfy the client. The client may have insisted that this marketing video had to be 25 minutes long and tell the viewer everything about the product or service, despite the producer's advice that a shorter video would be better.

When you view sponsored videos, ask about the client's role. You probably won't have to ask twice. Many producers of sponsored videos will not hesitate to explain how the video could have been better. Often they're right. But right or wrong, the client made the ultimate decisions. They did, after all, pay the bills. Your job is to judge the video, not the client. Is the video effective? Put yourself in the shoes of the target audience. What do you think?

A producer who wants your business will show you only the best excerpts from his productions. This is smart marketing and you'll be doing the same when you produce your video. You may, however want to see an entire video rather than just the best excerpts. If you request to see the entire video, you may encounter some resistance from the producer. If so, say you understand the compromises involved in sponsored videos.

If your candidate's video isn't just like the one you envision producing, don't let this prevent you from hiring a skilled person. A good marketing video is a good marketing video whether the subject is bagels or computer software. It's more important to ask if the video achieved its goal. Did it come in on budget? Has it helped the client's business? Rather than judge a producer on whether he or she produced exactly the video you envision, judge the filmmaking and marketing skills. Has this person produced a variety of videos in different industries? Since you may not be the target audience of any of these videos, try to imagine the concerns and interests of these audiences. Does the video address their needs?

We could continue dissecting sample videos, but we'll stop here. Your viewers will not study your video; in fact, they probably won't watch it more than once. Their conclusions will be drawn from their first impression. Similarly, your first impression of a video is also the most valid one. Trust your instincts. As in taking a test, your first answer is probably the best.

Ask about the budgets of the videos you see. The same script could be produced in different formats for different budgets. Instead of using an expensive format, professional actors and a sound stage, the same script could be produced in a less expensive format using "real people" in a borrowed office. With a big enough budget, it's fairly easy to produce a credible marketing video. The real test is what one can do with a small budget.

The cameraman's job is to help you achieve the highest production value at the lowest cost. That person's attitude and willingness to help you are the keys to achieving your goal. To do this, you'll need to go over the visuals of the script together. For this, the narration is not as important as the visuals: How quickly and easily these visuals can be photographed will directly affect your budget.

CAMERA EQUIPMENT

To film your script the camera person will need a camera, tripod, lights and microphones. Older video cameras used tubes for acquiring images; today they use computer chips. The camera used for your video should be a three-chip camera that can record in the format you choose. Most home camcorders have only one chip and should not be used for shooting your video.

Fluid head tripods are the professional's choice because they make smoother camera moves than the friction head tripods used by amateurs. A lighting kit with at least three or four lights will also be needed. This lighting kit will also contain extension cords and various hardware to bounce, deflect or soften the light. To record sound, there should be two types of microphones: lavaliere mikes which can be clipped on people's clothing, and shotgun mikes which are hand-held and can be quickly pointed to a sound source.

The Director of Photography or cameraman should supply all the production equipment as well as any other personnel, usually a production assistant and/or a separate audio person. The people and equipment he brings to the job are *his* responsibility. You are contracting his services as a package deal as you will see in the discussion on budgets later in this chapter.

PLANNING TO EDIT

When you choose a cameraman and a format, you need to plan for editing. If your cameraman owns editing equipment, you may not have to search any further. If not, he may suggest an editor or editing service. But first, you need an overview of the editing process.

Editing begins by making a list of all the shots on your tapes. This is called a Tape Log. You can't edit your source tapes until you know what you have. You need to know where each shot starts and stops as well as a description of what the shot is and how good it is. Without this log, you'd waste a lot of time trying to find shots and deciding what to do with them. And you'd never remember all the shots a month later. So, make a log of all the shots on all of your tapes. This can be done on paper which is both cheap and simple, or the log can be made electronically with a non-linear editing system which we'll explore later in the chapters on editing.

The window dub has a unique address of hours, minutes, seconds and frames

A vital tool in both logging and editing is a numbering system called *time code*. Think of time code as a street address to every single shot and location on your video tape. This time code never changes so anytime you want to get back to the exact place on the tape where that falling tree is just about to touch the earth, you can simply shuttle the tape to 03:21:02:12 and you are there. Time code may look like the tape counters on VCRs; however, it is quite different. The numbers you see on tape counters found in VCRs do not relate to a particular place in the tape. Since these tape counters can be reset at any time, they are not our friends, unlike time code which definitely is.

Tape Log & Cue

Page____ 8

Client:_____

Production:_"_The Boating Life"_

☑ SMPTE Code   ☐ Footage Counter   ☑ Scene Log   ☐ Edit Log

Scene	Title	Hours	Mins.	Sec.	Frames	Description	Rating
		04	02	02	−	B Roll — Wooden sailing ship in harbor	good
		04	03	10	−	Interview Captain Johnson	OK
		04	24	07	−		
		04	32	12	−	Interview 1st Mate while she is	V good
		04	47	21	−	Splicing line	

The log is a directory to help you locate every shot.

With the log of footage and the corresponding time codes, you could make a preliminary paper edit simply by writing the beginning and ending time code numbers of the best shots, as illustrated on the next page.

Tape Log & Cue

Page____1____

Client:_____

Production:____"The Boating Life"_____

☑ SMPTE Code   ☐ Footage Counter   ☐ Scene Log   ☑ Edit Log

Scene	Take	Hours	Min.	Sec.	Frames	Description	Rating
1		04	36	28	09	Interview 1st mate	
		04	39	12	01	begin " This boat has a lot of history..." end "... I love working here."	
1		04	02	02	11	B Roll of ship in harbor	
		04	02	04	14		
		04	39	17	28	Interview continues begin " We became a family..." end "...the ship saves our lives so she comes first."	

The paper edit is an inexpensive way to begin editing.

Let's say you've filmed 90 minutes of video to cover every scene in the script. Thorough planning puts you ahead of schedule so you had time to film an extra scene or two that supported the theme of the video. Some of these extras may be better than scenes you've scripted. The raw footage can now be edited (following your script) in as many different ways as there are editors. A clever editor will highlight the strong material and minimize or eliminate the weak. The editor can make or break your video.

Interview editors in the same way as cameramen by looking at sample reels, asking questions about their editing experience and collecting résumés. Since the editor's work is more invisible than the cameraman's, you may learn more about their skills by asking leading questions, like how they "saved" a difficult scene or improved the structure of a video. This is one way to begin a useful dialogue with a potential editor.

There are two distinct kinds of editing skills. One way or another they are both required for editing: the technical and the creative. Unless you have the technical skills to operate the editing system and make the edits you want, your creative skills will be stifled. The technical skills require competence in the use of a computer system which is configured or dedicated for video editing. At the very least the editor needs to be proficient in the use of an editing program such as Avid, Adobe Premiere Pro, Final Cut Pro, or Sony Vegas. The creative editing skills are about visual storytelling. On a basic level this may mean the editor knows various ways to put shots together to make a scene that tells a story and has an impact on the viewer. This is a fun part of film and video making and we'll spend some time exploring it.

Whether you decide to do a lot of the hands-on editing yourself or have your editor do most of it, choose an experienced editor who enjoys his work. Such a person is more likely to be a good partner who will help you improve your video. You'll be spending a lot of time together so the chemistry between you is an important part of producing your video.

BUDGETS

There are three parts to a video budget: *pre-production, production* and *post-production*. Pre-production covers all expenses up to the first day of shooting. Production covers everything you spend during the shooting. And post-production, often called *post* for short, covers all expenses incurred during the editing process.

Pre-Production

The script is usually the largest expense in pre-production. Other items include such things as location scouting and casting. If you're willing to roll up your sleeves, you can do the pre-production work yourself at little or no cost.

Production Budget

Most freelance camera people charge by the day; some will charge for a half day and others by the hour. Their rates, including camera equipment and personnel, will vary from $400 to more than $1000 a day. By studying your script, the cameraman should give you an estimate of how many shooting days it will take to film. Be sure to ask if there will be any additional expenses beyond the daily rate. These expenses may include transportation to the location, lunch for the crew, tape stock, and in some cases, additional equipment rentals.

After you've interviewed several candidates and decided upon one, sit down with this person and discuss the script and locations in more detail. This way you'll know what, if any, additional expenses may arise.

Insurance

Insurance is an unpleasant topic in video production because it's expensive. Some cameramen and production companies have insurance policies to cover liability or property damage during the shoot. If they do, their daily rate will reflect this expense. If not, the locations where you film may have insurance which would cover any accidents. You can sometimes buy a rider for an existing policy. I can't advise you, but I can report that many low budget videos are produced without insurance coverage. Insurance is an issue only during production because few dangerous accidents occur in the editing room.

Post-Production Budget

Hourly rates for editors with their own editing systems can range from $30 to $100 an hour, so shop around. A five to ten minute video that has been carefully scripted and photographed could take as few as 15 hours or as many as 50 hours to edit. Most of this time will be spent editing your footage, but there's more to post production than simply editing the raw footage. During this time you can also record and edit a "scratch narration" (a preliminary narration made by the editor or producer just to test timing), produce all titles and graphics, and finally, choose and edit music into the program.

If you have several hours of interviews or testimonials on tape, you may not want to pay your editor to sit with you and sift through it all. Instead, you could ask your editor to make you VHS or CD ROM copies from the original tapes. The only catch with this is that you'll need to see the time code or you'd waste a lot of time trying to find a particular place in the tape. The solution is called a *window dub*. Your editor should be able to make these tapes for you. If not, ask who could. The VHS Window dub is just a plain old VHS tape that can play in any VCR. What makes it different is that the time code from the original tape is permanently "burned" inside the picture area. (I'm using the word *burned* figuratively, of course, in the same way we "burn" CDs. None of the equipment should get very hot!) Anyway, as you're watching this VHS or CD ROM Window dub from the comfort of your couch, you note the best shots and sound bytes from the hours of interviews. When the interviewee says something interesting, note the beginning and ending time code numbers. Then, all you do is bring those numbers to your editor who can then edit the actual clips. See, editing isn't so bad!

You might want to take this a step further and try doing what some producers do on their way back from a shoot: They log and cut (edit) the show on paper by viewing tapes on a portable VCR or a laptop.

Estimating editing cost is a question of estimating the time involved. Assuming there are no animations or other computer- generated special effects to create, the editing of a typical eight minute marketing video can usually be completed in about 40 hours to 60 hours, including titles, recording narration, choosing music, etc. If your editor has quoted you a rate of $75/hour, you can expect to pay $3000 to $4500 in editing fees.

There are a few other items in the post production budget your editor can help with. For instance, your editor may be able to recommend a professional narrator. These performers can cost as little as $75 for a session. Recording narration can be done in any quiet room. It is not necessary to rent a sound booth. Music rights are usually supplied by the editor from his or her library of music. If your editor does not have a library of royalty-free music, he or she can suggest places to find it. Fees for using music can vary from zero, if the editor supplies music, to perhaps $100 if you need to use an outside music library.

You'll be spending a lot more time on each of these steps in later chapters, but now you've seen an overview of the essential steps to produce an effective video on a shoestring budget. Let's review the steps of an ideal situation.

You have completed your script. After diligently interviewing candidates and viewing many sample videos, you've hired a director/shooter/editor who owns a complete camera package and editing system. This person has agreed to the following deal:

1. She'll give you four hours of script consultations, including scouting the most important locations, finding props, and casting actors. During this time she'll make suggestions to improve the script and save production costs.

2. Together you plan the shooting day. She'll provide all the necessary equipment, supplies and personnel (often just one other person) for one day of filming at your business or other location.

3. If, after the filming is complete, there is a lot of interview footage, she (or a separate editor) will make VHS or CD ROM Window dub copies of the original footage.

4. You then watch these in your home and make a log of the best takes, noting the visible time code numbers. You write a paper edit which lists the best shots for every scene.

5. You work with your editor, who has agreed to give you a complete first rough cut within 30 hours of editing session time.

6. You take home a copy of this first rough cut to compare it to the script and to get feedback from a few friends whose opinions you trust.

7. A few days later, you return for another editing session with a list of things you'd like to improve or change.

8. This process continues over the next couple weeks until both you and your editor agree that you have an effective video that will accomplish your goals. During this time your editor has created all the titles and graphics, recorded and edited both the music and a scratch narration. The narration script has been rewritten as needed.

9. After listening to sample tapes from different professional narrators, you hire a narrator and record his or her final narration in the editing room.

10. Your editor performs the final video and audio edit. She makes a DV master as well as a backup master also in DV.

11.She makes a few video copies for your immediate use. She encodes the video for streaming and uploads it to your web site.

12. You take the seven and a half minute DV backup master to a reputable duplicator and order 35 DVD copies for $4.00 each and a

few additional VHS copies. They are delivered in one week. Meanwhile, you prepare a cover letter and mailing labels to send to a list of your most immediate prospects. When the videos arrive, you send them out. One week later, a prospect calls: "I just saw your video and I'd like to talk to you..."

AVOIDING MISUNDERSTANDINGS

Once you have narrowed the search for cameraman/director, down to one or two candidates, one problem may arise: the dividing line between a free consultation and an on-the-clock billable session. During a free consultation you are legitimately evaluating a persons's skills and ideas. On the other side of this line, he or she is working for you at an hourly or daily rate. This dividing line can easily become a problematic grey area.

This happens because *your* inclination is to pick his brain and get as much free advice as possible. *His* inclination is to get the job by proving how helpful he is. Gradually, he will feel that he is *working* for you. You, however, may feel that he is still *interviewing* for the job.

Avoid this situation. It can create bad feelings which will hurt your video and your budget. I know of one freelancer who took a client to small claims court on exactly this issue. Both parties probably shared some of the blame. The issue won't apply to your first interview with a freelancer, but on a second or third meeting with the same person, the potential for misunderstanding grows. Be clear from the outset about what is billable time and what is not and you will steer clear of this counterproductive situation.

The Letter Of Agreement

If this is a deal worth making, it's worth committing to paper. Here's the first page of a sample agreement that clarifies responsibilities, money and other issues:

Page 1
Video Production Agreement

Date:_____

Client:_____
Title:_____
Company:_____
Address:_____

Dear_____:

When signed by you and us, the following will constitute our agreement:

Acme Productions agrees to produce___1____ video(s) for your use. This video will have a running time of less than __8_____ minutes. We will provide the following services for this production:

__10____ hours of scripting & preproduction planning services. Your active participation in this process will help create an approved script that will be a blueprint for the filming and editing of your video. Additional scripting services are available at $60/hour subject to your prior approval. Changes to the approved script after filming begins will incur additional charges.

__1___ Day(s) of location filming based upon the approved script. We will produce this video in the DV format and will supply all necessary equipment and personnel. Additional filming days are available at the rate of $850/day.

We will provide a maximum of____40 hours____of post production to include all digital editing, professional narrator, text & graphics and music according to our approved script. Additional post production time is available at $60/hr. Your active involvement in the editing process will ensure that we produce an effective video on the budget that follows.

The bottom line is that the more people you interview, the more likely you are to hire the best. This process may take several weeks, but it's a good investment of your time. Ask their advice and listen carefully. Along the way you'll meet some interesting people, see a wide variety of videos and learn a lot.

GAFFERS, GRIPS AND OTHERS

You may be interested to learn what some of the people in those long credit rolls of feature films actually do. On a low budget production, all of these jobs must be performed by the cameraman and one or two helpers.

The *Director of Photography*, or D.P, as he or she is called, is responsible for the photography of every shot. The D.P. creates the look of a film or video through lighting, camera lenses and angles, moving dolly shots and much more. This photographer supervises a small army, the camera crew. This crew includes the *Camera Operator* who does the actual shooting and keeps shots properly framed and in focus. Two *Assistant Cameramen* change film and lenses and help the Operator.

The *Gaffer* is the technician who places, rigs and adjusts all the lights for the Director of Photography. *Grips* are technicians who handle, set-up and strike (take down and pack away) the equipment needed to photograph each shot.The *Key Grip* is in charge of this crew and works for the Director of Photography. A *Dolly Grip* pushes the camera on a dolly for those shots where the camera moves.

The *Continuity Director* or *Script Person* is the liaison between the editing room and the actual filming. His or her job is to ensure that the editor has all the individual shots needed to edit the scene.

The *Soundman* records sound at the location. Narration, music and sound effects are recorded later during editing.

In a low budget production, all of these jobs are performed by one or two people.

Chapter 6

Preproduction Planning
How To Beat Murphy's Law Most of the Time

THE NEED FOR PLANNING

A scene that appears on the screen for just one minute can easily take several hours to film. If a day of filming costs $700, efficient production planning clearly has a major impact on your budget. *When*, not *if*, things go wrong, your production budget can easily double, because you might have to bring the camera crew back for another day of shooting. Careful planning should help you shoot your video in one day.

Murphy's Law works overtime in video production. If something can go wrong, it will. Your only defense is planning. Planning will help you anticipate potential problems and solve them before that big day when your script is transformed into videotape.

Planning the logistics of shooting, i.e. getting all the people, equipment and props in the right place at the right time, is half the battle. To do this you'll have to work closely with your cameraman. Begin by going through the script together. Make a copy of the script and start making notes for each scene. This production copy is the place to list people, props, locations, and all the details you need to efficiently produce every scene.

The script is a blueprint that will help you and your cameraman work together. Make sure he or she reads and understands it. This includes knowing what shots to make and how to make them. Together, you should see the all places, people and props you will be photographing. Review how each scene supports the video's goal and addresses your audience. Ask for suggestions to make the message clear and compelling. Involving him or her at this level of filmmaking will encourage creativity and create a basis for a rich partnership between the two of you.

The most efficient way to film your scenes is probably not in the same order as they appear in the script. You want to minimize the number of moves the camera crew and equipment must make. If the people and equipment needed for Scene Two are in the room next to the one where you will film Scene Four, it is more efficient to film Scene Two and then film Scene Four. Scene Three can be filmed when you are closer to it.

If you and your film crew must travel 10 miles just to film one 30-second scene, see if you can bring the subjects of that scene closer to where your crew is filming most of the video. The fewer moves the camera crew makes, the more time they'll have for filming. If one scene is the most important scene in your video—the central idea—I find that it's best *not* to film that scene first. Let your team warm up a bit by filming a less important or simpler scene first.

LOCATION SCOUTING

The first step in the ideal scenario of Chapter 5 was script consultation and location scouting with your cameraman/director. Paying for his or her time to visit the locations with you is a good investment. This will help you determine what must be done to film each scene successfully and get the best out of each location. But the biggest reason to visit the sites is to discover and solve the inevitable problems inherent in any site.

Available Light

One of the first things your cameraman will need to know about each site is how it can be lit. If the site is already well lit with artificial lights, windows or skylights, the site may be OK with just a little additional lighting. However, "available light" can introduce its own problems:

During your location scout, you may notice a very pretty effect of sunlight coming through a window. Don't count on it being there when you return to film. Or, let's say that you're filming an important testimonial with a client. Behind the client is a wall of paintings and plants. Direct sunlight from a window creates a beautiful pattern of light and shadow on the background. While you're shooting the interview, black rain clouds suddenly obliterate the beautiful background lighting.

Later, during editing, you want to take a piece of the interview from the beginning and a piece from the end. When cut together, these two shots will look very different because the light on the background changed. This is a continuity mistake. The viewer's eye will go straight to this different-looking background, diverting his attention from the message of the testimonial and diminishing the effect of your video. To avoid this problem, many D.P.'s and cameramen cover windows or skylights and then recreate that lighting pattern with artificial lights. Now, no matter what happens with the weather, the lighting will be consistent.

On the other hand, a large factory with many skylights can actually make filming easier and cheaper, since skylights usually admit a diffused kind of light that brings up the overall illumination level of the scene. This ambient light helps you make that wide shot as written in the script without having to use 20 lights. You'll probably still be using some movie lights, but the lighting job is much simpler.

Electricity

Many scenes will require two, three or more movie lights. To simplify the math let's say each light uses 1000 watts of electricity. That's about the same as a hair dryer. Most home or office outlet circuits are rated for 15 or 20 amps. Each 1000 watts takes 8.3 amps. So a 20 amp circuit can safely handle two 1000 watt lights. (8.3 amps times 2, equals 16.6 amps.) A 15 amp circuit could only handle one 1000 watt light.

If each outlet were wired on its own circuit, you could safely plug one or two 1000 watt lights into each outlet, but this is rarely the case. Usually there are a number of outlets on each circuit. Knowing which outlets are on the same circuit helps you know where you can safely plug the lights.

Say you need four 1000 watt lights in one room that has only one 15 amp circuit. You can't plug them all into the outlets in that room —you would blow a fuse or even start a fire. Production grinds to a halt. A professional cameraman avoids overloading circuits by running heavy-duty extension cords to other circuits in other rooms.

When filming in a large plant or factory, introduce your cameraman to the house electrician, who can provide valuable information, such as how many watts each circuit can handle and the location of outlets, the fuse box or circuit breaker.

Other important points to remember: Movie lights generate heat. If placed too close to a ceiling sprinkler head, they might trigger flooding of the room. In a factory with dangerous chemicals or fumes, lights can create the danger of an explosion. Make sure the plant manager and the cameraman discuss any such potential problems. Explosions during filming can wreak havoc on your budget!

Sound

Sound is another production problem to investigate during your location scouting. If you are recording live sound that's important to a scene, perhaps an interview, make sure you're filming in a quiet area. It's easy to overestimate how quiet an area is, because we're used to ignoring much of what we hear. Take a moment and close your eyes. Listen carefully to all the different sounds you hear. You may hear birds chirping, a computer fan or a truck in the distance. Imagine turning the volume up. If you were recording an interview, these magnified sounds would be permanently recorded along with the interview.

The cameraman (or sound person, if you have one) must eliminate or minimize extraneous sounds so he or she can record a clean sound track. A location right under the final approach of La Guardia Airport will not be a good place to record clean sound. You'll continually have to stop for the roar of airplane engines. (The US Open Tennis matches are held there and the noise used to be so bad that TV announcers would stop talking, look up at the airplanes and resume only when the plane had passed. After years of this, the flight rules were finally changed.) The same problem can occur if you record during rush hour traffic. The noise from rush hour traffic can make sound recording difficult or impossible.

A more subtle sound problem is central heating or air conditioning systems in office buildings. You may not notice it during normal conversation until you stop and listen for it. Microphones will record this noise and you'll be surprised how loud it will seem on your sound track.

During your location scout, see if the system can be temporarily turned off. You can, of course, turn it on between camera takes. In some office buildings, these heating and cooling systems cannot be turned off. If this is the case, you'll have to go to plan B: cover the vents to minimize the noise. The easiest way to do this is to tape cardboard or posterboard over the vents.

Refrigerators and soft drink machines create even more subtle sound problems. They run intermittently and have a tendency to turn on automatically just when you're recording the most important sound bite. The solution is simple — unplug the offending machine, but please put a sign on the refrigerator reminding yourself to reconnect it when you're through filming. Make it a big sign like, "This refrigerator has been unplugged for filming—PLEASE REPLUG WHEN FILMING IS COMPLETED." You could do a lot of harm by unplugging computers or medical equipment. Check before unplugging equipment! Telephones have a way of ringing when you're recording once-in-a-lifetime sound bites. Again, unplug them when filming and insist that EVERYONE turn off their cell phones or beepers. Although you won't hear a peep out of them until you're filming, PA systems can be another subtle culprit.

Outside noises from lawnmowers, chain saws and jackhammers have delayed countless productions. The neighbor next door, or a road crew always seem to plan their loudest work on the day you're filming. You'll have to use diplomacy and imagination to solve these sound problems. (We've occasionally offered the operators of these machines $10 to take a break for 20 minutes so we could finish our work.)

Filming interviews in a large city will almost certainly put police and fire sirens on your sound track. There's not much you can do about this. If a siren is especially loud over an important sound bite, you may ask the subject to repeat what he's just said. (Of course, they never say it quite as well the second time!)

Location scouting helps solve many production problems beforehand and keeps your video on time and on budget. Many scenes in business videos can be filmed without sound. This is called M.O.S. for "Mit Out Sound," a phrase coined many years ago by a director with a heavy German accent who mispronounced the word "with." It's now a standard phrase in the business. Silent, or M.O.S. scenes, save production money because they are easier and faster to film than sound scenes. Later, in the editing room, you can add music and narration.

A few other potential problems to look for in your location scouting are microwave transmitters, high tension lines and nearby radio stations. Microphone cables and sometimes even your camera's video recorder can act as antennae for these unwanted signals which may interfere with the sound or video recording. When visiting a site, ask if any of these potential problems are close to the site. It wouldn't hurt to look around yourself and if you suspect a problem, shoot a test at the location with camera, mike cable and microphone. Then carefully check the tape for signs of radio interference on both video and audio. If the tape looks and sounds OK, you have one less problem to worry about.

If you do have interference problems, a last-resort solution is to wrap the video recorder part of the camera in aluminum foil. This may sound silly and it doesn't look very professional, but it does seem to work most of the time.

PLAN TO MINIMIZE DISRUPTION

Filming in a workplace is disruptive and generally means lost productivity for someone. When it is *your* workplace, the disruption is easy to accept. When filming in someone else's home, office or plant, formal permission should be obtained using a *location release form* which you'll find in the Appendix.

Be clear and business-like about what you'd like to film and how long it will take. Don't ask for carte blanche to film everything on the site. Your script should indicate the specific things you'll film. Be honest with the manager of the business and explain that you and your camera crew will disrupt the work to some extent. You'll be setting up lights and camera equipment. You may have to ask workers to repeat or stop an action for your filming. Of course, you'll want to make every effort to minimize any workplace disruptions.

If other camera crews have been there before you, you will hear about them. Especially if they were inconsiderate. You may learn what problems they had filming and how they solved them. All workplaces are subject to Occupational Safety and Health Administration (OSHA) safety regulations, so you'll want to film plant workers wearing any required hardhats, safety glasses or other equipment. Make notes about any required safety equipment in your production script. There are better ways to spend money than filming an industrial scene again a month or two later because workers in the scene were not wearing proper safety equipment.

Work with your cameraman and the plant manager to make this a good experience for all. After you film, leave the location cleaner than you found it. A thank you note and a copy of the completed video are a nice gesture. Sometimes a "special thanks" credit in the video is appropriate.

FILMING PRODUCT SHOTS

Some marketing videos promote only one product. Before you can shoot important product shots, you need to thoroughly prepare the product and setting. Don't wait until the day of filming to make the product look good and ensure that it works properly. If the product is not central to your video, you may be able to shoot an existing still photograph of it from an advertisement or brochure.

Study the product with your cameraman to see how to make it look good. This may involve painting or cleaning. If the product is to be filmed in operation, you will want to work with an expert operator. The day of filming is no time to discover a weakness that halts production until a part can be obtained from Taiwan. The expert operator doesn't have to be the on-camera operator. He or she could be off-camera coaching an actor who appears to be operating the machine. Rehearse the operation thoroughly until all of you are confident.

This should be done well in advance of the scheduled shooting day. It is a waste of money to have your camera crew waiting around while your actor learns how to use the equipment you want to film.

If many steps are needed to operate a piece of equipment, you might condense the process and show only those steps which clearly demonstrate benefits to your viewer. This is not a training video where you need to show every step. Marketing videos are not as literal as training videos, which we'll explore in Chapter 12.

Decide which close-ups would help your cause and note them in your script. When you photograph a close-up, you can throw the background out of focus as in the following photo. This can save a lot of work if the background looks old or dirty. The background can often be made to look like an impressionistic swirl of color when it's out-of-focus. But if you need just one wide shot, you need to make the background look presentable.

The background is a very important part of a shot and must be planned just as much as the primary subject of a shot. You may want the background or setting to make a statement, or to be at least a logical environment for the product. Picture a young woman using a cell phone at night on a cold desolate road standing in front of a steaming automobile. Now picture that same young woman using the cell phone in a shopping mall. See how the background alone makes a statement? Think about what kind of background, props or situation might promote the idea you want to sell in this video.

You can also create a "limbo" environment where the background seems to disappear. If the product is the size of a car, you'll need to do a lot of work to make a limbo background. Cars are filmed on special stages with a background called a cyclorama where the back wall, two side walls and the floor are connected to each other by gentle curves, unlike the normal 90 degree corners in a room. These four surfaces are painted the same color so that the car almost appears to be floating in space. The viewer's eye stays on the product.

COMPUTER MONITORS—A SPECIAL CASE

If a computer monitor plays an important role in your video, there are some special considerations. You can often use the camera to film the monitor directly, but you may encounter a problem—visible scan lines. You see this effect on news shows where they've filmed an office with a bunch of computer monitors in the background. Some of the monitor screens appear to roll. This problem is caused by the fact that the video camera and the monitor are scanning at different rates. The amount of preproduction work you do to solve the problem will depend on how important the monitor shot is to your video. If it's merely incidental to the message of the video, the solutions are pretty straightforward:

1.   Try changing the focal length of your camera lens by moving the camera closer or farther and then zoom in or out;

2.   Try substituting another monitor for the problem monitor; or

3.   Live with the roll, using only quick shots of the monitor.

However, if you were marketing a computer program, showing this monitor would probably be central to the whole video. In that case, it's important to shoot a test long before you plan to film. *Be sure to use the same camera, monitor and computer program.* (Some programs can change the scan rate of the monitor. If so, try setting the refresh rate of the monitor to 60Hz.) If the results of your test are unsatisfactory you have a couple of options.

1.   Try a flat LCD monitor

2.   Rent a scan converter. These things convert the computer's monitor signal into a video signal you can feed directly into a video recorder or camera.

3.   Rent a video camera that has a variable scan rate. This allows you to look through the camera at the monitor and dial in different shutter speeds until you see the offending rolling bars disappear.

Years ago I was faced with just this problem for a video I produced about a computer program. The program I was promoting did not use a standard PC monitor. It would work on a standard monitor, but was much more impressive displayed on a dual-page monitor.

Our first attempt to solve this problem was to find another dual-page monitor with a different scan rate. We found one—2000 miles away! And since my client was a good customer of this supplier, we managed to borrow the monitor by paying for shipping and giving the monitor company a Special Thanks credit. Unfortunately, that monitor didn't work either. Time was running out as our on-camera actress was leaving for Europe in two weeks. Finally we rented a camera with a variable rate shutter and that did the trick. The scan converter would not have worked in our situation because we needed the ability to shoot specific close-ups of details on the screen. Scan converters cannot do close-ups of a particular part of the screen. They give you the whole screen or nothing. This video later won an award as a marketing demonstration. Moral of the story: if a computer monitor is an important part of your video, shoot a test well before production day.

FILMING PEOPLE

Filming people is a lot more challenging than filming inanimate objects. Most of the people you film will be non-actors or "real people." They may be your customers, suppliers, clients or employees. Just as we obtained a location release for filming someone else's property, you should obtain a *personnel release* from the people you film. You'll find such a release in the Appendix.

In general, a release should be signed by anyone who is singled out for filming. People in crowds, or on public streets, don't need to sign releases. Anyone who speaks in your film should sign a release.

For any kind of Human Services agency, the release is very important. If your agency serves children, adults with disabilities or people with drug dependencies, the public relations department of the agency may already have releases from all clients. Often these releases were intended for publicity photos. Check that you have the releases and that they include video taping. A number of non-profit agencies have had to endure lawsuits because proper releases were not obtained. If there's any doubt, check with an attorney. Remember to photocopy many more blank releases than you'll need and bring them to the shoot.

You may remember our discussion on filming re-enactments from Chapter 2. Those guidelines are worth repeating for filming "real people":

1. Film real people doing things they do in real life;
2. Avoid writing a lot of dialogue for these folks. Let them re-create dialogue in their own words; and
3. Plan on filming these scenes several times until you get a take that is believable and to the point.

It is possible to film 40 separate testimonials in two hours. I know —I've done it. First you must organize the 40 people so that several of them are waiting in line at all times. The interviewer must have a printed list of questions including any special questions for particular individuals. His or her brain will go numb after about 15 interviews, so a printed list is vital. Choose an interview site where backgrounds can easily be changed a bit for each shot.

We've also filmed this many interviews in a few hours in press junkets for movie studios. Have you ever wondered how every TV news show in America gets to interview the star of a new motion picture? Well, it's called a press junket. Each interviewer gets exactly seven minutes with the star in a hotel room pre-lit by the camera crews. The entertainment reporters interview each star for their allotted seven minutes, but not a second more. These mass production techniques are grueling, but efficient.

When a non-actor, perhaps a company president, has to deliver more than 30 seconds of copy to camera, be prepared to shoot a lot of takes. Just because you've seen this a thousand times on television, don't assume it's as easy as it looks. I once filmed a church minister who spoke to hundreds of people every Sunday morning, but when the camera was pointed at him, he completely forgot his lines and became quite unnerved. It's not unusual for someone like this to show up completely unprepared. So don't you be!

Begin by asking non-actors to write an outline of what they want to say. Then, rehearse it with them and let them expand on the outline in their own words. When non-actors memorize word for word, they rarely sound sincere.

Teleprompters, Cue Cards and other Speaking Aids

Of all the speaking aids available, cue cards are the least expensive, but not the easiest. You may have seen cue cards used on Letterman, Leno or another of the late night talk shows. Cue cards are there to help the hosts deliver their monologues at the beginning of the show. When there's a mix-up, the cards often become the joke itself. These cue card mishaps have become a regular bit on live comedy shows where the cue card person and his cards unwittingly become part of the skit.

Cue cards have been around for quite a while. The first reported use was by a CBS page in 1949 on the Ed Wynn show. That page was Barney McNulty who went on to become known as the "Cue Card King." He called his freelance cue card business Ad Libs. Some of his clients included Bob Hope, Frank Sinatra and Milton Berle. Barney McNulty's story is available on the Internet at

www.letsmakeadeal.com/barney.htm

To make a cue card, write the script in large block letters on poster boards that can be read from a distance. Obviously the boards can't be placed in front of the camera so they are usually held to one side, close to the lens. This is one of the problems: it forces the speaker to look to the side rather than straight into the lens. In video and photography, looking straight into the lens is the same as looking straight into the eye of the viewer. Not looking straight in the camera's eye, makes you, the viewer, feel something's wrong, or that the person is not telling you the truth.

Rehearse changing the cue cards. When you go from card #1 to card #2, the speaker will need to see the second card quickly while you get ready to bring card #3 into view. This can all get pretty noisy which, of course, is recorded on your sound track. Two coordinated people who practice with the cards can make it work. Without practice you can end up with a Marx Brothers scene, which might make a funny commercial, but can wreck your shooting schedule.

A vast improvement over cue cards is the teleprompter. The teleprompter is a computer with a piece of reflective glass which projects the script directly in front of the camera lens. This way the speaker looks right in the camera and speaks to the viewer. Like a word processor, the teleprompter can easily accommodate last minute script changes. You can hire a teleprompter operator with equipment for about $500 a day. At those rates, buying your own soon becomes cost effective. (See the teleprompter hardware and software at *www.VideoUniversity.com*)

Whether you use cue cards or a teleprompter, rehearsals with the talent and teleprompter operator, or cue card person are essentials

Clothing, Makeup And Manicures

"Makeup!" the assistant director yells over the set when the star insists his makeup needs touching up. Unlike feature films, you won't need a special makeup room and a team of experts. In fact, most people you film won't need any makeup. The female president who will be on camera for 30 seconds or so is probably fine with any makeup she usually wears. A male president might need some light powder to smooth blemishes. Too much makeup or too many different colors can be exaggerated in a video close-up, so it is a good idea to ask the subject to tone down their makeup. TACTFULLY, of course.

Everyone, whether professional actors or real people, will perspire under the hot lights. The lights will make their noses and foreheads shine. To avoid this shine when filming, I carry a small container of face powder. The powder I use is a neutral translucent color that's hypo-allergenic and fragrance-free. A dark face, of course, requires darker makeup, but whether light or dark, the same makeup is used on both men and women.

The first time I used powder, I got it all over a man's navy blue suit and then had to waste time brushing it off. To avoid this, drape a towel over clothing and pat the powder on gently until you get the hang of it. Powder and occasional dabs with a Kleenex between takes will help keep the shine off the nose and forehead. The powder also evens skin tones and hides blemishes. That's all I know about makeup, I swear, and that's all you need to know.

I filmed a series of videos about the manufacture of computer chip wafers. Much of the footage consisted of extreme close-ups of these small wafers which showed people's fingers working with the wafers. Since the shots were so magnified, the appearance of the fingers became very important. We had to eliminate some otherwise nice shots because fingernails were dirty, the subjects wore too many rings, or nail polish was either chipped or an odd color.

If you're filming extreme close-ups of any small item where someone's finger enters the shot, a professional manicure the day before filming is worth the small investment. Use low-gloss, clear nail polish. All these details will contribute to a good-looking video, but they don't happen by themselves. That's why pre-production planning is so important.

COLORS AND CONTRAST

There are a few rules you should know about color and contrast before you shoot. The first is about filming white. This color is not especially good for video. Stark white may look great to the eye, but in video it often looks bland.

Video doesn't handle contrast well. If your subject has a very dark complexion and you film him against a white wall, the camera won't like it. To the eye this same dark face against a white wall looks fine, but it creates problems in video. If you expose for the face by opening the lens iris, the white background will overexpose. Conversely, if you expose for the background, the dark face will be underexposed and the face loses detail. A dark face with a white shirt causes the same problem. In this case the solution is to ask the subject to wear a darker shirt to lower the contrast. White shirts are hard to avoid in business settings, but, fortunately, only create a problem when the subject has a fairly dark complexion. In general, your video will look better if you can avoid scenes with great ranges of contrast.

A very saturated red color will often bleed in video, while a dark burgundy won't. People who appear in your video for longer than a few seconds should not wear bright red, or fine patterns like herringbone. These fine patterns sometimes cause a moiré effect so the pattern appears to dance on the screen. Even a chain link fence when filmed from a certain distance can create this distracting dance. Eliminate or minimize this problem by moving the camera closer or farther away and by changing the focal length of the lens (zooming to a closer or wider shot).

01:59:00:26

The white shirt and bright windows create
too much contrast with a dark face.

CASTING PROFESSIONAL ACTORS

James Earl Jones is walking through an aisle of computer operators saying, "The people of Acme are here for one reason—to
serve you."

Imagine the credibility you'd gain if Mr. Jones introduced your
company. The only catch is that spokespeople of his stature get
over $30,000 for a half day of work!(And no, you can't offer $125
for just one minute on camera.) Rather than taking out a second
mortgage, you can spend $100 to $350 and hire a local actor. He or
she won't have the national recognition, but can be just as convincing. You can hire skilled actors in your own area who have done other
corporate videos, plays, even Shakespeare.

They are easy to find. First, try the drama department of a nearby
college. Speak to an instructor who teaches advanced drama. Explain what you're doing and ask if she could help you by setting up a
casting session. To narrow the selection, you'll need to define the

character. Male, female, and age bracket are the first questions to address. You may want a corporate spokesperson to be in his or her thirties or early forties. Mention this early in the conversation because it often eliminates many of the instructor's students.

The first time I arranged a casting session at a college, the instructor was most helpful and invited eight actresses to read for the part. Since the role was corporate spokesperson, I wanted someone who was articulate, attractive and, in this case, able to handle some difficult technical language. The instructor set up a casting session that included some of her better adult students and other actors from the community. If your script calls for an actor to demonstrate a product or deliver technical language, be sure to include any of these challenges in your audition. I chose a scene with the toughest pronunciations of technical terms and gave the actors just a little preparation time. I also asked the instructor if she would read for the part. When I told her it paid $250, she was interested. I videotaped the auditions to show my client and to refresh my memory later. At home I narrowed the choice down to two and finally chose the instructor. She has since appeared in three of my productions.

Your community theater is another good source of local actors. Call the director and see if you can set up a casting session. If they are currently performing or rehearsing a play, you might want to sit in. You may be pleasantly surprised with the caliber of talent in your own backyard. Since 95% of all actors make less than $10,000 a year, you'll find them teaching, waitressing, and doing telephone sales to supplement their incomes. When word gets out that you're looking for an actor, you will get calls from friends, neighbors and strangers. They'll say things like "My son has always wanted to do this." Beware, you can't afford an inexperienced actor. If the actor you choose isn't available when you want to shoot, but is perfect for the part, consider changing your production schedule around the actor's availability.

Narrators

Most business videos don't need an on-camera spokesperson. An off-camera professional narrator can give your video that convincing voice of authority it needs. Since the narrator does not appear on camera, it's better to hire this person and record narration *after* your video is filmed and most of the editing is completed. There's plenty to do right now just to prepare for filming, but start listening to narrators on TV and radio. Later I'll show you how to hire and work with a professional narrator.

THE SCHEDULE

Your script should include an approximate running time for each scene. Most scene lengths can be determined by how long it takes you to read the narration for that scene. Go over the scene with your cameraman so he or she can estimate how long it will take to film.

Add all the estimates for filming the scenea, plus some additional time to move camera crew and equipment from one location to another, and you have an idea how much time it will take to film the entire script. On your production script, write a shooting schedule, e.g. shoot Scene 3 at 10:00 AM, Scene 1 at 11:15. Make lists of the props, people and any special requirements for each scene. The production script will keep you on or ahead of schedule.

If a scene starts taking longer to film than your schedule has allowed, decide if this scene has a high enough priority to justify changing the remainder of your schedule. If it does, could you afford to bring the camera crew back for another day of filming? If not, you'll need to find a quicker way to complete the scene.

Try to work ahead of the filming schedule, because you'll often find unscripted shots and scenes that are worth filming. When you're ahead of schedule, you can shoot these additions. Tape is cheap and it's surprising how often these unplanned shots end up in the final video.

Don't count on them, but do encourage these bonuses. Ask your camera crew and others who are involved to keep their eyes open for good visuals that might help your video. This will turn your ad hoc one-day production crew into a creative team, all dedicated toward making a better video. This kind of collaborative teamwork is found more often in documentary filmmaking than in big budget projects. A small dedicated group can move quickly which is quite valuable to the "guerrilla producer."It's also a lot more fun.

The scheduling of people, places and things must be viewed in light of their importance in your script. If you're filming 50 employees at work for a short "happy workers of Acme" scene, it's all right if some don't show up that day or if some wear bright red shirts. You'll still have plenty of choices. If, on the other hand, an important person or a particular computer monitor is vital to your video, ensure that they will be ready when you need them. As Woody Allen says, "Ninety percent of success is showing up." This is especially true in video. If Bob Smith is vital to scene 3, he must show up on time and be available for at least as long as you've planned. If he has to pick his child up at exactly 5 pm and you are still filming him at 4:45 because of an unexpected power shortage or another "Murphy trick," you have a problem. If the second shift comes on at 3 pm and you're not finished filming the first shift, it might be difficult to edit shots of these two shifts together.

Since you're on a tight schedule to complete your filming in one or two days, the punctuality of the people you film affects your budget and sanity. For example, we once scheduled filming a county executive who had a reputation for not showing up for meetings. So I planned an alternate who I knew was dependable. If the executive showed up, I would film them both. If she didn't show, I could still film my alternate. As it turned out, she didn't show so I went with my dependable alternate who did a great job. A backup plan helps you defeat Murphy's Law. Have some scenes in mind like "the people of Acme" or still photographs which you could film at anytime. So then when Murphy strikes, you're ready with some alternatives.

Does your schedule include a lunch break for your camera crew? It's amazing how many don't. *Taking care of your crew is an important part of producing.* This one production day is important to your project. You may be willing to skip lunch to get as much shooting in as possible, but your freelance crew does this work every day, so be considerate.

It's helpful if you can provide a secure and convenient place for your camera crew to store empty camera cases and extra equipment while they're shooting. They'll also need a place to charge camera batteries during the shoot. As soon as one battery dies it goes on a quick charger. If your cameraman started with a few hours worth of battery life, this continual recharging stretches battery power to a full day of shooting.

One last camera note. Virtually all of the feature films and high budget commercials you see were shot with filters in front of the lens. These filters are commonly used to soften and romanticize images. We use soft filters primarily for human service agency videos because they help sell the "people helping people" message. Industrial videos, on the other hand, rarely call for this soft filter look. Ask your cameraman to show you what a Pro Mist or similar filter would do for a scene.

PUBLICITY

Whether your customers are local, national or international, you will want to get as much free publicity as possible for your company. And it is a certain way to grow your small business, corporation or non-profit. There are many good books to help in this work. One is *Six Steps to Free Publicity — and Dozens of Other Ways to Win Free Publicity for You or Your Business* by Marcia Yudkin available from her web site *www.yudkin.com*

If you produce videos for others, you will want to see the *Video Producers' Automatic Newsmaker System* available at *www.VideoUniversity.com/newspr.htm*

A local video production can be a great news story that many local newspapers and magazines will publish. Mention *video production* and many people conjures images of Hollywood sets with camera, lights and other "glamorous" show biz stuff.

Shooting a business video is a golden opportunity for free publicity and now is the time to plan for it. Start thinking about the most newsworthy or interesting angle of the video you're making. How is the product, service or idea going to help people? If you have a friend in the news business, give him or her a call and ask if you can buy your friend a cup of coffee to pick their brain. Be sensitive to the fact that most journalists would be insulted if they thought you were trying to bribe them.

Launch your publicity campaign by making a list of newspaper and magazine editors in your region. Then send each one a well-written press release about your production. Sending photos of the production can increase the odds your story will be published. *Be sure to read a lot about press releases before you write one.* If you don't send photos or if the editor doesn't care for them, he or she may want to send their own photographer to shoot your production company at work. If so, you'll want to choose one of the more visual scenes you're planning to film and then set a convenient time. The photographer will undoubtedly want a shot of your cameraman filming something interesting. Give some thought to how you and your product or service can be a natural part of that photograph.

Publicity shots will slow your production so allow the photographer to shoot just the one scene you've selected. Granted, this publicity does take some effort. Is it worth it? You bet it is! Consider why you are doing the video in the first place. This publicity can help achieve the same goal and costs you nothing.

Preproduction planning takes a lot of work. While a lot of the work is in the hands of the cameraman, it is *your* planning and attention to details that control the ultimate quality and cost of your video.

Chapter 7

Shooting/Production

E ven though you've hired a professional camera person to shoot your video, learning more about the craft will help you and your cameraman work together to produce a first-rate video. This chapter is intended to help the first-time producer understand the work of the professional cameraman or camerawoman. It can also help you shoot better videos, whether for home movies or in-house training. All the shooting techniques described in this chapter assume the raw footage will be edited.

CAMERA BASICS

Color Bars and Tone

Professional cameras can electronically generate a pattern of color bars as well as a tone of sound. These color bars and tones are recorded at the beginning of each new video tape for at least 30 seconds before the camera shoots anything else. Later in the editing room, color bars and tone give the editor a consistent color reference and sound level throughout all phases of post production.

White Balance

To keep colors consistent from one shot to the next, the camera has a function called *white balance*. On home cameras this is automatic, but not completely dependable. That's why some shots in home movies look too red or too blue. White balance is how the camera adjusts to different colored lighting. Even though the eye may not appreciate the color difference between sunlight and indoor lights, the camera does. White balance corrects this difference so that a white shirt is the same color outside as it is inside. The professional cameraman doesn't take a chance with an automatic white balance, so he or she manually sets the white balance every time the light changes. This simple procedure is fully explained in the camera's operating manual. The producer doesn't have to know how to do color bars and white balance—you just need to know that they have been done.

The Zoom Lens

The camera's zoom lens has three important controls: *focal length, exposure* and *focus*. **Focal length** allows the lens to change the size and framing of the shot without moving the camera or subject. Zoom in and you have a close-up. Zoom out and you have a wide shot or any shot in between. A lot of zooming in and out *during a shot* is an unmistakable trait of an amateur. The professional cameraman rarely uses the zoom during the actual shot.

The lens also controls the **exposure** of the shot by opening or closing the aperture. This admits more or less light to produce a well exposed shot.

The third and final job of the lens is to **focus** the image. Through the small viewfinder, it can be hard to tell whether a wide shot is actually in focus. So, before filming, always zoom into a close-up of the subject, adjust the focus and then return the zoom to your intended shot.

The viewfinder shows slightly more of the picture than the viewer will see on a home TV set. Unfortunately each TV set does not show the same amount of the picture. The lost areas around the edges are known as *TV cutoff*. To ensure that no important detail is lost, keep all important details away from the edges of the viewfinder. About 90% of the viewfinder area is safe for all TV sets. Most professional cameras define this safe area with electronic frame lines that are superimposed over the viewfinder image. If the viewfinder does not have frame lines, assume that 10% of the edges will be lost to some viewers. If you use a video monitor to watch what the camera sees, you should know that a monitor, like a viewfinder, also shows about 10% more of the picture than a TV set. The advent of Hi Def further complicates the issue of TV cutoff, but you now have the basics.

TV Cutoff. On the left is what the camera sees, but on the right is what most TVs will see.

Before the action starts, the camera should record for three seconds. This "preroll" allows the camera to get up to proper recording speed. Without this preroll time, you may not be able to use the very first part of the shot. When there's a separate director, cameraman, and actors, the director calls "roll camera." The cameraman then calls "speed" (after three seconds of recording). This tells the director the camera is ready to record. Then the director cues the actors with "action!" When the shot is completed, the director calls "cut." Before cutting the camera, the cameraman lets the camera roll for another three seconds. This additional running is called *post roll*, and is vitally important so that the final bit of the shot is protected.

Since your cameraman will be shooting and directing, you usually won't need this "roll camera," "speed," "action" and "cut" sequence. He or she will start the camera, wait for it to get up to speed and call "action" and then "cut." Sometimes, the cameraman will need your help to cue an action that may be visible to you before he or she sees it.

When the camera's recorder stops, some recorders backspace the video tape a second or two to prepare for the next shot. This erases that last second or two, which is why it's wise to keep the camera running for a couple of seconds after "cut" to avoid losing the very end of the shot.

Slates

In large-scale productions, filmmakers identify every shot by a scene and take number. This information is written on a clapstick, or small slate, which is photographed at the beginning of each shot thus saving time for the editor, who is rarely involved in scripting and preproduction planning. Slates take some of the guesswork out of editing.

During preproduction planning, you and your team should have already seen everything you will shoot for each scene. And since you will be in the editing room, it is not usually necessary to identify each shot with a slate. On most low-budget productions, shooting a slate for each shot is probably not worth the production time it takes.

If, on the other hand, you were shooting a hundred historical photographs in a library, you might want to use Post It Notes® as slates to identify each one and note which scene each photo belongs to. Weeks later in the editing room, these slates and notes could save a lot of time.

Camera Platforms

Ninety-nine percent of the shots in a business video should be made on a tripod rather than handheld. The tripod makes a shot "rock-steady" and pleasing to the viewer. The fluid head in a professional tripod also helps the camera move smoothly when a camera move is desired.

Handheld shooting is appropriate only if the shooter is skilled at it (remember the sample reel) and it's the only way to capture a fast breaking documentary situation with a lot of unpredictable action. In these cases, handholding the camera is faster and more flexible than using the tripod. It can spell the difference between capturing a once-in-a-lifetime event or missing it.

The trick to making steady handheld shots is to stay close to the subject and keep the camera's zoom lens at a wide focal length. This works best when the subject in the shot is moving. That motion helps mask any slight camera shakiness. A static shot, without any motion, will emphasize even the slightest camera movement.

The worst handheld shots are shot far away from the subject with a long focal length. This always results in a shaky shot, which is OK for TV news and home movies but not for a business video. Shaky shots can induce seasickness among viewers. Seasick people won't buy your message. The tripod takes longer to set up, but it's worth it.

Another platform is the camera dolly, typically a wheeled vehicle that is pushed on a special track.. The moving dolly shot can be a good way to capture all the elements in a long row of things like an assembly line. Professional dollies are expensive to rent and take time to set up and rehearse. Large productions have a *dolly grip* whose job is to set the dolly track and then move the dolly to get a perfect moving shot. An improvised dolly shot can sometimes be made with a hand truck or even an office chair on wheels, but this only works on a very smooth floor. It's a waste of time to try on any other kind of floor. Discuss this with your camera crew. If you can't make an improvised dolly shot work in a couple of tries, abandon it and move on to the next shot.

Camera Moves

There are two basic camera moves: A *pan* moves the camera from side to side. A *tilt* moves the camera up or down.

Any moving shot like a pan, tilt or dolly shot, should start and end with a well-composed static shot. This gives the most editing options. The editor could choose to use the static shot before the camera moves, or the static shot and the move which follows, or just the moving part of the shot. For a pan or tilt, a rule of thumb is that it should take at least five seconds for the first object that passes through the frame during the pan to reach the opposite side. Any faster than this can be unpleasant to watch.

One pan that's a lot faster than the five-second pan is the *swish pan*. This camera movement is so fast that the subject is blurred and was a common technique in the old *Batman* TV series. It was used as a transition between scenes.

This swish pan shot would be a good transition
between scenes for a Pop Art style.

Subject Moves

Moving pictures or "movies" are just that. We are like animals in the sense that our eyes are attracted to motion. When something moves, we look and we keep looking until the action is completed. Movement holds our attention. A still or static shot without movement will not hold viewer attention for long. Any motion will catch the viewer's eye. It also leads to an expectation that something will happen. Give the viewer that payoff by showing the climax or result of the movement.

Shots with motion will edit together very well. A scene that's all motion shots is fun to watch, especially when it's cut to music. With these motion shots, you can condense an action and hold the viewer's interest. To see examples go to *www.movies.com* and watch a few trailers—those short films advertising coming attractions. We'll play with this editing style in the next chapters.

THE 3 C'S OF SHOOTING: COMPOSITION, COVERAGE AND CONTINUITY

Composition

Composition is the art of arranging the subject of a shot and the camera's view of that subject. This view could be wide, medium or close-up. To make one of these shots, either move the camera closer to or farther from the subject, or leave the camera where it is and change the focal length of the lens by zooming in or out. Just don't zoom during the shot; it usually looks amateurish.

Since TV is a close-up medium, you'll want to shoot more close-ups than wide shots. The best close-ups are often made by moving the camera and subject closer together rather than just zooming the lens from a great distance. Shooting close to a subject with a wider lens gives the subject a more three-dimensional look as opposed to the flatter look created by a long lens. It's also easier to keep the subject in focus when the lens is wider.

Composing a video shot is similar to composing the elements in a painting. Many of the same principles apply even though video records movement. A good composition directs the eye towards the subject, usually the dominant element in a composition. By removing unnecessary clutter in a shot, you simplify the composition and direct attention to the subject, whether it's a landscape, a person, or a small object.

Lines of perspective give a composition depth. A head and shoulders close-up of a person placed in front of a wall looks flat and uninteresting. Place that subject in a hallway that recedes in the distance and the shot becomes more interesting because it has depth.

When shooting an object, try to show as many surfaces as possible. The classic car shot shows the front, one side and some of the top. This ¾ view enhances the look of any sized object whether a car, sugar cube or a building. It is more interesting than a straight-on view showing only one surface of the object.

All shots have a background. Whether it is a recognizable environment or an unrecognizable limbo, you'll want to control the background through composition and lighting. Sometimes, placing an object in the foreground will improve the composition. In a landscape, for instance, this foreground could be a bit of foliage from a nearby tree or some other prop that is natural to the setting. Of course, a foreground object shouldn't hide your subject.

The subject doesn't have to be the only thing in the frame. Props or other people could be arranged around the subject of the shot. Deciding what to include, how it is arranged and the camera's position is the art of composition. Cameramen and photographers often study the great masters of painting to improve their composition skills.

Another element to consider in composition is the superimposed graphic. Let's say during editing you want to superimpose a name and title on a shot. You need to allow room for this text when you compose the shot of the person or object. This superimposed name and title is called a "lower third" because it occupies that part of the screen. The cable news shows have taken this to an extreme by filling most of the screen with superimposed graphics, perhaps in an attempt to make their TV shows look like web pages. They even scroll unrelated news stories across the bottom of the screen which you're supposed to read while you're listening to the interview. To me that says the interview is not very important.

The shot on the left was composed with enough room to superimpose a "lower third title." The close-up on the right wasn't.

Coverage

How thoroughly a scene is covered with different shots determines the options for editing that scene. Imagine a wide shot of two people talking. If that were the only shot you had of the conversation, your editing options would be very limited. You could use any one section of the shot, but if you wanted to edit two separate pieces of the shot together you would have what's called a "jump shot." The positions of the people will jump from one shot to the next. Your audience would shake their heads. We'll discuss the jump shot in the chapters on editing but for now, just remember that a jump shot will create problems later in the editing room. Here's a better way to cover that same conversation with three different shots:

#1 MEDIUM SHOT OF TWO PEOPLE TALKING.
CUT TO #2 CLOSE-UP OF "A" TALKING.
CUT TO #3 CLOSE-UP OF "B" TALKING.

This kind of coverage of a scene provides many editing options.

You've seen this kind of basic coverage in movies and television. Here's how it's done. First, film the entire scene with a wide shot. Then shoot the entire scene (or at least the important parts) over the shoulder of B so that A is seen talking.

Before you shoot the reverse angle of B talking, continue shooting A so that you get some footage of her just listening to B. This shot may show a corner of B's shoulder as he is presumably talking to A. Or of him listening when she is talking. You could shoot this listening shot even if B has gone to lunch. Just make the shot a little closer so the viewer can't tell that B's shoulder was missing. These listening shots are called "reaction shots." A should be reacting to what B is saying. If it's funny, A is laughing or smiling. The visual aspect of the listening shot can be enhanced by having A nod her head slightly just as one does when listening.

Now shoot the entire scene again, this time over the shoulder of A so that you see B talking. By filming this scene three times, you've given the editor a great many options. Not only can the editor cover the entire conversation with any number of shot combinations, he or she could also cut out entire paragraphs of the conversation and change the meaning by rearranging the order. The editor can transform a long boring conversation into a short interesting one that makes a few important points. This kind of coverage is essential in effective filmmaking.

Having lots of editing choices is a very good thing. After you become really confident in your directing abilities, you may not need to have so many editing choices so that your shooting ratio becomes more economical.

Clever use of one camera can make it appear that the finished scene was filmed with two or more cameras. Why not just film the scene with two or three cameras? In some ways that would be more efficient, but it also costs two or three times as much. By changing the camera position and repeating parts of the action, you accomplish the same results at lower cost.

Single camera coverage of an interview or other scene where sound is important does require the recording of "room tone." This "room tone" is recorded immediately after the interview before anyone has left the room. The audio person will ask everyone to be silent while the audio is recorded. Recording "silence" only seems silly until you are in the editing room. Then you realize that true silence would stick out like a sore thumb in those spots where you have removed some of the sound from the interview. True silence does not exist in many real locations.

This kind of single camera coverage introduces another potential problem—continuity.

Continuity

If you shot half of the above takes with actor A's glasses on but shot the other half without them, you've severely limited your editing options. In fact, it may be impossible to edit the scene. Glasses are a pretty obvious example of a continuity mistake. A more subtle mistake is hand position. If the three shots of this scene show the actors' hands, the position of their hands must be kept fairly consistent. You don't want the viewer thinking, "Wait a minute; her hand was by her side a second ago. Now she's holding her hands together. How did they get there?" The logic and consistency of these hand positions need not be precise, but they must be in the ballpark. You'll be surprised at how much you can cheat in the editing room if your subjects maintain somewhat consistent physical positions.

Professional film actors have learned to duplicate their actions through many takes of the same shot. Stage actors and "real people" aren't trained to do so. In filmmaking when budgets permit, a "Continuity Director" works with the director and watches continuity to ensure that the editor receives only shots which can be edited. On a low-budget or guerrilla production, the cameraman and producer must do this job.

INSERT SHOTS

If two people discuss a prop which one of them is holding, shoot close-ups of that prop in all the positions it goes through during the scene. These close-ups are called inserts. They're extremely valuable for editing. They could be edited or inserted almost anywhere during the scene. An insert shot allows you to contract or expand the length of the scene. You can also use it to focus attention on the prop at a significant point in the scene.

If the scene shows a machine in operation, shooting close-up details of the machine provides the same sort of inserts. These details might be a dial that's measuring pressure, or a digital counter. In either case, shoot a variety of different readings so the insert shots can be used anyplace throughout the scene.

CUTAWAYS

Shots outside the immediate action are called "cutaways." For example if you were filming two people talking, a good cutaway shot might be a shot of a bystander who is observing the conversation. The cutaway shot can give you as many editing options as the insert shot. One famous use of the cutaway is in the film *High Noon* with Gary Cooper. The filmmakers repeatedly cut away to a clock on the wall. This famous cutaway not only provided many editing options, but actually served to structure the film.

Another cutaway is the reverse shot of an interviewer while the interviewee is speaking. The interviewer may only be nodding as one does when listening, but this short cutaway could hide an edit which eliminated 30 minutes of the interviewee's conversation. The audience won't have a clue they're missing so much.

THE DRAMATIC AXIS

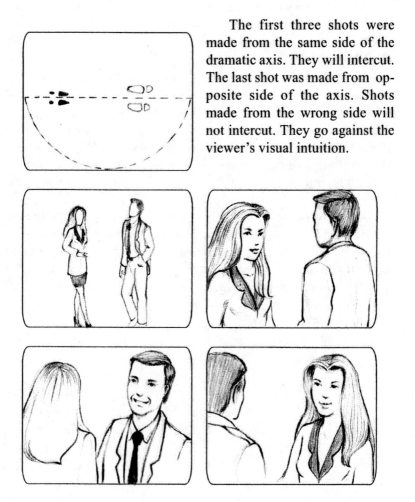

The first three shots were made from the same side of the dramatic axis. They will intercut. The last shot was made from opposite side of the axis. Shots made from the wrong side will not intercut. They go against the viewer's visual intuition.

The dramatic axis is also called the "180-degree rule" or the "action axis." Draw an imaginary line through the two subjects. For the first shot, place the camera on one side of this line. All subsequent shots must then be made from the same side of this line. Any shot made from this side of the line can easily intercut with the other shots. But, changing the camera position to the other side of the line after you've made the first shot is called "crossing the line." None of the shots that crossed the line will intercut.

Eye Direction

By keeping the camera on one side of the dramatic axis, all subsequent shots will show the actors looking in the proper direction, left or right.

Screen Direction

The dramatic axis also applies to moving objects like cars or assembly lines. Say you're shooting a car moving from left to right. If you crossed the road and shot the same car, it would then move from right to left. Cutting these shots together would make it appear that the car had turned around and is traveling back toward itself. You could use either shot, but not both. To maintain all your editing options, do not cross the road (dramatic axis)!

CLEAN ENTRANCES AND EXITS

When shooting a person or object that moves across the frame, it's better to start the shot with the subject out of frame, let the subject walk into the frame and finally exit the frame on the opposite side. This allows for more editing options than if the subject were filmed already starting inside the frame.

GOOFY PEOPLE

When shooting people at work or anyone who is not talking to the camera, ask them not to look directly at the camera. You've seen this in TV news when kids in the background wave and make "goofy faces." Even when the subjects aren't this obnoxious, their eye contact with the camera can be unsettling to the viewer.

SHOOTING FOR THE EDIT

The point of all of these shooting principles is to give the editor the greatest flexibility to construct each scene. In a nutshell, here's what you have to do to shoot raw footage that will be easy to edit.

- Cover each scene thoroughly and give the editor a variety of shots with as many editing options as possible.
- Change the angle and framing for each shot. If you make two medium shots of the same subject from only slightly different angles, these shots will not intercut. They are too similar and will usually make a poor edit. The angles or sizes of shots must be changed more significantly so the shots will intercut.
- When filming an individual "talking head," i.e. a testimonial or interview, you need to plan for editing. Odds are good that you'll want to cut or rearrange parts of the speech in the editing room. An easy way to prepare for this is to change the frame size every time you ask the subject a new question. Different sized frames (wide, medium or close-up) make it easy to edit sections of answers 1, 2 and 3 together. While you can't edit a close-up to a close-up, you could edit a close-up to a wide or medium shot. You'll at least have some editing options. Unless you vary the frame sizes, all the shots will be the same size and none of them would intercut. To edit part of one shot to any other shot, you would have to cover the edit with a cutaway, insert or reaction shot. This approach takes longer to shoot and may leave you continually searching for new cutaways or inserts to hide these problems.
- Remember TV is a close-up medium so shoot plenty of close-ups.
- Be generous in shooting cutaways, inserts and reaction shots for each scene. When it's time to edit, you'll be grateful.

THE ESSENTIALS OF LIGHTING

There are two reasons to light the scenes you shoot:
1. Sufficient **exposure** of the camera image.

Too little light produces a dark and muddy image. Too much light and the image seems to burn out.

2. To enhance the **appearance** of the image.

Lighting can draw attention to the subject and make it interesting, appealing, or dramatic.

Most video cameras warn you when there is insufficient light for a good exposure. When this happens, you can change the camera's gain switch to a higher sensitivity so the image can still be recorded, *but this increased sensitivity can introduce a grainy look to the shot and should be avoided whenever possible by adding more light to the scene.*

Four Lights

Lighting to enhance appearance is one of the primary skills in the craft of camera work. The classic lighting setup uses four basic lights: *key, fill, kicker* (or *hair light*), and *background light*. These can be used to light a person or an object.

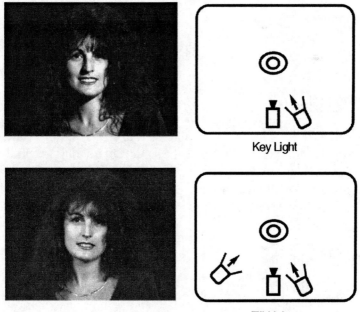

Key Light

Fill Light

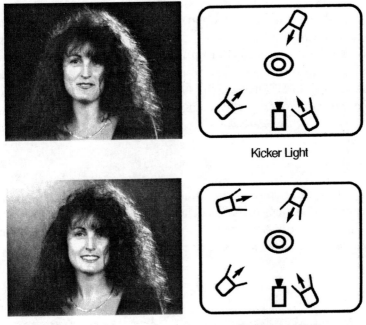

Kicker Light

Background Light

Key Light

To light a person (or an object) for filming, begin by making the room dark. This way you can add the four lights, one at a time, and easily control the results. Since the subject of a shot is generally the brightest element in that shot, start with the key light, the primary light. The key light is usually placed above the subject anywhere from straight on (same angle as the camera) to about 45 degrees to either side of the camera.

Hard and Soft Lights

The quality of light from a key or any other light can be either hard or soft. A sunny day with no clouds is an example of hard light. This kind of light is brilliant, but it creates harsh shadows. An overcast day, on the other hand, produces soft light with very soft shadows, sometimes none at all.

When you set a key light for a person, an unmodified hard light will create dark shadows under the nose, chin and eye sockets, resulting in a harsh look. To lighten and diffuse the shadows, you can soften the effect either by placing a heat-resistant lighting gel in front of the light or by bouncing the hard light into a special umbrella or white surface like a poster card or white wall. A wide variety of special lighting gels are available for modifying light.

Hard Light   Soft Light

Soft light, especially for people, has a more pleasing natural look than hard light. It is easier and faster to make a soft light look good. Hard light produces a more dramatic look and takes longer to fine tune.

Fill Light

After the key light is set, the second light to set is the fill light. This should also be a soft light. It goes on the other side of the camera from the key light. The fill light is not as bright as the key light. It fills any shadows or dark areas cast by the key light. If you've used a very soft key light, you may need little or no fill light because shadows from this key light produces very soft shadows. More about this later.

Kicker or Hair Light

After achieving a pleasing look with the key and fill lights, a third light called the kicker or hair light may be set behind the subject. It is aimed at the top of the head. When viewed from the camera position, it makes the hair glow, almost like a halo, giving the subject a glamorous look. Setting this light properly takes some time. The hair light was originally developed for black and white photography. Since all the surfaces were shades of grey, something was needed to separate the person from the background. This light contrasted the outline of the head from the background. In color photography, however, because the different colors between the head and the background often provide enough separation, the hair light is not as important as in black and white photography.

Background Light

The fourth and final light to set in this classic approach is the background light. This light is kept off the subject so it illuminates just the background. A shot with a large area of background may require two or more lights to adequately light the surface. On the other hand, some backgrounds, because of their color and the amount of existing light, may look fine without the addition of a separate background light.

All lights, stands and extension cords must be kept out of the shot or hidden in some way.

Lighting Tricks

An old lighting trick from the early days of Hollywood evolved from the box office power of popular leading ladies. These stars could insist on hiring their favorite Director of Photography whose lighting skills they found especially flattering. This cameraman's trick was a special light he had built "just to compliment Miss Smith's beauty." The construction and use of the light was a closely guarded secret. "Bring Miss Smith's light over here. Be careful! That light's irreplaceable." Miss Smith's box office clout ensured that this photographer with his special light worked on every picture she made. In reality, these "special" lights were nothing more than big soft lights which would make anyone look terrific. Since the light was so big and soft, it often required no fill lighting because it created virtually no shadows.

Using one big soft light gives the subject's face a soft, pleasing two-dimensional look with surprising ease. On the other hand, the classic four-light approach gives the subject more three-dimensional depth and modeling. On a low-budget, guerrilla production where you must light many subjects quickly, a big soft light is ideal. But instead of using a special custom-made light, you can use ready-made lights with umbrellas. One such light is the Lowell Tota-Light with an umbrella, illustrated on the following page. The umbrella reflects the hard light from the Tota-Light and transforms it to a large soft light. The light, umbrella and stand are lightweight and can be easily carried from one set-up to the next.

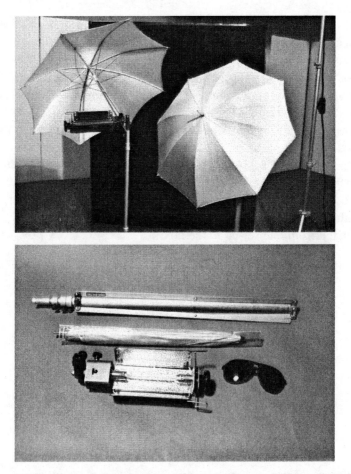

Two of these Lowell Tota-Lights with umbrellas and 750 watt bulbs can do most, if not all, of the lighting for many productions. They are lightweight and produce a soft, easy-to-use illumination.

In video production, time is money. As a guerrilla producer, your challenge is to get plenty of good-looking shots quickly. Arranging the lights for each shot and then making the shot takes time. The trick is to keep the lighting simple. These portable soft lights help you do that, especially when lighting people. When you're moving quickly and must shoot a lot of quick shots, you may find it efficient to have one person finding outlets and running extra extension cords for the next shot while you are shooting the current shot.

Is there a difference between lighting for DV video and lighting for other film or video formats? The only difference is in the light sensitivity and contrast range of different formats and cameras. Modern DV cameras are generally more sensitive so they require less light, but there's a lot more to it than simply providing sufficient illumination. Regardless of camera sensitivity, the art of lighting has as much effect on the beauty and impact of a shot today as it did 50 or 100 years ago. A video camera that is very sensitive in low light situations can produce acceptable images, but it is the skilled use of lighting, composition and direction that creates a memorable shot.

USING A PORTABLE MONITOR

A portable monitor or small LCD TV set can be connected to the camera to help in composing and lighting a shot. The monitor is useful in keeping track of a difficult continuity issue. However, it is one more thing to carry and set up at each location site. It takes more time to use the monitor and it encourages a "committee approach" to shooting.

This is a sure way to increase production costs. On big budget commercials, it's alright for every agency vice president to watch the monitor and give his or her opinion of how a shot might be improved. On a guerrilla budget it isn't. You can't afford it. That's why you spent so much time hiring a good cameraman. Trust his or her judgement and use a monitor only when absolutely necessary.

When interviewing people on camera, a monitor may inhibit your subjects if they're allowed to see what they look like. Politely tell them you'd rather show them after you've completed their interview. Even this takes away from production time so only offer it if necessary. Another danger in using a monitor is the temptation to rewind the tape and look at what you've recorded. It is easy to make a mistake and erase part of your valuable tape. So avoid rewinding the tape unless you need to check that the camera was recording properly or that there were no problems in an important shot.

SHOOTING OUTDOORS

Murphy's Law is still waiting to ambush you when you work outdoors so, no matter how sunny the forecast, always bring a couple of garbage bags to cover the camera in case it rains. When shooting for a long time in hot sunlight, a dark camera can absorb lots of heat which may damage the video tape. Cover the camera with an umbrella or another light-colored shade. If you're shooting in the cold, batteries can die quickly. Bring extras and keep these extras warm until they are needed. If you bring a cold camera into a warm room, there will be a lot of wet condensation which forms on both the inside and outside on the camera and lens which can cause damage. To prevent these problems, put the camera in a plastic garbage bag while you are still outside. Close the garbage bag with a twist tie and then bring it into the warmth. Put the camera aside for about an hour and you will see the wet condensation form on the outside of the bag. When the camera has reached room temperature (in about an hour or so) you can safely remove the camera from the bag.

SOUND RECORDING

The microphone is to sound recording what the lens is to picture recording with one big difference. The lens sees only where it's aimed. The microphone, even when it's aimed at a particular sound, records to some extent every sound in the area. The built-in microphone on most cameras will record many extraneous sounds. For home movies this quality of sound is good enough. For a business video, it's not. You need a separate microphone.

Separate external microphones can minimize or eliminate extraneous sounds. A separate mic that can be positioned close to the subject and still be hidden from the camera produces a much cleaner sound. There are two basic types. The *lavaliere* is most commonly used for recording "talking heads." Named after the jewelry pendant that is worn around the neck, the lavaliere mic is small and can easily be clipped to the subject's clothing where it is unobtrusive if not invisible. It has been used for decades by CBS'S *60 Minutes* and other shows. Like other external mics, the lavaliere is plugged into the camera. Its thin cable can be hidden from camera view by running it under or behind the subject's clothing.

The second type is called a *shotgun mic*. The shotgun mic is much larger than the lavaliere and is generally handheld by a sound man or production assistant. It records in a very directional pattern.

When carefully aimed from a distance, it isolates and magnifies a particular sound source while minimizing extraneous sounds. Because it has a long reach, it can be handheld completely outside the camera's view.

Even though the shotgun mic has a much longer range than the lavaliere, the best results are made by keeping this mic as close as possible to the subject, but just outside the edge of the camera frame. This mic can be especially useful when filming a person talking in a noisy environment. When carefully aimed, it does a remarkable job of isolating the one sound you want from those you don't. The shotgun mic can also be connected to a boom. This is a handheld collapsible "fishpole" usually held over the subjects so it is close to them, but just above the camera's view.

A great deal of other sound equipment is used to record sound on location. Radio mics, for instance, use radio signals rather than wire to send the sound to the camera's recorder. The mini disk recorders are an alternative to the radio mic. They are small, inexpensive and record digital audio. But radio mics and other equipment add complexity and cost to your production. You can avoid the additional expense by careful preproduction planning with your camera crew. In some cases the camera's mic will be sufficient, but leave this decision to your crew. That's why you hired them.

To record clean sound, begin with silence. No one should be talking, slamming doors or starting cars while you are recording. Unless the sources of these sounds are seen by the camera, they probably don't belong on your sound track. When filming an interview, you may have to wait for an airplane or truck to pass. It may be helpful to post a sign in a noisy hallway, "QUIET PLEASE—Sound Recording in Progress." Occasionally, you may need to post a person in a loud area to shush any noisy innocents.

Wind is another conspirator against the quest to record clean sound. To the naked ear, wind might not sound very loud, but through an amplifying microphone it can sound like a hurricane. Most microphones have accessories called *windscreens* which are designed to minimize wind noises. When even windscreens fail to do the job, you can sometimes move the microphone or the subject so that a building, person or other object blocks the wind.

Wild Sounds

It's not rock 'n roll, nor is it the sound of a cheetah snarling in the night. Wild sounds are those which are recorded independently of the picture. Say you're filming a scene showing the complete process of using a copy machine. You film wide shots and lots of close-ups of every step in the process. You have all the shots you need to edit the visuals into a complete scene that tells the story. But the sounds of these shots were all recorded from different perspectives and distances. The sound edits probably won't match because they are too different.

The solution is to record wild sound. Re-enact the entire scene from beginning to end. This time place the microphone fairly close to the copy machine and keep it there. Roll the camera. It doesn't matter if the microphone is in the shot. You only want the sound. In the editing room you can replace the original sounds with this clean consistent sound. The result is a better sound track.

And as discussed earlier, when you've finished shooting an interview, ask everyone to be quiet so you can record 30 seconds of room tone or quiet.

Some producers put most of their effort into the visual camera work and give sound recording a backseat. The truth is that sound recording and editing can make an enormous contribution to the success of your film.

THAT'S A WRAP

This chapter is by no means a complete instruction on shooting, lighting or recording sound. This is only the tip of the iceberg. There's a lot more to good camera work than most people realize. And whether it's just the two of you or a crew of 20, this production phase of filmmaking is a collaborative effort aimed at a common goal. The production techniques I've outlined here are proven by years of work on a variety of productions, but they are only a starting point. Your camera crew may suggest better ways to achieve high production values on a low budget. Work with them and ask for their ideas; a creative partnership makes a better film and in the process you'll all have more fun.

FINAL WORDS

Over the years, my freelance friends and I have filmed riots, airplane stunts, whitewater rafting, and war zones. But the biggest danger we've faced (aside from too much fast food) is something you probably do everyday—driving. No matter how much or how little driving your production requires, use common sense and slow down. It's too easy to get caught up in the moment when talking about your film and forget about safety.

If you're leading a caravan of cars to a shooting location and you're the only one who knows where that location is, keep track of the cars that are following you. Don't risk anyone's safety by crossing several lanes of traffic to avoid missing an exit on the highway. Those who follow may not be able to safely make that exit. Think of the cars that follow you as a long trailer you're pulling. Better yet, give each car a detailed map. *Keep safety in mind for the entire shooting day.*

And wear comfortable clothes and shoes. You will be on your feet for a long time and you may be carrying camera equipment. After today, you'll be sitting.

ABSOLUTELY FINAL WORDS

When finished shooting a tape, ALWAYS PULL THE ERASE PROTECT TAB! This tab prevents you from accidentally recording over and erasing your tape. Remember, a lot of work went into this $10 tape.

Chapter 8

The Nonlinear Edit System

In this chapter you'll learn about the equipment, general procedures and technology used in nonlinear editing. (We'll cover the artistic side of editing in the next chapter.) But before you can be creative, you need to master the basics of using a nonlinear editing system. Nonlinear Editing (NLE) is video editing on a computer as opposed to linear editing which uses fancy VCRs. Whether you intend to do the editing yourself, or are planning to hire and direct an editor, this knowledge should, at the very least, help you communicate with others to ensure that your video is the best it can be without costing an arm and a leg.

Today's nonlinear editing system is light years ahead of tape-based edit systems. You can move elements at will just as you can with a word processor. You can zoom out so you see the entire program on one screen, or zoom in to see one individual frame. You can start an edit two frames earlier or one frame later. You can change your mind and see if you prefer to see the Close Up before the Wide Shot. It's easy to do on the NLE's timeline. You can add more video tracks and make special effects. You can change a shot to slow motion or speed it up to faster motion. You can make cuts, dissolves, fades and wipes. You can correct colors in a shot where someone forgot to white balance. We could go on about the virtues of nonlinear editing, but let's get into the real deal and see how to harness this power.

The Editing Computer

A nonlinear editing system (NLE) consists of a computer with a video capture card, a nonlinear editing program, hard drives for storage, and one or more monitors. You'll also need a DV VCR (also called a deck), DV drive or DV camera to play and record the DV tapes and transfer the video into and out of the computer.

Ideally, it's wise to have a separate, dedicated computer that is designed for and optimized strictly as a video editing system. If you're planning to buy an editing system piece by piece, *don't buy the computer first.* Each of the capture cards and editing programs have specific requirements for the computers that will house them, so do your homework carefully, then first choose the NLE, which will consist of a capture card and editing program—often bundled together. Build your computer system around them.

You need a computer with lots of hard drive space. DV creates 3.6 to 3.7 Megabytes of data per second. One minute, 222 Megabytes. 10 Minutes: 2.2 Gigabytes. A 90-minute, feature-length video would take 20 Gigabytes of hard drive space—and that's just for the final edited file. You'll also want a good monitor. A 19" monitor set at 1028 x 768 resolution is a good starting point. Two monitors, side by side, give even more "screen real estate' to display your timeline. Flat panel LCD monitors can be easier on the eyes than CRTs.

A few of the popular systems include a Mac with Final Cut Pro (if you're used to Macs) or a PC system with Sony Vegas, or Adobe Premiere Pro and a DV capture card . You'll want to have at least 200GB of video storage and you should consider adding a DVD burner and authoring software to deliver your projects on DVD.

When you choose your card and software first, then build your computer system around that choice, it's easy to follow the manufacturer's guidelines for building a stable, efficient computer designed to edit video. In nonlinear editing, good preparation is half the battle. You'll find that using a dedicated computer just for video editing makes computer stability. If, on the other hand, you used the same computer for editing video, browsing the Internet, downloading and installing games and the like, you may be creating an unstable system that does not do any one thing reliably. This can create that special kind of frustration caused only by computers, airlines, and tech support phone lines.

Editing software and cards change so fast I can't advise you which one is best. What I can tell you is that for most purposes the DV format—and therefore a DV card— is your best choice. While you can only capture DV footage with this type of card, you can still transfer older analog footage to DV tape and bring it in that way. This strategy works just fine and can sometimes actually make older footage look better than it did as analog!

There are two basic types of DV video cards: Under $50 card that simply transfers DV video from your camer a or deck to your computer. Many computers now come with built in IEEE 1394 (also known as Firewire, or iLink) ports for DV. The second type of card provides hardware acceleration for "real time" editing and playback. These cards are generally bundled with editing software (and may be limited to only one program). They can cost around $1,000, but if you are going to do a lot of editing, they can speed up your work flow.

For up-to-the minute information and help on these issues, check out the www.*VideoUniversity.com* Community Forums. These busy forums are full of helpful people who know the ins and outs of the latest cards. They won't hesitate to share their honest opinions—good, bad or indifferent!

Don't worry too much about your gear becoming obsolete, because it's going to become obsolete no matter what you do or how much you spend. There's no avoiding it. Obsolescence is a fact of life built into all computers. Also don't believe in the idea of a computer that is upgradeable. Ha! By the time you're ready to upgrade, there's usually nothing in your computer that's worth saving except the data.

Rather than building the computer from scratch, it can be a wise investment to buy a ready-to-edit NLE system from a well-known computer video reseller. This way you'll avoid the buck-passing syndrome if there's a problem with the system.

Good Computer Habits to Develop

Over the long run you may be dealing with thousands of files, including video clips, graphics, music, narration and more. One of the keys to successful editing is good organization. You can get off to a good start if you give some thought to the conventions you will use for naming your files and directories. Mac and Windows handle file names differently. So study your operating system before you decide on a file naming system.

• Don't use symbols that aren't letters, numbers, or underscores.

• Don't use spaces in your filenames.

• Use underscores to separate words instead of spaces.

• Make your filenames descriptive. If your company is the Acme Corporation and you are producing a first video, a folder or bin called Acme Video Clips may seem logical enough. But what if six months later, the boss says to produce three more training videos? Acme Video Clips would no longer be such a helpful name for a bin. AcmeVideoClips2005Aug might be more helpful.

• Get into the habit of doing regular backups of your system, software and configurations. When working on a project, save the project files often. And as extra protection, it's wise to save different versions with different names and or numbers. This is an extra safeguard in case a project file becomes corrupted. In addition to saving the project files, you may also want to save an Edit Decision List (EDL) of your project. For more information on creating an EDL, see your software manual. Saving should be an automatic reflex you do all the time. Just remember; the question is not *if* your computer will crash, but *when*. Save your work often.

Master Your Tools

If you are buying an editing system, the purchase is the easy part of the investment. More difficult is the investment of time and work you devote to mastering it. Yet, this work and mastery of the tools are crucial, for without a mastery of your system, you will likely waste a lot time in frustration and inefficiency. To achieve any kind of proficiency, you must study the manual and any tutorials that come with the system. Forgive me if this sounds obvious, but it is one of the main reasons people have difficulty with NLE systems. Go through the entire manual thoroughly. And then practice, practice, practice. Then go through the entire manual a second time. Yes, this will take you weeks or months, but until you master your tools, you can't make good videos, nor will you be efficient in your work. In addition to the training materials that came with your system, there are quite a few after-market books, videos and information products available for most editing systems. See *www.VideoUniversity.com* for recommendations

Good Housekeeping is more than a magazine. Your hard drives will periodically need to be cleared of old projects before you can start new ones. Think of this as Good Housekeeping for Survival and Sanity. So, before you need to, learn the right way to clear your hard drives of past projects and learn how to archive EDLs and all other project information so that years down the road you could, if necessary, put the entire project together again without having to repeat all the work.

And, finally, beware of computer ergonomics! Ouch! That was my thumb reminding me that all this computer stuff can be painful over the long run. In fact it can be downright dangerous to your health. Many of the most talented people I know now have severe wrist and thumb problems caused by using keyboards and mice. A good task chair, proper desk height, and correct arm and wrist position will help a lot. There are also ergonomic keyboards and mice that may help prevent or reduce problems. Finally, there are alternate interface devices such as jog/shuttle controllers or digitizing tablets that many users find more comfortable and convenient. Learn how to avoid problems that can cause you a lot of pain and ultimately put you out of business. For more information see "Ergonomics and Video Editing" at *www.VideoUniversity.com/ergo.htm*

Logging And Reviewing Raw Footage

We're finally ready to edit! Begin by logging and reviewing your footage as we saw in Chapter 5: Producing the Script. Make sure your monitor(s) are set up correctly with Color Bars. You can find detailed instructions for doing this at

www.VideoUniversity.com/tvbars2.htm

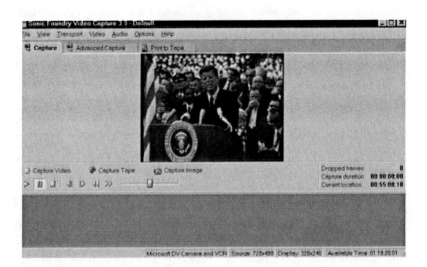

You'll need a DV source machine whether it's a tape deck or your DV camera plugged into your computer with a firewire cable. Then access the logging function of your nonlinear editor. The logging process is generally combined with capturing or transferring the best shots and clips to your computer. The log and capture window may look something like this:

How To Log Your Footage

If you were logging your tapes the old-fashioned way— on paper, you would write down the time code addresses where each good shot starts and stops. But with a computer you don't have to write it down

There are two basic approaches to capturing and logging. One way is to capture an entire tape to your hard drive. Then, it's quick and easy to run through and select just the portions you want to keep. You can always go back and use some of the "deleted" footage later since it's still there on the hard drive. But remember, this method will eat up about 13 GB per one-hour tape. The second way is to select from the tape only those clips you want to capture to hard disk and then create a "batch capture" list. Given this list, the computer will take control of your deck or camcorder and shuttle to each clip in the list, capturing only the selected footage. One advantage of this method is that it forces you to properly name and organize your clips.

When using this second method of capturing, the nonlinear editor will record time codes as you log and capture your selected shots. Just press a key where you want to start the shot. Starting at that point the system captures the shot to the hard drive and records the time code of that starting point. Watch the video carefully as it is being recorded to the hard drive. Then, when you see the point where you want to end the shot, you press another key. *But leave yourself a generous extra margin in setting both the start and stop points.* Later, when you're editing, you'll fine tune the exact start and stop points.

So, now the capture has stopped and the ending time code has been grabbed by the computer. A logging window appears where you can type a description of this shot you've just captured. You will want to devise a descriptive name that will be helpful months later e.g. "Raymond writes SALES INCREASED on blackboard." If the next shot you log is simply another take of the same subject, you could keep the same name and let the system automatically renumber the "Raymond writes SALES INCREASED on blackboard #2". This way you can easily find and compare the two or more takes you have of the same subject. You might also want to note any camera movements or other important visual elements that would be helpful in editing.

An accurate written description of the shot can prove invaluable months and years later. Even though you could always just watch the entire shot to see what it is, a good written description would save you a lot of time. You will find that being extremely organized in the logging process pays big dividends in editing.

Here are some more tips for developing a useful logging system.

Give every tape a unique identification number or code and then list it on a master list or even in a database of all your tapes. Several years from a now when you have hundreds of tapes, a database and an organized system of labeling and describing can be worth their weight in gold. OK, so technically a database is just electrons with virtually no weight, but you get the idea.

Standardize your abbreviations and terms, e.g. CU for Close Up, XCU for Extreme Close Up, etc: as we saw back in Chapter 4: Writing the Script. Be thorough. Log any shot you might need. These shots may be useful to you in other projects, but they only have value if you can find them! Organized logging is important and you don't have to be a lumberjack!

Some individual sounds are also worth a log entry. A unique sound may be useful to you in other parts of your project, or even in other projects. There are times I wish I could find that loud cow mooing we recorded on a farm. If you have lots of interviews or talking heads, you may want to hire a typist to make a complete transcript of every word and its corresponding time code. There are companies that specialize in this work. You'll find them advertising in the video trade magazines. I've also used local typing services and court reporting services. Most of them will need to work from an audio tape, but ask first.

If you have to do a lot of logging for a busy production company, you may want to investigate one of the handheld logging tools, or find one of the shareware/freeware palm-logging programs which can be used during the shoot. However, these products have never really caught on enough to gain a foothold in the industry. I think the reason is that most logging is done in post-production or if done in the field, is easily handled by a simple palm pilot database.

Time Code

We've talked a little about time code and frame rates throughout the book, but now we need to delve deeper since it is very important to our editing process. Time code generally reflects the normal frame rate of 30 frames to the second. On the web and on some CD ROMs you will sometimes see non-standard video that is 15 or even 10 frames a second. This takes a lot less bandwidth, which is one of the web's limitations. Just keep in mind that 30 frames a second is the normal frame rate for video. 10 frames a second is about the minimum rate for showing a smooth motion. Less than 10 frames a second and the video looks jerky, more like a slide show on steroids.

If you're working in DV you will use what's called *DV timecode*. Here's the good news. You don't have to know much about time code as long as your tapes have time code and your editing system can read it.

Oh, there's one final thing before we leave time code and that has to do with television. There are two classes of time code. They are *Drop Frame* and *Non Drop Frame*.

• **Drop Frame** is a type of time code designed to exactly match the real time of regular, everyday clocks. To accomplish this, two frames of time code are dropped every minute, on the minute, except every tenth minute. This corrects for the fact that video frames occur at an actual rate of 29.97 per second, rather than an exact 30 frames per second as I've described. Sorry for lying to you, but it was for your own good. This Drop Frame time code system is used in television to insure that broadcast times coincide with real time. This is important when a "30 minute" TV show must start and end exactly on time to make room for commercials and station breaks. DV uses drop frame time code as its default standard. No video frames are dropped when using Drop Frame time code. The time code merely skips a number when assigning the value to the next frame.

• **Non Drop Frame** time code counts a full 30 frames to the second even though that's not exactly accurate. Consequently Non Drop Time Code does not exactly match real time. Some professional DV camcorders and decks give you the option to use NDF time code.

For more information on the various types of time code see Adam Wilt's article on the DVformats on our web site.

The Straight Cut Edit

Video editing is based on one primary procedure called the *straight cut edit*. If you can make a good straight cut edit which propels the story and then make another good edit and another, you have most of the skills you need to edit a feature film, TV commercial, sitcom or documentary. The fact is that 99.95% of all the edits you see in movies and TV will be straight cuts, with the remaining .05% being dissolves, fades or wipes. The general procedures for making a straight cut are similar among the popular nonlinear systems; however these procedures are just different enough that we can only look at the general situation. For more specific step-by-step how-to guidance, read the manual that accompanied your NLE system.

When you previously captured the shots onto your hard drive, you set in and out points which defined the beginning and ending of that shot. You purposely set these in and out points to include much more than you would use to give yourself great latitude in making the edit work. So when you bring this shot into the timeline, you can fine-tune the edit by watching it a number of times, adjusting a few frames here or there until the edit feels just right.

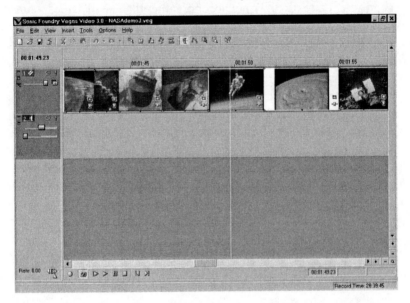

The timeline is the window where most of the heavy lifting of editing takes place.

The timeline window is where most of the heavy lifting takes place. This is where you can most easily see your options for making a straight cut edit. The most common way of making a straight cut edit is called the *three point edit*. This means that as you place a new shot in your program, you are going to specify only three of the four points in that edit. The four points are the in and out for the new shot and the in and out points in the program. The durations of the shot and the in and out of the program would need to be exactly the same length or the edit would not work. So, by specifying any three points, you let the edit system do the math to determine the fourth point. This approach saves you from the tedious job of calculating that fourth point so the shot fits exactly in the space allotted for it. The computer can do it for you and still give you complete control over the edit.

The transition you choose to go from one shot to the next is another creative choice you will make every time you make an edit. Fortunately the vast majority of these transitions will be the straight cut. The *fade up* and *fade down* to black are transitions you'll also need to master. You'll usually begin and end a program this way. The fade down doesn't always need to be black. You could fade to white or any color.

The *dissolve* is a transition that can indicate a change of time or place, or it can simply take the edge off and smooth transitions between a series of still photographs. There are also *wipes* and other fancy 3-D transitions you will use occasionally. If you spend your time mastering the straight cut, fades, and dissolves, you will have the lion's share of transitions under your belt.

Audio Editing

In Chapter 10 we'll discuss how to choose and edit four types of audio: dialogue, narration, sound effects and music, but first we need to understand the technical aspects of audio editing. Audio clips are handled in much the same way as video clips in most systems. When you capture any audio, you will first need to decide which *sampling rate* you'll use for capturing. Sampling rate is the number of samples or snapshots taken of, in this case, an audio signal in a given period of time. DV camcorders support a sampling rate of only 32 or 48 kHz audio, not 44.1 kHz which is CD quality. So you need to choose 32 or 48 kHz when capturing audio to your hard drives. I recommend capturing audio at the higher sampling rate even though 32 kHz may be fine for most video situations. The higher quality audio will be appreciated by viewers who watch your video on a home theatre system with excellent audio capabilities.

In most cases your video clip will have a synch sound track which was recorded along with the picture. Many of your audio edits will be straight cuts of the audio and the video. In other cases you may want what's called a *split edit*. This is where the visual and audio start or end at different times. There are two kinds of split edits:

- One is called an *L-cut*. The audio and video start together, but then the audio continues playing past the video. For instance if one person is talking to another, you might cut the video of the speaker, but let the audio continue. Over that audio, where you removed the video, you could place a silent shot of the other person listening. This is a very common kind of edit. You will see it often in TV interviews, movies and other films.
- The other type of split edit is called a *J-cut*. Here, the audio starts before the video. In this edit the audio plays over the silent listening shot and then continues as we cut to the video of the speaker.

Nonlinear editors all have some built-in audio tools to help you "sweeten" the audio tracks. That's a vast subject in itself. The primary skills you need to acquire in audio editing are

- Changing the gain or volume on parts of an audio track and
- Fading the track up or down. As you add additional audio tracks for music, narration and more, you'll want to be consistent in which track you use for music, narration, etc.

Eye Candy - Titles and Graphics for Video

Ready to add some great looking titles? For most situations your NLE's built-in titler which includes hundreds of fonts, colors and sizes is all you need. In the old days video titles were created with a separate black box called a Character Generator or CG. The Chyron Corporation made the industry-standard Character Generator so the Chyron name became the generic name for CG's. This company continues to provide television broadcasters with graphics equipment.

The CG or titler, works like a typesetting or publishing program, but compared to other media it has a very low resolution. In fact, the resolution of video is much less than this page of paper you're reading. Motion picture film has a much higher resolution than video— at least until digital High Definition video is the norm. The bottom line is that video titles cannot be designed the same way you'd design for print. Video titles must be BOLDER than titles created for paper, or even motion picture film. The fine lines in some type styles tend to disappear in video. Any thin horizontal line is a big problem in video. Text on a video monitor is usually much easier to read if it has drop shadows, especially when the text is superimposed over a video shot. For these reasons, text or graphics which were intended for print may not always work very well in video without some doctoring.

Unlike a computer monitor, a TV set does not display the entire video image. There is a small area around the edges of the screen where part of the image may be lost on some sets. This means you'll want to keep important visuals like titles or actions away from the very edges of the screen. This is called the SAFE TITLE ZONE and it's defined as 80% of the screen area measured from the center. It is actually within another area called SAFE ACTION ZONE. This latter zone is 90% of the screen where it is considered safe to frame all actions. When creating any titles or graphics for video, always keep them within the SAFE TITLE ZONE. Your NLE will have a way to show title safe areas. At VideoUniversity.com you'll find Title Safe files you can download and use if you are creating titles or graphics outside of your editing program.

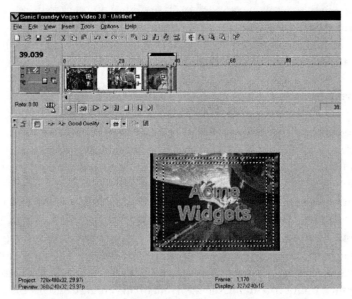

Safe Action and Safe Title Zones in Sony Vegas

Adobe Photoshop, a powerful graphics program originally designed for the print world, has become a standard for the creation of those special titles and graphics which are beyond the reach of the built-in titling tools found in most nonlinear editors. Photoshop is a complex program that some feel is overkill for use in video, but it does have a number of features specifically designed for video.

When you create graphics for use in the DV format, you will want to create them on a screen that is 720 x 540 pixels and in 24 bit RGB color or 32 bit color if you want the graphics to be partially transparent. The DV screen size is actually 720x480 pixels, but those pixels are not square. They're actually a bit taller than they are wide, so you'll have to resize your final image to convert from the square pixels of your computer to non-square NTSC video pixels. Photoshop has some tools to make this process easier. For PAL countries the screen size is 720 x 576 pixels, and no resizing is needed.

On TV I'm sure you've seen those small, semi-transparent, and subtle graphic logos usually in the lower right or left portion of the screen. These logos are called "bugs" and they are typically created in a paint program such as Photoshop. There's no reason you can't use a bug in a business video even though that video may never appear on TV.

Graphics for video is a fascinating, complex and quite addictive craft, especially when movement is added to the mix.

Two Basic Types of Computer Graphics

The first is bitmaps. Bitmap Images are made up of pixels .The word "pixel" is a contraction of "picture" and "elements." The resolution and sharpness of an image is defined by the number of pixels in the frame. One DV video frame is 720 pixels wide by 480 pixels high in NTSC countries. PAL DV video is 720 x 576 pixels. Each pixel has a color value which in video is usually one of 24 possible values.

Bitmap images come in formats like Pict, JPEG, GIF, Targa, TIFF, BMP, Photoshop and more. All digital video is based on bitmap format graphics. Bitmap images cannot be enlarged without losing quality and suffering obvious "pixelation". When you enlarge a bitmap image too much, the invisible pixels enlarge and become visible until you lose all detail and are left only with stairstep blocks of color.

Programs that work with bitmap images are generally known as 'paint' programs such as Photoshop, Paint Shop Pro, Commotion, Painter and Corel Photo Paint. The advantage of bitmap images is that they are more lifelike. That's why they are used for retouching photos as well as for video editing. The disadvantage is that they are made up of pixels which cannot be enlarged or reduced without distortion such as pixelation.

The second type of computer graphic is called Vector Graphics or Structured Graphics. These graphics are objects which are definitions of lines, shapes and fills. These lines and shapes define what the picture is so that it can be enlarged as much as you want without losing quality. These structured drawings are created by drawing programs like Abode Illustrator, Macromedia Freehand, and Corel Draw. Vector graphics are not easily used in digital video, but they can be converted to bitmaps through a process called *rasterizing*. Bitmap images form lines (rows) of adjacent pixels—referred to as "rasters" in the same way that a video image is made up of rasters of images - lines of images.

The Alpha (Transparency) Channel

Using an alpha channel is like painting on glass. For example, say you painted a circle using thick, heavy, yellow paint on glass. Behind this glass is paper drawing. This glass or "alpha channel"with the painted yellow circle would be opaque. The picture from behind the glass that was covered by the yellow circle would not show through. You would only see the yellow circle. But if instead of a thick yellow, you used a thin watery red paint to paint the circle on glass, the alpha channel would be more translucent and you would see both the drawing and the red circle.

The virtue of this technique is that you can completely cover the picture behind the alpha channel, or you can let most of the picture shine through the alpha channel. This alpha channel concept is what makes it possible to do things like superimpose titles over live video. You can also vary the transparency of your alpha channel. Another way to think of the alpha channel is as a mask or masks of different parts of your image. These marks can be more or less transparent.

Let's say you created a bug (or corporate logo) in Photoshop or another photo program. You want to superimpose it over the lower corner of your video. You'll make this graphic on a frame that is 720 x 480 pixels so the scale is correct. The rest of the frame is just background which must be a transparent alpha channel. Otherwise the background would completely cover the entire video frame when you only want the bug to cover a small area in the lower right of the frame.

Adapting Print Graphics for Video

At some point either a client or perhaps your own art department will give you a graphic file, perhaps a logo, to use in your video. To your eye this graphic may look just great, but if this file was created for print, you could have trouble with it in video. To avoid that, there are some rules both you and the art department must know about using graphics in video:

1.   Use bitmap graphics rather than vector graphics.

2.   Avoid very thin lines, especially horizontal thin lines, or you may end up with a line with "interlace flicker." You can see what this looks like by making a horizontal line that's only 1 pixel high, particularly with high contrast to adjacent colors.

3.   Avoid very large files. bitmap images for print are typically in the 200-400 dpi range, while video only requires 72 dpi.

4.   Use Video colors. Not all colors are "legal" for use in video. The term legal refers to colors which will reproduce on your TV set. Some computer-generated colors are called illegal because they don't display properly on TV sets. Photoshop and other paint programs have a tool which makes your colors legal for video. In general, avoid colors blacker than about 17,17,17 (256 step RGB scale) or brighter than about 235, 235, 235

5.   Use an alpha, or transparency, channel.

If you can work with the graphic artist on these issues beforehand, you will be way ahead of the game.

Chroma Key, Luma Key and Video Magic

Want to fly through the air in a death-defying feat like Drew Barrymore when she *appeared* to jump out of the jetliner in the first *Charlie's Angels* movie? Or maybe you just want to make an electronic weather map appear behind you like the TV weather man does. Both effects are called *chroma key*. The backgrounds in both the Drew Barrymore and weatherman shots are plain walls which are painted a highly saturated blue or green. The computer can make this (or any color) transparent. So when you place a second video on the timelime under the Drew Barrymore shot, the transparent areas reveal the second or background shot. Magic!

What is this thing called keying?

Chroma keying is the process of matting out or making transparent specific colors in a frame of video. The NLE looks at each frame and finds every single pixel containing the color you have chosen as a key color. The pixels with that color become transparent. It's very much like the painting on the glass we did earlier. If you now add a second layer of video underneath that first layer, the second layer will only show only through at those transparent pixels.

So go ahead and paint a wall a saturated color of green, then put your friend in front of the wall. Now look around for a second shot you can use as background, perhaps a shot of a formal ball at Buckingham Palace. In your editing program you put the shot of your friend in front of the green wall on Video track #1 in your timeline. Right under that you put the Buckingham Palace shot on video track #2. Now you click on Chroma Key. (The exact steps will be differ in each NLE.) With an eye dropper type tool you choose a color you want transparent in the first shot. You choose the saturated green you had previously painted on the wall. When you click on that green, the entire wall becomes transparent which at the moment looks black. Click it again and the Buckingham Palace shot fills the entire transparent area. Your friend is attending a ball at Buckingham Palace!

Now, if you were wearing a shirt the same color green as the wall, your shirt would also become transparent and the lords and ladies would now be on your chest. Green or blue are the most common colors used for Chroma Key, but you can click on any color and make that color transparent. Green is better than blue because, for one thing, sunlight is full of blue so any sunlight would create a problem. You can buy special Chroma Key paint or background cloth and, of course, they are a lot more expensive than buying the same paint or cloth in a regular store. However, you can do it yourself by getting a bunch of green paint swatches and shooting a test shot of them. You might first use a paint program and make a solid color printout from the RGB values of 0,255,0 (green) or 0,0,255 (blue). At your local paint store ask for some paint swatches close to the green printout. Take 'em home and shoot a test to see which shade of green gives the cleanest Chroma Key in your NLE. Buy a gallon of that color and paint your background wall with two coats.

Tips to get the best Chroma Key results.

Lighting is a critical element. You need to control the light. If even a little stray daylight strikes your background or subject, you can forget about fooling the audience into thinking your subject is somewhere she's not. Make sure the background is evenly lit. You will need to use at least two lights on either side of the background. The subject also needs to be well lit. It's important that there's no light bouncing or spilling from the background to the subject. If any reflected green light hits your subject's face, that part of his or her face would become part of the key. Is that the Duke of Edinburgh in your cheek?

Lighting continuity between the subject and the background is important. If your background shot is lit by the sun coming from the left side of the frame, the subject in the other shot should also be lit by "sunlight" coming from the left. Make sense?

Lens perspective is another thing you'll want to match. If the background shot was shot with a wide lens, you'd also want to shoot the subject with a wide lens.

Chroma Key is simple to do and can be fun, but it requires some practice and experimenting for best results, especially when working in the DV formats. Just don't promise an important client you can make her appear to be speaking to the Congress until you know what you're doing. For an extensive two part tutorial on Chroma Key see the Free Library at www.*VideoUniversity.com*

Key Frames

The concept of key frames is important to your mastery of NLE. A key frame is a snapshot of how the scene looks at one point, often at the beginning or end of a sequence of frames. This frame is a reference point for change over the sequence of frames. A key frame can define a color change, a morphing process, or a motion over a precise amount of time. For instance, it can define the motion of an animation, a title movement, or other added motion within the video frame.

Let's say you want to move a title "Free Lunch" from the upper left corner of the frame diagonally down to the opposite right bottom corner of the frame. You want this movement to take exactly one second. 30 frames in a second, right? To accomplish this movement you could place this title in 30 different positions on the 30 frames starting at the top left through the bottom right, but that would be a lot of work and it would be very difficult to perfectly align the titles and evenly place them. By setting a *beginning* key frame and an *ending* key frame on frame #1 and frame #30, you are defining the motion path of the title and how long it will take. Two key frames is all it takes to define that motion. If you wanted it to move twice as fast, you could start the first key frame on frame #15 instead of frame #1. Then the title would move from frame #15 to frame #30 and this takes only half a second rather than a whole second moving from frame #1 to frame #30.

You could also define a motion that was more like a bouncing ball title. To do this you'd define a bunch of key frames where you wanted the "Free Lunch" title to bounce to. Those undefined frames in between are called "in between" frames and the process of creating them is called "tweening." This term is used in animation to describe the process of generating all those in-between frames. In traditional animation work, tweening is done by hundreds of human artists. In computer animation and nonlinear editing, the computer calculates the frames in between the key frames you specify.

The Offline and Online Editing Strategy of Yesteryear

(Feel free to skip this section if you just want to get on with editing your project.)

In the first edition of this book there was an entire chapter devoted to the Offline and Online editing strategy, but today that strategy is nearly obsolete. It began back in prehistoric times when video was analog and you had to edit by trying to precisely copy part of one video tape to another tape. The biggest problem with this kind of editing was that the copying created a very ugly defect called *generation loss*. For the high-end edit systems using Betacam and 1 inch video this generation loss was hardly noticeable, but it was a problem on editing systems using more affordable formats like Hi-8 and SVHS. The offline edit strategy was a good way to minimize expense while getting a high-end final product.

In a nutshell here's how it worked: You would start by making window dubs of the original camera tapes. These could be VHS tapes and the time code from the original tapes was "burned into" into these inexpensive VHS copies so that the time code was always visible on the screen. Then, using these window dubs on a cheap VHS or SVHS editing system, you could do a "rough cut" edit until all the edit decisions were perfect. You could read the exact edit decisions right on the screen because the time code was visible on the tape. This rough cut was the ideal way to make the creative decisions about each edit. But because you were copying a VHS tape, the generation loss would become worse each time you changed an edit on tape, though that wasn't really a problem because the goal of this rough cut was to make a list of all the edits rather than to make a final master tape. The list is called the *Edit Decision List* or EDL.

The next step in this offline/online process was to go back to the original tapes and edit them on a high-end edit system which was typically Betacam to 1 inch. These were the exact same edits you had made in the offline master and recorded in the EDL. The good news was that the generation loss in this system was negligible and the resulting edit master was very high quality suitable for broadcast. The catch was that a full-blown Betacam to 1 inch editing suite with all the bells and whistles might RENT for $100 to $300 an hour!

So, when editing an eight minute marketing video, I might spend a few weeks working on the inexpensive VHS/SVHS offline edit system. Usually I worked closely with my client and would show new versions of scenes and finally the entire offline master. Then, when my client and I were both happy with the offline edit master, I would book an online edit session for six to eight hours so I could make those exact same edits I had made in the offline system, but this time at a very high resolution without generation loss. Think of the *offline* edit as the *creative* part which is done on inexpensive equipment, and the *online* edit as the *technical* part which is done on high- end, expensive equipment.

This kind of offline/online editing is disappearing from the scene. Now that DV formats are so good and so affordable, there's no real reason to do a separate offline edit and then do an online edit. With DV you just do one edit. Of course, you still go through many rough cuts and improved versions, but it is all done on the same editing system.

Before DV became so popular, there was another offline/online process which involved editing a low resolution version of your original tapes on an Avid NLE at a highly compressed ratio, then editing those tapes again on a better, higher resolution Avid platform with no compression at all. This was much like the offline tape strategy above, but worked with digitized footage on AVID and other editing systems.

Today, you can buy an amazing DV nonlinear editing system for less than the cost of the VHS/SVHS offline system we used in the Stone Age, just a few years ago. With DV, all editing is online editing. There's no need for offline editing; there's no generation loss, the shots are available to you by random access and so on. The advantages are overwhelming. There is no longer any reason to consider buying a new linear editing system; however the concept of offline and online editing may be useful as you progress to even more sophisticated and expensive projects such as Hi Def.

I know this chapter has been a little tedious. You deserve a reward, so in the next chapter we're going to have some fun and get creative.

Chapter 9

The Art of Editing

WRITING WITH PICTURES

Video editing is somewhat like writing—you decide which word to use and where to put it. Carefully chosen words or edits add to the meaning of a sentence or a scene. Each choice you make can be revised or rearranged for greater clarity and impact. Just as writing can often be improved by cutting unnecessary words, videos can usually be improved by condensing or eliminating extraneous shots. The goal of both good writing and video editing is to clearly communicate a thought or feeling.

You'll probably find that editing your video is easier than writing. In video you start with a structured guide, the script, and then film the shots needed to build this structure one scene at a time. Your log shows where to find each shot. Then, by editing, you put these pieces together. It's like putting together a jigsaw puzzle, but instead of having just one solution for this puzzle, your video has many possible solutions. You can continue to make changes by re-editing the video until you are completely happy with it.

When you're editing a business video, there is usually money and work involved—either your own or your client's. This brings another dimension to the work. This video has a focus and a specific goal, as well as a detailed road map in the script. It has a timetable and often a completion date by when it must be delivered. When there's a client involved there are at least two hands to get the work done, think through solutions and collaborate on the production. There are also expectations and contracted obligations.

These are all good things if you approach it the right way. And this team—you and the client—can and hopefully will, have a lot of fun with the editing process. It's an interesting process because it is storytelling with moving pictures. I've had a number of clients who have been quite taken with the editing process and have asked to do some of the hands-on editing themselves. Often with less instruction than I've given you, these clients have been able to do some of the editing themselves. Having a collaborator whose goal is the same as yours—making an effective business video—can be quite helpful. Since you've been through the scripting and shooting with this person, I'll assume you've already developed a good working relationship. In fact, you *have* to make it a good working relationship.

Editing is a creative challenge that can be both satisfying and fun. And if you have fun with it, your audience probably will too. While there is a script, as well as the footage you produced for that script, there are still many different ways to edit this same footage. Editing is a good time to experiment with a scene that might be done different ways. The worst that could happen is that you'd have to re-edit that scene. You might, for instance, try some interesting editing structure you saw in a TV commercial. You can save different versions of the scene if you like.

But since there's a client and money involved here, it is *your* responsibility to get approvals from anyone with the power to say, "You'll have to change this. You should have checked with me before you finished it." While the client you are working with may be quite pleased with the work, this same person (unless she is the company president) must undoubtedly answer to others. It is these hidden bosses who must approve of the work. Get them on board early in the game.

Now, let's start editing! Here's a log sheet of a scene from a promotional video. The video's goal is to convince non-college-bound high school students that they'll need some technical education beyond high school to qualify for fun high-paying jobs. This scene is set in a TV studio run by students.

SHOT #1
Wide shot in TV studio. From behind we see the backs of two camera operators shooting a student announcer. The studio is full of lights, video equipment and a monitor that shows a close-up shot of the announcer talking to the cameras.

SHOT #2
Medium shot from the side of the two cameras with student operators.

SHOT #3 AND #4
Close-up of the monitor showing the announcer. After a few seconds the camera pulls back and pans to a medium shot revealing the student announcer sitting close to the monitor. This continuous shot could be used as one shot from start to finish. Or it could be treated as two separate shots: one using only the close-up shot before the camera moves; the second shot using only that footage after the camera moves.

SHOT #5
Close-up of the zoom lens on one of the cameras as the zoom barrel moves.

SHOT #6
Wide shot of the studio from over the shoulder of the announcer showing the room, cameramen and equipment.

SHOT #7
Wide shot from inside the adjoining control room. From the side we see a row of students operating buttons and knobs. They are wearing headphones and watching a row of monitors that show the student announcer in the adjoining studio. Above these monitors is a large picture window through which we see the studio.

SHOT #8
Over the shoulder of one of the control room students we see two monitors. One has a close-up shot of the student announcer. The second has a medium shot of the announcer from a different angle.

Let's first edit this scene without sound. Later we'll add narration and music, but the sound track can be a crutch in editing. Television sitcoms rely heavily on the sound track to tell their story. Try watching one without the sound. You probably won't have a clue what's happening. Instead of taking this "illustrated radio" approach, let's see how much we can do with a "silent movie" approach where the pictures alone tell the story. Even though the scene was scripted, there are still many options for editing the same footage. Here's one.

FIRST TRIAL CUT

This is a fairly conventional way to begin cutting this scene. By using the wide establishing shot at the beginning, we let the audience know immediately where they are and what's going on. Following is another way to cut the same scene.

SECOND TRIAL CUT

This second trial cut is just as valid as the first. By starting with a close-up of the lens, we let the audience know this has something to do with a video shoot, but not yet what. Beginning with a close-up is like starting the scene from "inside." In the first trial cut we began the scene from "outside" with a wide shot. Either way can work.

By editing the scene without sound, you'll be better able to judge how well it stands by itself, without the distractions of a sound track. The script indicated that this MOS (silent) scene would be cut to music. When you edit a scene that will later have music or narration, make it work first as a silent scene. When you're happy with the silent version, the addition of a sound track will only strengthen it.

Even though this was an MOS scene, we recorded the live sounds and voices when we filmed. Some editors use these sounds with their pictures even when they're editing an MOS scene. To keep from being distracted by the sound, they just turn the volume down. Later when the picture editing is completed, they listen to see if there are any interesting synch sounds that might be worth keeping. If not, it's easy to delete or silence the audio on that part of your timeline and replace it with music and/or narration, e.g. "Students who study electronics can go on to exciting jobs in the television industry." After you create an effective scene without sound, consider some of the options for your sound track. You might, for instance, use different sound bites over the scene like, "One year of tech education helped me get a really fun job"; "With this job I bought a new car!" These are but a few editing possibilities. The commercials and other videos you see on TV will reveal even more editing styles and structures you can use. Keep an eye out for styles that might serve your goal and audience.

EDIT WITH THE SCRIPT

Before you start cutting, read your script again to recall the idea or feelings you intended to convey. How does the scene support these intentions? Does it address your audience?

In this case our audience was high school students. To win their attention we designed it as a music video. The message was simple: here are some of the fun things you can do with just a little additional education. Rather than conveying hard information, the video was intended to dazzle the eye with cool images that support the message. There is a little narration, but most of the important ideas are conveyed in other parts of the video by sound bites, or short testimonials by young adults such as, "I got this neat job because of my technical education." The hard rock music track keeps the audience hooked.

When a scene in your script has narration, the visuals of that scene must be edited to run at least as long as that narration. If narration for a scene takes 40 seconds, the visuals must run for at least 40 seconds to accommodate that narration. I say "at least" because wall-to-wall narration is not the best way to go. A scene with no narration can be edited to run as long or as short as you wish.

LISTEN TO YOUR INNER VOICE

How do you know when your scene is right? This is the art of editing. It's right when it feels right. Or, as Duke Ellington said about music, "if it sounds good, it is good."Make a trial edit, then sit back and watch the scene— as a viewer, not an editor. How does it make you feel? Trust your instincts and listen for the little voice that says Shot #2 is too long or Shot #3 is in the wrong place. Try moving Shot #3 to a different place. If that doesn't work, try eliminating Shot #3 entirely.

When editing, I continually ask two questions: "What's wrong with this scene?" and "How could it be better?" If you have a nagging feeling there's something wrong with a scene, you're probably right. Identify the problem and change it.

You may be tempted to ask for an outside opinion. That's a good idea, but it's premature. Your own instincts are already better than you realize. Like your audience, you've probably grown up with television, so you've been a film and TV critic for 20 or 30 years. Our high school audience is the MTV generation and they have short attention spans. Think like your audience. Remember how you felt as you watched other business videos. You probably know more about what works and what doesn't than you consciously realize. The time to get other opinions about a scene is *after* you've made a first pass at editing the entire video.

As a viewer, you'll feel impatient with a scene or a shot that runs too long. Bring this same sensibility to your role as an editor and you'll realize that short scenes and short shots are generally more palatable to your viewer.

BEGIN BY MAKING ONE EDIT

The first choice in constructing a scene is to choose a first shot to edit. Your decision where to start and end this shot will determine its length. You'll make these two decisions for every edit. Each one needs an *in* point and an *out* point. Set the out point a little longer than you really want and you'll have more options for ending the first shot and beginning the next one.

After you've made the first edit, you need to find a second shot to edit. What would your audience want to see next? If you started with a wide or medium shot of a machine, the audience might want to see more detail in the next shot. Give them a close-up or a different medium shot that logically shows the next step in the process. The second edit should be from a different angle, or one with the subject a different size so the edit is not jarring.

In addition to choosing a start and end point for your second shot, consider how the beginning of the second shot works with the end of the first shot. Carefully watch how the end of the first shot cuts with the beginning of the second one. Hopefully you've practiced using your NLE enough so you can now focus on the craft of storytelling rather than the mechanical and technical aspects of editing. Play the video and start it a little before your edit and let it run a bit after your edit. Ask yourself "What's wrong with this edit? How can it be better?"

Keep adding shots until your scene feels complete. Then sit back and watch it. Are the shots in the right order? If you want to change the order, you may need to change the individual start and end points for some of the shots. This is not as complicated as it sounds: Actual editing is easier to do than reading about it!

Remember how we lit a scene for filming by starting with darkness and adding just one light at a time, each with a specific purpose? Think of editing in the same way. Start with black and silence and add just one shot at a time. Choose shots that contribute something important. There are no neutral shots. Each one either adds something worthwhile or it doesn't.

Since I shoot many of the videos I produce, the cameraman in me sometimes falls in love with a particular shot. These are tough shots to eliminate, but when a pretty shot doesn't fit, I have to be ruthless and cut it. *A shot belongs only if it helps the scene.* It's either part of the solution or part of the problem. No matter how great a shot is, if it doesn't help the scene, it doesn't belong.

Ideally, the shots you choose will be the most visually striking of all your takes, but it's much more important that these edited shots build a scene which tells a concise but complete visual story.

MANIPULATING TIME

It's unlikely your audience will want to watch a scene that runs for 10 minutes in real time. You can almost hear them say, "Just show me the essence." Could you show the essence in ten seconds? Five? Arrange those five or ten seconds-worth of shots into a logical order.

Here's Step One, Step Two, then the conclusion or payoff. Could you go straight from Step One to the payoff? You may not even need Step Two.

Condensing events like this is very common in editing, perhaps the most common form of manipulating time. You can radically abbreviate a scene by eliminating entire steps and/or condensing those steps you show. You can also change the order of events to suit your needs. Occasionally, you will want to extend time. Perhaps you want to show how strong your pickup truck is, so you decide to show it being dropped from the top of the Grand Canyon and surviving. Let's say this takes 1.9 seconds of real time and the actual moment of impact is even shorter. You would probably have to do several drops until you get one that your truck actually survives.

If the audience blinked, they'd miss the one good take of this moment of impact and you'd have spent a lot of money for nothing. The same problem may occur in a guerrilla video which demonstrates a high-speed stamping machine where the "money shot" happens too quickly.

One way to extend the screen time of both the truck and stamping machine is to use a slow motion shot. This can extend the screen time as much as 100 times longer than the real time. The easy way to do slow motion is simply to use your NLE. The software creates slow motion by adding frames to a shot. This can look great. The limitation is that there is only so much slow motion you can do with 30 frames a second. At some point it becomes more like a slide show than slow motion. To do even slower motion you may need to rent a specialty high-speed camera. To shoot slow motion the camera must capture more frames than usual. That's why it's called a high-speed camera. There are industrial high-speed cameras made by Kodak, Redlake and others. The broadcast quality slow motion video cameras systems sell for over $200,000 and rent for over $2000 a day. At these prices, I would personally go with a high-speed *film* camera and just transfer to video. The expensive video slo-mo camera system can only shot at three times the normal video frame rate while film cameras can easily do 10 – 100 times the normal rate.

A cheaper way to extend the screen time of a fast event is to make a number of different shots of that event and edit them together as if you were showing just one event from several perspectives. The audience won't know that you cheated and filmed the same event several times. When you edit the scene, you can extend some shots a bit longer than the real time event would justify. You can also use cutaways and inserts to prolong the screen time. While these techniques won't enable you to add ten seconds to an event that only lasted for half a second, you could probably extend the time by another half second.

You could also use a still shot in the middle of a process and hold this as long as needed. Over this still photo you might superimpose a title, graphic or even a simple animation. Or you could insert a title, without a video still-shot, between the steps of the process.

The second and third shots are a simple animation which was used to extend the screen time of a quick action. A title card would achieve the same result.

You can stop time in a scene by using a still photo from the last shot. I did this recently in the opening scene of a video about suppressing Electro Magnetic Interference or EMI. Lightning is a dramatic example of EMI and helped us explain what it is. I had obtained shots of lightning from a NOAA (National Oceanic & Atmospheric Administration) video , but I only had a few seconds of lightning shots from the NOAA tape. Editors generally try to avoid reusing shots unless they can fool the audience into thinking they haven't seen them before. In this case, the lightning shots were so quick the audience couldn't tell that I had repeated two of them.

But I still needed more screen time, so I extended the last shot of lightning by freezing the last frame and holding it for a while. I continued the sound track of thunder underneath the still and gained a couple of seconds so we could complete the narration while holding audience attention with the striking visual images of lightning. To learn how to freeze a frame you will need to read your NLE manual.

CUTTING AROUND PROBLEMS

Say you've got a problem in the middle of an otherwise great wide shot. Perhaps the camera was bumped or someone in the background made a coarse gesture. You might cover the problem area with another shot, perhaps a close-up insert or a cutaway. Once you're past the problem area, you can cut back to the original shot. Use the original sound throughout to mask the interrupting additional shot.

The editor can use this cutaway to slightly lengthen or shorten the time between Shot #1 and Shot #3. When you can't cut around a problem, you may be able to get away with using it if it passes very quickly. You'll see it, but if the audience doesn't, what's the difference?

#1, #2 and #3 are one continuous shot. #4 is a separate cutaway which can hide the problem you see in #2.

CONTINUITY PROBLEMS

What to do when an action in one shot doesn't match the action of the next one? For instance, in one wide shot the actor is pointing to a map with his right hand, but in the next shot, a close-up, he is pointing with his left hand. This is a flagrant continuity mistake. Many are more subtle. Individually the shots are fine, but edit them together and the mismatch is conspicuous. Sometimes you can solve the problem by using the offending shot for just a split second. It's so fast the audience doesn't notice the mistake. Another solution is to put a cutaway shot or insert shot between the two. In the case above, you might cut away to someone else who is looking at the map. This may be enough to distract the audience from the problem.

THE MATCH CUT

To make a match cut, you need to have filmed an action twice using different angles or framing. The action of these two shots must overlap and the continuity must be consistent. Here's an example:

Shot #1   Medium shot of woman at computer. She picks up a pencil and points to to a particular spot on the monitor.

Shot #2   Close-up of the screen. Her hand and pencil enter the shot and point to exactly the same spot on the screen as in Shot #1.

You can cut these shots together at any point where the position of the hand and pencil in Shot #1 is the same as it is in Shot #2. Match cuts are fun to edit. They make it appear that you have filmed the action with two cameras.

THE JUMP CUT

The proper definition of a jump cut is an edit which cuts out part of a continuous shot and joins the remaining pieces together. Consider a zoom shot that starts wide and slowly zooms into a close-up. Cut out the middle and join the beginning and end of the shot together. The result is jarring and the audience sees that something in missing.

The term jump cut also refers to any abrupt cut that shows missing action even when that cut joins two different shots, rather than joining two parts of the same shot. Not long ago the rule was to always avoid jump cuts, but today that rule is routinely and deliberately broken. I remember a national commercial that was all jump cuts where the editor had taken a zoom shot and cut many pieces out of it. The result was that, instead of smoothly zooming into the close-up, the viewer was stepped into the close-up by "stop-and-go" jumps. The effect was emphasized with very rhythmic music. Most editors try to make their editing invisible, but in this case, the jump cuts created a riveting style that's as much visual content as the shots themselves. Generally, you want the viewer to follow your story, rather than your style of construction. Experiment with jump cuts, but don't get carried away, because unless it's done skillfully, a jump cut will disturb the audience. The subject of jump cuts often arises when editing an interview:

If you edit these two shots together, you'll have a jump cut.
Inserting the sea gull shot between them hides the jump cut
without jarring the viewer.

By inserting a quick shot of the sea gull between these two nearly
identical talking heads the jump cut is hidden. This insertion also lets
us cut seven seconds out of his speech. Instead of the seagull, we
could use shots of whatever he was discussing. If we had a shot of the
interviewer asking a question or just listening and nodding, we
might have used that instead of the sea gull to mask the jump cut. Or
we might have used a different sized shot of the subject. What he said
in that shot would have to make sense between his statements in
Shots #1 and #2. If, on the other hand, we had nothing at all to insert,
we might try using the two shots in different parts of the video so
they would not be next to each other. Isn't it nice that this jigsaw puzzle—editing—has so many solutions?

CUT ON MOTION

To cut on motion means that the subject in Shot #1 is in motion at the *out* point of the edit and another subject in Shot #2 is in motion at its *in* point, so that both subjects are in motion at the edit point. Cutting on motion can cover a multitude of editing problems while keeping the audience glued to the screen. I just finished a 12-minute manufacturing video with hundreds of edits where virtually each one was a cut on motion. The sound track was classical music with only minimal narration. My clients love it and even people who don't care at all about manufacturing find themselves hypnotized by the interesting motions driven by Wolfgang Amadeus Mozart.

A nice thing about cutting on motion is that you can cut from any motion to almost any other motion. For example, take shots of a red ball bouncing down the stairs in your home. Then make shots of it bouncing into the street outside and then down a few blocks to a store and finally landing in a whole rack of identical red balls. Even if you had only ten shots, you would find hundreds, if not thousands, of edit points where you could cut on motion. One cut might be of the ball bouncing high in the air against a background of blue sky. In the next cut, the ball seems to fall from its last bounce. The background is apparently the same blue sky, but as the ball falls, an entirely new location is revealed.

You can take a lot of liberties with continuity by cutting on motion. The red ball could bounce out of the frame in one shot and into a new location in the next shot. This technique of cutting on motion can help you edit any kind of scene with motion. It will speed your editing work and produce a dynamic scene that grabs your audience.

Is it beginning to seem that the primary goal of editing is to fool the audience? Some would say we're just rearranging things a bit to present our own interpretation of reality, but anyway you look at it, yes, we are manipulating the viewer. Call it Machiavellian, but that's filmmaking.

JOINING SCENES FOR A SOPHISTICATED AUDIENCE

Now that you've edited a complete scene or two, you'll want to consider how to join two scenes together. Beginning editors often think they need to show events and account for time more literally than is necessary. Consider a story that moves from Dallas to Washington. The heroine in Dallas is fed up with taxes and bureaucracy and decides to go give 'em hell in Washington. In the past, the director would inevitably film an airport scene with a shot of a plane taking off and then show the heroine departing that plane at Dulles and taking a cab to the Capitol. Today's audiences don't need nearly that much explanation. You can cut straight from the office in Dallas to the floor of Congress without losing your audience.

Many directors routinely use a dissolve to indicate the passage of time. In the 1960's, a movement of French directors challenged this and other editing conventions. Francois Truffaut, a leader of this "New Wave" movement, questioned the need to show time passage at all. He used the straight cut as a transition. So, instead of using an airport scene or even a dissolve to go from Dallas to Washington, he used a straight cut. The audience followed.

PARALLEL CUTTING

Parallel cutting is a storytelling technique editors have used since the silent film days. It tells the stories of two different scenes simultaneously. Instead of completing Scene #1 and then starting Scene #2, you can alternate parts of #1 and #2. Scene #1 begins, then cuts to Scene #2 and cuts back to Scene #1 again and so on. The viewer can be in two places at once, as in "Meanwhile back at the ranch..."

FLASHBACK

Charles Dickens' *A Tale of Two Cities* begins with a flashback. "It was the best of times, it was the worst of times..." He's about to tell you what happened in years past. This storytelling technique is generally specified in the script, but it can sometimes be imposed after the fact. The 1941 film *Citizen Kane* is considered by many to be the best film ever made. In that film, director Orson Welles makes extensive use of the flashback and other time-shifting techniques.

MONTAGE OR RAPID CUTTING

The "People of Acme" scene is a montage. You've seen the montage in TV commercials where hundreds of photographs of products are fast-cut in just 30 seconds. In one scene of a business film, I used quick shots of more than a hundred people from three different states. Each shot lasted a second or less and music tied it all together.

THE ONE SHOT, ONE EDIT SCENE

The one shot, one edit scene is called "mise-en-scène," a French term for staging. A perfect example of how complex this staging can be is illustrated in the 1948 Hitchcock film *Rope*. The story is adapted from a play that takes place in one room. In the film, both the subjects and the camera move to effect the dramatic emphasis and pacing you would ordinarily achieve by setting new camera positions and editing.

Each shot in this film lasts for ten minutes, the amount of film in a movie camera (both in 1948 and today). To make a close-up, Hitchcock either had the actor move closer to the camera during the shot or he dollied the camera into the actor. It's also interesting to see how he gets from one ten-minute reel to the next. In one of these transitions he has a character walk in front of the camera just before the film runs out. The actor's dark suit fills the frame like a fade to black. The next ten-minute shot starts with the same black suit. You don't notice the jump cut because the darkness from the suit fills the frame. The dialogue continues without interruption and the actor walks away from the camera, revealing the scene again.

This film is remarkable as a directing exercise. It works because the actors and camera crew rehearsed their movements over and over again. Every detail was meticulously planned in typical Hitchcock style. The only editing required was to cut the entire Reel #1 to Reel #2 for a total of seven edits in the film. Rent the film and see if you can identify Hitchcock's methods. He proved he could construct an entire film in the mise-en-scène style, but it's worth noting that he never repeated it.

It's possible for you to do your entire film this way, but you'd probably conclude, as Hitchcock did, that it isn't worth it. The standard techniques of shooting and editing yield better results and are easier to control. However, a short, easily controlled scene might be worth doing this way.

The storytelling structures we've just examined—parallel cutting, flashback, and montage—are directing techniques which can usually be constructed after the fact in the editing room. The mise-en-scène technique, however, can only be employed if it had been scripted and filmed as such.

These advanced techniques are more properly the domain of scripting and directing rather than editing. Like most aspects of film and video making, however, the three principal disciplines of filmmaking—script, production and editing— are interrelated and cannot be viewed in isolation.

WHAT TO DO WHEN A SCENE JUST DOESN'T WORK

Occasionally, you'll have a weak scene that doesn't improve no matter how many times you re-edit. Rather than keep a weak scene, my advice is to eliminate it. Remember, your film is judged only by what you show. The so-called editing room floor has been the final resting place of many scenes that were *almost* good enough. If your editing room floor is clean, you're not being ruthless enough in your edit decisions!

But what about a weak scene that has some important narration? You know you should cut the scene, but its narration is too important to lose. Try moving the narration to another, related scene. This may take some rewriting and editing changes, but it often works. Or try adding a text screen that makes the point of the lost narration in a concise headline.

THE FIRST ROUGH CUT

Keep editing until you have a complete rough cut of the video. Then, save the project with a version number and date. Sometimes it's wise to get away from the project for a while so you can see "the forest for the trees." Then you may want to show it to a colleague or two whose good taste you trust. You'll want to know if they find any parts of the video boring or unclear. Make a list of all the things you want to change, then brainstorm solutions for these problems.

When you're ready to make version #2, load the last version into your NLE and immediately save it with the next version number. Then you can easily move scenes around, or recut a scene as you wish. If you need a little more of a shot than you first captured, you'll have to go back to the camera tape and recapture it, but with time code that is very easy.

Chapter 10

Sound Editing and
Advanced Graphics

CUTTING SOUND

So far we've concentrated on cutting pictures without sound. But the fact is that the sound is often more important than the video. For instance, the TV show *60 Minutes* can be heard on many CBS radio stations, but what good would the video be without the audio? There are four types of sound you will edit: *dialogue, narration, music* and *sound effects*.

Dialogue is typically edited simultaneously with the visuals that accompany it.

Sound effects are usually edited later.

Narration is best edited after the picture editing is completed.

Music is generally the last to be edited.

Your NLE will have many audio tracks available to you and you will want to keep the different types of audio on their own separate tracks. Dialogue and any live sound should, of course, have their own tracks. Narration, music and sound effects should each have separate tracks.

Dialogue

If you have a lot of on-camera talking, say an hour of testimonials or interviews, a written transcript will make this material more manageable. Many secretarial services and court reporting firms routinely create transcripts from audio cassettes. You can copy your video to an audio cassette by simply placing a cassette recorder next to your TV's speaker and recording the spoken parts of the video. This can save a good deal of time when you're dealing with extensive dialogue.

Editing speech often involves precise cutting between words. Some people speak so quickly their words run into each other, making it hard to find a frame or two of silence between words. Speakers who give you just a tiny bit of silence between words are easier to edit.

An unusually loud breath or other unwanted vocal sound can often be eliminated or diminished by using the "rubber bands" on the audio tracks of your NLE timeline. By pulling down the rubber band on a particular section of audio, you can easily lower and raise the volume just for that moment.

Remember when we filmed the two-person dialogue in the production chapter? We filmed close-up "listening shots." These reaction shots allow dialogue to be condensed or rearranged, and provide great editing flexibility. Without reaction shots, you may be forced to find a different size shot of the speaker to enable you to cut some of his dialogue.

The Scratch Track Narration

Since your edited project will probably go through many changes before it is completed, it would be premature to hire and record a professional narrator at this stage. It's better to wait until editing is completed, because even though your narration is already written in the script, it is likely to change during editing. The footage you envisioned when you wrote the script will be somewhat different from the footage you actually filmed. Some things will work out better than expected: others won't. Rather than lock yourself into a final narration now, use a temporary narration, or scratch track, so you can continue to revise your edit decisions.

The first step in creating a scratch track is simply to read the narration aloud as the video plays. Rewrite it as necessary until it sounds good and flows well. Then, put together a small audience. Read the script aloud while playing the video. If the narration is too long for a scene or if it isn't as clear as it might be, you can change it. After you've refined it this way, record the narration and edit it onto the timeline on a separate audio track.

Think about the easiest way to record your own voice as a scratch track and then bring that scratch track into the timeline. You may want to use the camera and a mic since this will record directly to DV tape. Just don't use one of your valuable camera tapes to record the narration. As you watch this version of the video with your new scratch track, you may see other ways to improve the narration script before you spend money on a professional narrator. Don't record the professional narrator until you've "locked" this version of the video.

Sound Effects

Remember the lightning scene? Lightning without the sounds of thunder isn't particularly dramatic. Unfortunately, the NOAA film where I found those lightning shots did not have thunder I could use because the narration and music tracks had already been mixed with the thunder. I found the isolated thunder sounds I needed in an unrelated New Age music tape. The first 30 seconds of this tape consisted only of thunder sounds. After that the music faded up, but those 30 seconds were all I needed. More elaborate sound effects, such as footsteps or squealing tires, are rarely used in low-budget videos. If needed, you can find vast sound effects libraries on CD or the Internet.

MUSIC

The power of music in video can be astounding. The right music can spell the difference between a video that's just OK and one that moves your audience. Finding the perfect music can be a challenge, but it's one that deserves your best efforts. I don't hesitate to ask others for music suggestions and as a result, I've found outstanding music ideas from unlikely sources, including people I've filmed and others who were not involved in the editing. The *VideoUniversity.com* forums can be a good place to ask for music suggestions especially if you can give a web address where people can see your video. This technique has helped many find the ideal music for a particular scene.

Choosing Music

Before you explore the aesthetics of music selection, first determine how many minutes or seconds of music you need. Does the music play for just a couple of scenes or throughout the entire video? Using one piece of music throughout your video is easy and gives the video a unified style, but the music must run at least as long as the video. If your video is five minutes long but the music is only two-and-a-half minutes, you could simply repeat it. This can work in some situations.

Rather than making a straight cut where the music repeats, it's better to fade the music down before it ends. Set another in point just after your fade and make a second music edit, this time fading the music up. This works pretty well if the place you choose to do it has some other sound like a synch sound from the scene, dialogue or narration. The technique isn't perfect, but if you experiment, you'll find you can hide the cheat pretty well.

Music with lyrics should only be used when there is no narration or dialogue, because the lyrics compete for the audience's attention—you want them listening to the message of the narration, not humming the lyrics of a song. You can, however, use lyrics over scenes with no narration or dialogue.

Choose music with a mood and tempo that suits your message. The mood might be pleasant, happy, hot, thoughtful, or uplifting. Finding the right tempo is a little easier. A fairly fast tempo will help move the video along and is appropriate for most industrial videos. Videos that make an emotional appeal, like those produced by non-profit agencies, may do better with a slower, more emotional tempo.

You'll also need to choose a style such as rock, classical or something in between. TV commercials have used every style in the book, but the choices are quite deliberate. Some commercials use pop music of the '60s because they have identified their customers as baby boomers who have fond memories of '60s music. Luxury car ads are aimed at an affluent audience who may respond better to jazz, classical or opera. Keep an open mind. Even if you hate opera, you've probably enjoyed commercials with operatic music.

You'll see some commercials where every beat of the music is synchronized to a picture edit or movement. With a fat budget, you could edit the picture first and then commission original music composed so that each beat synchronizes to your edits. But even without a big budget, you can still make cuts on the beat. One way is to lay the music down first and then edit the visuals so they fall on the beats. This can take a lot of work.

Another approach is to again make all your visual edits and place the music on a separate track. Randomly choose a starting point for the music. The results may surprise you. There will be a number of serendipitous intersections between the music and video, places where the music and picture work together beautifully. Some of these will knock your socks off, but don't expect these magic points of synchronization to remain until your editing process is locked.

MUSIC SOURCES

Copyrighted Music

All music you find in a record store, on the internet, in your CD collection or anyplace else is protected by Federal and International copyright law. The use of copyrighted music requires written authorization. Securing copyright authorization can be expensive and very slow. It is not unusual to take six months to receive all of the paperwork and releases. There are different rights which must be obtained from different entities. License fees for music are based on a sliding scale, depending on use. A feature film, TV commercial or "industrial video" might have very different fees for the same piece of music. Some music publishers offer music on a "laser drop" basis (per-use of piece) or on a blanket license basis (a number of CD'S for a specific time period). License fees can easily cost thousands of dollars.

For more information on music copyright and licensing see National Music Publishers' Association (NMPA) *www.nmpa.org*

For the above reasons most producers opt for what is called "buyout music." A buyout music library is a collection of music which is sold to a producer for a one-time fee, including unlimited use, usually in perpetuity. A number of buyout music libraries are listed in the Appendix and you can find many more on the Internet.

Some producers believe it's OK to break the copyright laws, unless their video is for sale, will appear on TV, or be mass distributed. Many feel that if they're only distributing 30 or 40 copies to business prospects, the law does not apply. Legally, they're wrong!

I was amazed when I saw a cable TV commercial with music from a major motion picture. The commercial was obviously produced on a very low budget so I am sure the music rights had not been cleared. You, too, will see these copyright infringements, but don't even think of doing it yourself.

Years ago, when I produced my first documentary film about a seventh-generation blacksmith, I had my heart set on using bluegrass music for a couple of scenes. ASCAP fees were too expensive so I went to a small music shop that specialized in independently produced folk music. I looked for obscure- sounding labels of small music producers and bought a few likely albums. When I found music I liked on one of these independently produced albums, I asked the publisher to license rights to use the music in my film. It turned out that the publisher was a one-man company operating from his kitchen table. He agreed to accept $100 for limited rights to his song. The film played for several years on television and won a couple of awards. It's listed in the Appendix.

Buyout Music Libraries

Buyout music libraries are collections created specifically for use in film and video. They're available s or on the internet as MP3 downloads. They cost more than regular music CDS, but the one-time fee gives you unlimited legal rights to use the music in any video or film you produce. This music is composed with rhythms and structures that are ideal for video editing. Do a search on the Internet for "buyout music library" (including the quote marks) and you will find hundreds of web sites where you can listen to and purchase a wide variety of production music at very affordable prices.

In the old days you could always recognize the "canned" sound of library music in a video, but today many of the buyout libraries have spectacular music that can help any video. I remember hearing a radio ad for the *New York Times* which used the same music I had just spent the morning editing in a marketing video. I couldn't help thinking what good taste they had!

Ralph Rosenblum, editor of six Woody Allen films, writes in *When the Shooting Stops ... the Cutting Begins* that a colleague who worked with World War II propaganda films claimed he could cut any film to the following five selections:

1. Tchaikovsky's "Sixth (Pathetique) Symphony"
2. Stravinsky's "Firebird Suite"
3. Moussorgsky's "Pictures At An Exhibition"
4. Tchaikovsky's "Fourth Symphony"
5. Rachmaninoff's "Second Piano Concerto"

Rosenblum says that he, too, came to depend on these pieces when editing films. If you're stuck on music, look for these selections in a buyout library. To this list I would add the fourth movement from Mozart's "Jupiter Symphony #41 in C" and Pachelbel's "Canon in D."

Popular music can also be quite effective in marketing videos. For example, "Mission Impossible" from the TV series and movie; the Dolly Parton song "9 to 5", and black gospel music have all been used effectively. Naturally, the videos were directed toward very different audiences.Copyright issues must be negotiated.

THE PROFESSIONAL NARRATOR

When your editing is complete and you've decided to make no further changes to the visuals, save the project with a new name or version number. Now it's time to hire and record a professional narrator. Don't be tempted to use the scratch track narration you made in your own voice or to use your neighbor who has always wanted to try narrating. A professional adds a lot of value at little cost.

A good narrator is much more than a trained voice. He or she communicates the ideas of your script the way a good actor does. A skilled narrator can make difficult copy sound natural and compelling. The narrator enunciates each word clearly and emphasizes particular words to express subtle meanings. The narrator's job is to sell the ideas in your script.

A common narrator style is "corporate spokesperson as the collective voice of your company," e.g. "We at Acme are here to help you." Some call this "The Voice of God." Listen to James Earl Jones say the tag line, "This is CNN." He gets my attention every time.

One of the narrators I use is a man in his fifties whose background is live radio. Not only does Gene have a great voice, but more importantly he knows how to communicate and sell. From his days in live radio he's used to doing just one take. In our sessions he usually does several takes, but his first take is often the best. An experienced narrator like Gene can save you from doing a hundred takes and a lot of editing. One style I avoid is the "Top Forty Disc Jockey." To me this voice sounds phoney—the last thing I'd want in a marketing video.

You can find skilled narrators from a number of sources. If you're working with an editor, ask her. Other producers will often have a collection of audition tapes from narrators. In addition you may find what you need from local theater groups, radio stations and even the Internet if you're willing to work long-distance. As you listen to different narrators and audition tapes, listen first for a great voice and delivery. If you're talking to other producers who may have worked with a certain narrator, ask if the person needs a lot of takes to get a good one. Finally, determine if the narrator lives close by. Who cares where the narrator lives? Your checkbook does. If the narrator is closeby and you can promise that the session will last only a half hour, you might offer $75 or $100. You can easily pay more, but you won't necessarily get more unless, of course you hire a "name" actor. You don't have to work with the narrator in person. You can always find a narrator on the internet and work with and direct them over the phone. The narrator records his or her voice as a AIFF or WAVE file and then sends the file to you as an email attachment or MP3 download. This will cost a lot more than the in-person strategy outlined above, but it can be much quicker and give you a larger group of narrators to choose from. To find narrators on the Internet go to the Usenet newsgroup *rec.video.production* and search for "narrator" without the quotes.

We once persuaded a famous Broadway actor to do our narration for free. I can't reveal his name, but I can say the video he agreed to narrate promoted a worthy cause for a non-profit agency. To make it easy for him to say yes, we went to his home and recorded him in his living room. I brought a camera (to use as a recorder), a lavaliere mike, headphones and the script. The entire video was produced for about $3000 and has won a number of awards, partly because this man was a master storyteller.

Poorly written narration will be difficult for your narrator to read, but worse than that, your audience won't make the effort to follow it. Write narration in a natural speaking style, as if you were talking to one person. Don't use "ten dollar words" and complicated sentence structures. The object is to communicate, not to impress people.

To prepare for the narration session, you'll need two copies of the script. If any of the narration has to be read quickly to fit the visuals, you'll also need a silent stop watch to time it. It's a good idea to get a signed release from your narrator. See the Appendix.

You can easily spend several hundred dollars to rent a recording booth, but if you do, your narrator may well negotiate a higher fee. A quiet comfortable room can work just as well. Turn off computers and any other subtle noises-makers and then listen. If you hear trucks or airplanes in the distance, wait for them to pass. Have your narrator sit in a chair that doesn't squeak. Place a glass of water near his script to avoid dry mouth. Write phonetic spellings for any words or names that might have several pronunciations. With your headphones, listen carefully to the reading, and for subtle problems like the narrator rustling pages of the script, hitting the microphone, or turning away from the mike while reading. After the session, make a log of the tape so you can easily find the best takes of each narration.

Invest your energies in finding a great narrator and writing a clear and effective narration script. When you're working on a guerrilla budget, these are much better investments for your money than an expensive recording booth. When you're importing and editing the professional narration, it's wise to give it a separate audio track. You may also want to keep the scratch track narration on its own track until you've completed editing the new professional narration.

Audio Editing and Sweetening Software

While today's powerful Non Linear Editors typically include all the audio editing features you need to produce an effective video, a digital audio editing program like Sound Forge by Sony can add a lot of power. The best way to get good clean sound is, of course, to record it properly in the first place. But say, for instance, an unavoidable noise occurs in the background. A program like Sound Forge, Adobe Audition, or the shareware program Gold Wave may be able to equalize some of the particular frequency that hopefully carries only the noise and so improve the audio. These programs, however, are fairly complex and/or expensive so before you commit to one, it would be wise to fully explore the audio capabilities of your NLE, or consider finding an audio engineer in a radio station and/or music studio.

Study a Master of Sound Editing

Want to study an amazing film sound track? Buy or rent the DVD of Robert Altman's 1975 film *Nashville*. The film was created as an homage to country music, but it is also a tribute to the 24-track sound technology that dominates the music industry. It's no coincidence that the film also revolves around 24 characters, each with his or her own sound track, making it just as much an ode to the sound mix and the engineers behind that mix. For a fascinating analysis of the sound editing in this film see "24-Track Narrative? Robert Altman's *Nashville*" by Rick Altman, Ph.D., who teaches at the University of Iowa. This article appeared in *Revue Cinémas Vol 1 No 3* published by the Université de Montréal. It is available on the web at *www.revue-cinemas.umontreal.ca/vol001no03/08-altman.htm*

Robert Altman's innovation and mastery in sound is just one part of his genius. You cannot go wrong watching the films of Robert Altman. You'll find it a great pleasure and a wonderful education in filmmaking.

Animation & Motion Graphics

Much of what follows in this section will not directly apply to your early productions. These are advanced techniques which require serious budgets and skills. Nonetheless, this amazing world of motion graphics and animation may very well became a vital part of your productions and business.

Let's define some of the terms. The overall field is called **Computer Graphic Imagery** or CGI. This a fast-growing field as you can tell by the stunning pace of visual effects in movies and TV commercials. Each season of new movies has more digital dazzle or eye candy than the previous season. CGI is changing so quickly that it can be a bit hard to define. In the purest sense CGI refers to images that have been *created* in a computer, not those that have merely been *manipulated* by a computer. In other words, objects that have been modeled, animated and rendered in a virtual environment.

Another area of filmmaking that has become digital is **Character Animation**. This brings a new character to life by creating an illusion of personality, life, and character through great writing and drawing. Walt Disney pioneered the concept of animated cartoons when in 1928, he created the character Mickey Mouse in *Steamboat Willy*. Walt did the voices of both Mickey and Minnie in the early cartoons, including *Steamboat Willie*, which was the first cartoon with sound. Then, in 1938 he introduced his first full-length animated cartoon, *Snow White and the Seven Dwarfs*. Today's digital work stations now give the animator great powers, but it is still the writing and the art which make the character come alive. As Disney animator Glen Keane says "Animation alone may move drawings, but it will not move an audience."

Clay animation uses stop motion photography to film a clay puppet just one frame at a time. Before each shot one or more parts of the puppet are moved just a little then the next frame is filmed. So, after some very tedious work, you can run these frames at the normal rate of 30 frames a second and magically have a puppet in motion. (If shooting in film rather than video, you'd be working at 24 frames a second, or 25 frames if you're in a PAL country.)

An excellent example of clay animation is the 2000 feature film entitled *Chicken Run*. This clay animated film has been described as a remake of the 1963 film *The Great Escape* but this time with animated chickens. And this film is not just for kids. It's full of visual and verbal jokes many of which refer to films from *Modern Times* to *Star Trek*. When the hens, following inept flying instructions, are launched into the air only to fall flat, one of the characters moans, "It's raining hen."

In addition to an intelligent and entertaining story, the DVD version includes commentary by directors Nick Park and Peter Lord, production notes, NBC'S *Making Of Chicken Run* as well as HBO'S *Hatching of Chicken Run*. It's like going to animation school! I urge you to rent this DVD. These kinds of extras are one more thing that make DVDS so superior to VHS tapes.

Animatics

An animatic is a test version of a scene also called previsualization, a term which for me is another sign of the decline of our civilization. It seems to me that you either visualize something or you don't. Like how do you preboard an airplane? But I digress. An animatic is an animated storyboard on video. Think of a storyboard with motion and sound. Animatics are commonly used in big budget TV commercials and complex feature films and animations. They can map the actions of real people as they will appear in the finished version. They can also show a simple version of what will become a more complex animation. The animatic has a lot less detail than the finished animation. George Lucas uses animatics to plan every shot of his *Star Wars* movies. Animatics are typically produced with a sophisticated storyboarding program such as Storyboard Artist.

Compositing

If you've ever used Adobe Photoshop or a similar program you have probably used layers to create a composite photo. This technique lets you put yourself in the same picture with Marilyn Monroe. It's the same thing in video. Compositing means to superimpose a still or moving video over one or more other video layers, resulting in a composite shot. These layers can be keyed (transparent) or matted (opaque). In the previous chapter we discussed Chroma Key as it's used for the weatherman and map shot on TV. This is a composite shot. Different effects can be achieved with various compositing and alpha channel combinations. One of the milestones in digital compositing for the big screen was the 1994 film *Forest Gump* where Gump appears to be in the same room with President Lyndon Johnson and other historic figures. This is another DVD that is worth renting just for all the featurettes which explain the technical aspects of this film.

For compositing and motion graphics, Adobe's After Effects is one of the industry-standard programs used in broadcast TV and Hollywood feature films.

Rotoscoping

Rotoscoping was originally used in animation and was patented in 1917 by Max Fleischer. Rotoscoping enabled animators to give their characters realistic human-like movements by starting with the movements of a real animal or person.. For the Disney film *Snow White*, they filmed a pretty young dancer who acted out the graceful movements of Snow White. This film was then projected onto an animation table one frame at a time which allowed the animator to trace some of the movements of the real person onto the cartoon character. This same approach is used today to give computer generated characters and animals life-like movements.

Rotoscoping has evolved from hand-tracing to the process of using hold-out mattes to make certain elements of the frame invisible. A hold-out matte is a process which obscures parts of the frame, for instance everything but a person.This is similar to the Chroma Key process we discussed earlier. The difference is that rotoscoping does not use a color to define the area of the hold-out matte.

Many of the bird attack scenes in Alfred Hitchcock's 1963 film *The Birds* were created with a Rotoscope camera. For instance they could matte out the sky in the original shot and replace it with a sky filled with hundreds of menacing birds.

In Hitchcock's day Rotoscoping was a painstaking process that required skilled artists. As technology improved, the process was later employed to create cheap but very human-like animation which is generally reviled by classic animators. Rotoscoping is an important tool in both traditional animation as well as live-action visual effects. Today, software makes this work a breeze compared to the old days.

A stunning advance in rotoscoping can be seen in a 2001 animated feature film entitled *Waking Life*. The NY Times called the film " a technological coup: it transforms photographed reality into a sophisticated cartoon world by superimposing brightly hued digital animation on live-action digital video...In the expressionistic landscape of *Waking Life,* nothing is static. The images are continually rippling and heaving in a way that lends an extra meaning to the concept of animation by suggesting how the universe and all matter are in ceaseless flux."

The underlying film was shot entirely with DV camcorders and actors. The resulting DV tape was then transposed by Bob Sabiston's Rotoscoping software, then the images were revised by a talented band of artist-animators. This is like a painting that has come to life. Buy or rent this DVD.

Some other software you will want to explore for animation and motion graphics includes:

Macromedia's Flash

This powerful animation program was primarily intended for multimedia content for web sites and CD ROMs. Since video, the web and multimedia are all converging, Flash is a program you should know about. With it you can mix video, audio and motion graphics on the web and provide interactive content to the user. It is often used to create web advertisements with movement and video and to put interactive video commercials on CD ROMS. Many people think Flash is the best program for making a multimedia document both portable and interactive. Flash has a significant learning curve.

Adobe Acrobat

You undoubtedly have some acquaintance with Adobe PDF (Portable Document Files).Your computer probably already has the free Adobe Acrobat Reader program which is required to open and read PDF files. However, many people do not realize that PDF files can be much more than documents with text and pictures. These files can also contain video. The Adobe Acrobat program is not free but can create PDF files with video in one easy step. In fact, you can insert videos and create navigation links between them.

Newtek's Lightwave 3D

This powerful 3D animation program has been used in feature films such as *Titanic, Jurassic Park, Men in Black, Black Hawk Down* and scores of others. If you have the time and talent, this program can create people, places and things which appear to be real, but exist only on the screen. Newtek is the company that started the desktop digital video revolution with the 1990 introduction the Video Toaster.

Before you get into the more complicated software, be sure to thoroughly explore the capabilities of your own NLE. The manufacturers of NLE systems are very competitive. They are always trying to outdo each other. Every few months they add powerful new features and power to their NLE software. Your NL editor, or its newest version, may already have the capability to produce the effects you envision.

Final Words

As you can see, this area of digital video is an industry in itself. Back in the old days of Amiga video, I produced a number of animated projects for business videos and TV commercials. I did some of the hands-on work myself with a wonderful Amiga program called Deluxe Paint, but my skills were limited. For most of these jobs I would hire skilled freelance animators to do the real work. Even though I was not doing the actual animation, just working closely with some of these very gifted artists was a lot of fun. It was also profitable for the animators, my clients and me.

If the graphics side of video holds a special appeal for you, download a trial version of one of the programs discussed above and see how you do with it. For many people this can lead to an entirely new career.

In either case it is worth learning about the programs that can create such magic. At some point in this business, you may well have the opportunity and the budget to include animation or motion graphics in a business video you produce. When that time comes, you'll find it can be very interesting to work with a professional animator or a motion graphics designer. To find such people in your local area, network with other video producers in the region. You can also check out sites like Animation World Network on the web for their job listings and a free directory listing hundreds of animation schools and resources *http://www.awn.com* You may find both pros and advanced students who would be ideal for your project.

To learn more about the world of visual effects visit *www.vfxpro.com* Also take a look at the Industrial Light & Magic company founded by George Lucas. This company has created special effects for eight of the top 15 box office hits of all time. According to their web site *http://www.ilm.com* ILM is the largest digital production facility in the world. There are also many dynamic smaller companies in this field and they are well-represented on the web. The web and visual effects software are a natural combination.

In the context of video production I think of animation in much the same way I think of composing and performing original music. It can be a lot of fun, but may not be worth attempting unless you are willing to make a major commitment to learning it.

CONGRATULATIONS—YOU'RE NOW A PRODUCER!

Before you pop the champagne, be sure to pull the erase protect tab on your online edit master and label it with its length and format as well as your name and address. Now make a copy of it in the same or a higher format. This "protection master" could be invaluable should a disaster strike your edit master. Now you can send the master out for mass duplication!

Chapter 11

Cable TV and the Web

EXTREME CLOSE-UP OF A THUMB ON A TV REMOTE "From Washington today the House voted..." *click* "Daren, I left my husband for you..." *click* "Rub this cream on your belly and watch the fat melt away..." *click* "Detective, the bust is going down now..." *click* "The crunch that wakes up your body and your mind..." *click* "For only 3 cents a day you can feed an entire village..." *click* "Elect me and I promise to cut your taxes..." *click*

Ready to get your message on TV? Before we do, there's one term you can't escape.

BROADCAST QUALITY

The term "broadcast quality" refers to a set of engineering specifications the Federal Communications Commission requires of any video that's broadcast on television. This term creates a lot of confusion because many consumer DV camcorders can create broadcast quality video unlike the early days of broadcasting when the equipment required to meet broadcast quality standards cost so much that only the original three TV networks could afford it.

Now, the technical distinctions between consumer, industrial and broadcast equipment have blurred to the point that some of today's consumer camcorders produce technically better results than the expensive "broadcast" equipment used in the early days of television.

To show how confusing this can be, you might shoot footage with a ten-year-old VHS camcorder and edit or copy that footage down five generations. The resulting footage would look terrible and test equipment would reveal that you could not legally broadcast it. However, if you took the same fifth generation copy and bumped it up (copied) to Betacam sp or D2, the new copy of your footage would be legal to broadcast (even though it would still look like a mess). That's how shows like *America's Funniest Home Videos* and the network news shows can use footage that was made with a consumer camcorder.

The footage you've shot and edited in the DV format is broadcast quality; however, before you submit a tape for broadcast on a local TV station, always ask which formats they can accept. These days most stations can accept DV tapes, but there are probably still a few who can only accept Betacam, in which case, talk to one of their engineers and see if you could bring your DV camera or deck into the station and pay them to make a Betacam SP dub. In addition, most stations will also have individual broadcast requirements such as those found at *www.VideoUniversity.com/bcstreq.htm*

GUERRILLA TV MARKETING

Television advertising is the titan of marketing, responsible for selling billions of dollars of goods, services and ideas. It is a complex business that, until the advent of cable TV, was beyond the resources of most guerrilla marketers. Think of it as the business of renting viewers to advertisers.

Rating services like Nielsen Media Research *www.nielsenmedia.com* report the numbers and types of viewers who watch individual shows and networks. A rating is the percentage of TV homes watching a show in a particular universe of possible viewers. This universe can be national, local, or a demographic like women in a particular age group. All TV homes in that universe are included, whether their sets are on or not. Rating points translate to number of viewers.

Share, on the other hand, is a percentage based solely on those homes actually watching TV. Share compares a show to its competition. For instance, in a remote area that only receives two stations, the show with less than a 50 share is doing poorly. Of everyone watching TV in that area, less than half are watching that show.

One of the all time top-rated TV shows was the final episode of M.A.S.H which aired in Feb, 1983. This CBS show received an amazing 60.2 rating and a 77 share.

These terms—*rating* and *share*—are at the heart of the television industry. Both are percentages. A *rating* is a percent of the universe that is being measured, most commonly discussed as a percent of all television households. As such, a rating is always quantifiable, assuming you know the size of the universe (TV households, persons, women 18 – 34, and so forth). the 60.2 rating above translates into 50.15 million homes.

A *share* is the percent of households or persons using television at the time the program is airing and who are watching a particular program. Thus, a share does not immediately tie back to an actual number, because it is a percent of a constantly changing number—TV sets in use. Shares can be useful as a gauge of competitive standing. The numbers of this final *M.A.S.H.* episode are very unusual. Most of the top ten TV shows get a rating somewhere between 6 and 9 and a share between 12 and 16.

A 30-second commercial in one of the top ten shows can easily cost $250,000 for a network buy including all CBS stations, or as little as $300 in some small markets. Buying time on a market-by-market basis is called "spot TV" which is a bit confusing because the terms "commercial" and "spot" are often used interchangeably.

Cable TV advertising, however, can be a low-cost way to target the communities a cable system serves. And within these cable communities, you can, by choosing specific shows or cable networks, target the kind of viewers most likely to be your prospects. According to media strategist, Chris Hackenbrock, cable advertisers can buy prime time slots for as little as four dollars each. But before you run down to your local cable system with four dollars in hand, you should know that one advertising slot, or even ten, probably won't do a thing for your business.

Successful cable advertising requires a longer approach based on GRPS or Gross Rating Points. One GRP equals one percent of all the TV sets in a region. Some experts recommend a media buy of at least 150 GRPS a month for three months just to give your spots a reasonable shot at success.

The cost of a GRP is based on the number of viewers, the quality of the audience, competition and the time of year. The Christmas season, accounting for 50% of all retail sales, is more expensive than summertime when there are fewer viewers and less purchasing frenzy. Most direct response advertisers (those who want you to order their product from TV) find that their most profitable advertising is during the first quarter of the year. The next most profitable period is the third quarter. Many pull their ads during the less profitable second and fourth quarters.

A GRP in a rural area might cost only $15 while in a major market (defined as one of the 50 largest TV markets) one GRP can command $1000's. Cable stations list the prices of advertising on various shows and packages of shows in their "rate cards," but these official prices are highly negotiable. Rather than attempting the negotiations yourself, hire a professional media buyer. Their fees range from 8% to 15% of your total media buy, but this fee usually pays for itself in savings. These specialists use demographic research to target your specific audience. They also negotiate, purchase and place blocks of advertising at substantial discounts.

If you're in a small to mid-sized market, you won't find media buyers listed in the yellow pages. In these markets, ad agencies usually do the media buying or they subcontract it to a media buying service. Call the Small Business Development Center in your area. These state-funded agencies offer free advice and can help you find media consultants. You might also check with your chamber of commerce, or call local companies which advertise heavily on your stations. Look for a media buyer with a successful record of negotiating ad rates and ask for references.

Producing The Low Budget Commercial

Once again, the script is the key to producing an effective TV spot. The script below is modeled after a commercial for cookies. The original version was produced for about $1500. It was so successful the advertiser withdrew the commercial because he couldn't keep up with the demand.

TWO MEN FACING CAMERA. TED IS HEAVY, HAROLD IS THIN	Ted: Hello. I'm Ted and this is my friend, Harold. We'd like to show you why Acme Chips have more chocolate.
HAROLD SMILES UNTIL HE IS CALLED A COOKIE.	Ted: Let's say Harold is a cookie.
TED POURS A HUGH VAT OF MOLTEN CHOCOLATE OVER HAROLD	Ted: Now pour chocolate over the cookie .
CLOSE-UP OF HAROLD'S FEET. A POOL OF CHOCOLATE RUNS ONTO THE FLOOR. DISSOLVE TO:	Ted: Most of the chocolate runs off. Here's how Acme makes cookies.
TED LIFTING A CLEAN HAROLD INTO A BATH TUB FULL OF CHOCOLATE.	Ted: We put the cookie in the chocolate.
AS HAROLD'S HEAD EMERGES FROM THE TUB OF CHOCOLATE, MORE CHOCOLATE IS POURED ON HIM	Ted: Then we pour more chocolate over it and let it set.
DISSOLVE TO: HAROLD STANDING FROZEN IN CHOCOLATE.	Ted: (beaming)Now we have a cookie with more chocolate .
TED HOLDS A PACKAGE OF ACME COOKIES IN FRONT OF HAROLD'S FACE	Ted: Acme cookies have chocolate in them, not just on them.
HAROLD, FROZEN IN CHOCOLATE, TRIES TO MOVE HIS HEAD.	Ted: Don't you agree, Harold?

Unless you plan to produce an original commercial like this one, the shooting you've done for a marketing video may provide most of the visual elements you need to produce a commercial. It's a fairly simple matter to re-edit your footage and add new titles, music and narration. That's how I turned the marketing video for high school students described in Chapter 9 into a 30-second Public Service Announcment. I re-edited footage I already had and added a new title screen, music and narration. While not all marketing videos can be re-edited so easily, many will contain elements you can use for a commercial.

If you are starting from scratch, talk to your cable system. Their business is selling air time and to do this many of them will produce a commercial for as little as $250 (sometimes even for free) just to sell the air time. The trick to getting an effective commercial at these prices is for you to control the process just as you did when you produced your marketing video. Write your own script, then supervise the filming and especially the editing.

Be sure to ask which format the cable station needs. You also need to ask the station about their broadcast requirements since each station may have different requirements. Tapes for broadcast should generally use Drop Frame Time Code. The following are typical broadcast requirements: Every tape should have bars, tone and slate or BTS. Start with color bars and and a 1 Khz tone for 30 seconds and then have 20 seconds of a slate or text screen which includes the production company/ad agency's name, the name of the client, the name of the commercial, the length of the commercial from fade up to fade down, the date, and an identifying code number. After the slate is a countdown which lasts less than 10 seconds. In addition audio should be mixed Mono or Stereo on both channels 1 and 2. Video levels should not exceed 100 I.R.E. and blacks should be no less than 7.5 I.R.E.

Don't assume that your commercial must be either a 30-or 60-second spot. It could be 15, 90 or even 120 seconds. If it's a direct response commercial, 90-and 120-second lengths are more likely to get your phone ringing. Whichever length you choose, make your commercial is 15 frames (½ second) shorter than the nominal length. While most stations will air a spot that's exactly 30 seconds, it is safer to produce one that's 29 seconds and 15 frames, so there's less danger the final few frames will be chopped off when it airs.

Label the tape and case with program title, producer or ad agency, name of the spot and total running time.

TWO TV OPTIONS FOR NON-PROFITS

Public Service Announcements

These spots, called PSAs are given free (or discounted) air time to promote worthy causes and charities. When air time is free, the broadcaster or cablecaster decides when and if the PSA will air.

The causes most likely to get free air time are for non-profit agencies dealing with health, safety, education, drunk driving, alcohol and drug abuse, crime prevention, child abuse, families and social relations. Local agencies tend to get more free air time than national agencies. You've probably seen national PSAs from the Ad Council. Their ad campaigns have used lines like "Friends Don't Let Friends Drive Drunk"and many other memorable lines. Some of their ads have become part of our culture. The Ad Council is the most visible organization in the field and they don't pay for air time. You may want to explore the possibilities with them. Start by logging onto their web site at *www.adcouncil.org* And if you are producing a PSA, you can learn a lot by watching some of the PSAs on their web site. In fact even if you're not producing a PSA, I urge to visit this site and study some of the PSAs as you will find a collection of masterful commercials for worthy causes. PSAs are not only for television. There are also print, radio and Internet version of PSAs.

But free air time might not be worthwhile for a small non-profit which doesn't have the clout of a national organization like the Ad Council. While many stations will donate free air time to a worthy cause, a Public Service Announcement that airs once a month at 3 in the morning, isn't going to do much good. To insure that your PSA works, you'll have to buy air time. Most stations give non-profit agencies a discount, but each cable system has its own policy regarding PSAs, so talk to the people at your local system or, to a media buyer.

Also, check with the national public relations department of your agency to see if they have generic PSAs specifically designed so you can add your local agency's name, address and phone.

Linda, executive director of a local Literacy Volunteers of America, did just that. But she thought the generic PSAs looked dated and decided to produce her own. She developed a concept and then approached the advertising representative of her cable TV system. Their policy was to give non-profit agencies a 50% discount. Linda agreed to buy 400 slots at $2.50 each for a total of $1,000. Her spots would air locally for six weeks on the community news show as well as on cable networks like ESPN.

After striking the deal, her ad salesman sent her to a production company which produced her 15-second spot for $100. The PSA sought to recruit volunteers to teach people to read; these volunteers are the backbone of literacy organizations. From her ad campaign, Linda enlisted 40 new volunteers, each agreeing to stay with the program for a year. That's a lot of volunteer hours from a small investment.

Telethons

Telethons can raise most of a non-profit agency's annual income. Josephine Todaro, a producer who specializes in telethons, advises non-profits that the key to success is to find a producer with a track record of producing telethons. The reason is that a telethon is live television, a very different proposition from a marketing video where events are easily controlled. In live television, just a couple seconds of dead air time can seem like an eternity. So when an entertainer doesn't show up as planned or the host suddenly gets laryngitis, the telethon producer needs to improvise quickly on the spot.

Even though they air for just a few hours, telethons require thousands of hours of preproduction planning. The easiest are those where a parent agency produces the national show and a local agency broadcasts a short segment every hour. For example, Gloria, director of public relations of a county-wide Cerebral Palsy Association, says her agency succeeded in raising $40,000 from the local segment of the national telethon produced by United Cerebral Palsy.

Gloria's telethon was shared with one other sister agency. Each paid $2,500 to a local TV station. The national show was hosted by well-known actor and ran from 10am to 7pm. Every hour the two local agencies got ten minutes of air time to broadcast their live segment. From their rented TV studio they had their own host and a bank of volunteers from an Elks Lodge, which accepted pledges from local callers.

In some of their ten-minute segments, they showed taped interviews with clients who explained how the agencies had helped them lead independent, full lives. These testimonials had been carefully planned to show viewers just what their pledge money could do.

To make these ten-minute segments successful, Gloria worked full-time for three months before the air date. One of her first tasks was to solicit volunteers to help with the vital preproduction work. Gloria and her volunteers spent thousands of hours on three distinct goals:

- finding sponsors for the local telethon,
- raising consumer pledges and
- raising business pledges.

They raised a total of $40,000, but only $8,000 was pledged during the telethon. The balance was raised before the event. The sponsors pledged a part of this and, since their company names were involved, they also had a stake in promoting the telethon and helping it succeed.

Gloria credits the success of the telethon to an extensive mail campaign and many phone calls. Next year she plans to produce a short documentary to use in some of their ten-minute segments. This might be a day-in-the-life video about a client showing how the agency enabled this person to achieve a life of independence. The message to viewers is not simply that their pledges will help a person lead a more fulfilling life, but that independent people contribute to society by holding jobs and paying taxes. Gloria advises that a successful telethon must be entertaining because it's competing with national entertainment shows. She believes that without the support of the national telethon, producing one would be very difficult.

Another PR Director from a human service agency told how her agency joined forces with four other sister agencies to co-produce a local telethon. They shared the work and the rewards, but they did not have the support of a national telethon. It took the agencies six months to prepare for the show. Like Gloria's telethon, this one raised most of their pledges before the event. They, too, had an experienced producer, many volunteers, and donated entertainment. They paid for a TV studio and several hours of air time. Despite all their work, the telethon was not nearly as successful as Gloria's. In fact, this PR Director believes it was a bad investment and does not plan to repeat it. If you're contemplating a telethon, talk to your parent agency and see if they can share some of the risk.

VIDEO NEWS RELEASE

The Video News Release, or VNR, is a public relations tactic which can be used by both businesses and non-profits. Both the VNR and its print counterpart, the news release, are presented as story material to TV, radio, newspapers and magazines for publication or broadcast. The goal is get the company name or product mentioned in the media, hopefully in a positive light. The problem is that the media are not interested in promoting your business. They'll tell you to talk to their advertising departments.

What news directors and editors do want is news their viewers want to hear. As a former newspaper editor myself, I can tell you that news people are continually bombarded with "news stories" that are poorly disguised attempts to get a company in the news. Most of these attempts fail.

The few stories that are published or broadcast are either educational, informative or a public service—newsworthy stories. It helps if the story is one that's not readily available to the news producer. It is entirely his or her decision whether your message is newsworthy, no matter if you are a regular advertiser. The two functions, editorial and advertising, are scrupulously separated in most organizations.

A video news release that repeatedly shows a company logo or overtly promotes the benefits of a company will probably not be used by a news director. Nor would a director be likely to use narration you provide. They want "B roll" which is footage they can voice over from an accompanying fact sheet containing all the pertinent information about the story. Sound bites you supply may be used by the news producer who can rearrange the material and write his own voice-over script.

Back in 1993 sales of Pepsi Cola plummeted because several consumers found syringes in their drinks. Pepsi sales stopped cold. To stem the disaster, Pepsi produced VNRs showing how secure their manufacturing process was. The VNR also showed hidden camera footage of a person in a store tampering with an unopened can. Finally it demonstrated how consumers could check the integrity of a can. Pepsi hired Medialink, *www.medialink.com/vnr.htm* a VNR specialist, to distribute thousands of the VNRs to TV news shows. Over 3,000 were broadcast and in just one week, millions of Americans once again trusted Pepsi. Most viewers never suspected that this "news" was in fact a massive public relations coup.

VNRs are best handled by a public relations firm or a VNR specialist. Look in the yellow pages or ask your Small Business Development Center. You'll want to see examples of their successes and ask for references. To see examples of VNRs you can do a search on the Internet for "Video News Release" (Be sure to be use the quotes.) You'll find many examples of VNRs. But keep in mind that VNRs you find on an organization's web site have probably not appeared on TV in the same form. In fact, many of them may never have appeared on TV at all. There's certainly nothing wrong with producing a Video News Release and putting it on your company's web site. It's a logical place to start. It could also be put on a CD ROM or DVD.

PUBLIC ACCESS CABLE TV

Want to produce your own cable TV show? Public access is the place to start. And if you think public access TV is like the zany 1992 film *Wayne's World* starring Mike Myers and Dana Carvey, you would be partly right. Like Wayne and Garth, you can produce your own show for little or no money (usually after taking a very inexpensive production course at the local station) and, within some pretty wide guidelines you can do most anything you can conceive. Now, you may think the audiences for most access shows are minuscule or non-existent and you're right most of the time. At the same time there is more to it than just an ego trip. Here's an actual pitch I found on a web site. I've changed the names so I won't have to talk with any attorneys.

SPIRIT VIDEO AVAILABLE FOR
LOCAL ACCESS CABLE TV

A new videotape by Rev. Jones-Smith is now available to public access cable TV shows nationwide. In this tape, Rev. Jones-Smith presents the Spirit Awake program as a profound, innovative, scientific method for creating world peace.

Contact your local cable company to request that this 28-minute video be aired on your cable system. Once you've made the contact, Rev. Jones-Smith will send a free copy of the video to you for each station that agrees to play it.

HOW TO GET THE VIDEOTAPE BROADCAST

To get airtime for the tape, contact the business office of your local cable company listed in the Yellow Pages and ask for the public access channel office. As a local citizen, you generally have the right to air any tape that you want, as long as it is a not-for-profit tape. So be sure to approach your cable company as a local citizen representing the Spirit Awake program.

Ask what video format is required for the tape. Since each local public access station has its own rules, you will need to get the guidelines for submitting a tape to that station. You may also need to fill out an application, which you will submit along with the tape.

The pitch above is very close to the actual web page I found. The organization and personality are well-known, probably one you'd recognize. You could apply this same type of pitch to other, more honorable ideas.

Public access stations are created when a cable company negotiates a franchise agreement with a local government. Not all franchise agreements include public access channels. Some have access channels just for local governments where you can watch town meetings and other government functions. Others are educational, e.g. a school district with its own channel. Another is local origination where the cable company serves the community by producing local news and sports shows. The public access channels, sometimes called Community TV, allow citizens to produce and broadcast their own shows.

The mission of public access channels is to encourage the widest spectrum of local programming and to provide ordinary citizens with access to the tools for producing this programming. These channels can be a great resource. For instance, the New York Staten Island Community TV channel offers a 20-hour video production course for $60 that's open to anyone in Staten Island. You won't find a better price anywhere. In addition, they offer studio or location production and editing packages.

Rules vary by community, but most require that programs be non-commercial. According to Lance Armstrong, the Outreach Director for Staten Island Community TV, a business could produce an informational show about their industry as long it's not a sales program. Ask your own access channel about their requirements.

There are hundreds of public access stations throughout the country. You can find them by calling the local cable station or watching the preview channel on cable TV. If your cable system does not have a public access channel, look into other nearby cable systems. The residency requirements are not always carved in stone. Sometimes all you need is a local resident to sponsor you. You'll find that the public access people try hard to be accommodating.

There are thousands of interesting and worthwhile cable shows appearing every day on every topic you can imagine. To find public access stations near you go to

www.VideoUniversity.com/resource.htm

and click on the list of Access Stations. You can also discover the amazing range of Public Access shows by doing a search on www.*Google.com* for "Public Access Cable TV" (include the quote marks). You will find tons of show descriptions from all over the world. For books and more information on producing shows see the The Alliance for Community Media *www.alliancecm.org/* Their national headquarters are listed in the Appendix.

LEASED ACCESS

The Cable Act of 1992 gives independent producers like you the opportunity to lease cable air time in half-hour segments for commercial use. If your cable company has at least 36 channels, the law requires that they set aside 10% of their channels for leased access (not to be confused with public access, the non-commercial air time). The current law says that one half-hour of leased access time should be calculated at $0.40 per thousand viewers. So a half-hour of time on a cable system with 30,000 subscribers should cost $12.00, but it can vary depending on the time of day, with prime time being the most expensive.

Unlike public access shows, there are few restrictions on leased access shows. There is no prohibition against business-related shows, and commercials and/or infomercials can be aired and sold on leased access.

Some cable companies have been accused of using a variety of tactics to prevent or delay independent producers from leasing air time so inexpensively. And most cable companies seem to charge a good bit more than the prices cited above. The result is a good deal of contention between independent producers and cable companies.

But before you assume an adversarial role, first arm yourself with information. One place to start is with the Federal Communications Commission's (FCC) rate regulation Report and Order (R&O) and the FCC's *Report Concerning Leased Access.*

With leased time, you could produce your own cable show, sell a pay-per-view program where the cable system collects payments for you, or start a home shopping club. You could even have your own channel on one of the new 500-channel networks.

To learn more about Leased Access study publications such as *Broadcasting and Cable* and *Cable World.* You will also want to study the laws which are available through the FCC. Contact the Cable Services Bureau at (202) 418-7200, or visit the FCC web-site at *www.fcc.gov*

You may also find help through organizations such as The National Cable and Telecommunications Association *www.ncta.com/* and The Cable Television Advertising Bureau *www.onetvworld.org/*

Infomercials

You can be rich, thin or beautiful. At least that's what these late night, 30-minute programs claim and if you're not satisfied, most will give your money back. Infomercials are a billion-dollar-a-year industry. Ever see the ones that ask you to spend $4 a minute so a psychic can tell your future? (The skies parted. Wait, it's coming...I think I can see...yes! I predict these infomercials will gross $10 million a month.) Amazing isn't it? That'll be $4, please.

While many small businesses try their hands at infomercials, the business is dominated by companies which specialize in these direct marketing programs. The key to their success lies more in finding the right product rather than in buying the right air time or producing the right infomercial.

If you're considering an infomercial, here are some questions you'll need to ask:

1. Is the product unique? If it's already available in stores or there are a number of competing products which do the same thing, you may be in for an expensive uphill battle.

2. Does the product appeal to the masses? This means it must be the kind of product nearly everyone would want. If it is a niche product intended for a specific target audience, then direct response television is probably not the way to sell it.

3. Can the benefits of using this product be clearly demonstrated? Some products lend themselves to visual presentation. Think about the long-running infomercials you've seen. They are easily demonstrated on TV.

4. Can you mark the product up at least three times over the cost?

Not all successful infomercials have followed the above guidelines. As in all direct response testing is a vital part of the game. The George Forman Grill is one of the most successful infomercial products of all time. But its success came only after a number of unsuccessful tests.

A legend in the business is Ron Popeil. Be sure to visit his web site *www.shop.ronco.com/* I was pleasantly surprised to find the Popeil Pocket Fisherman still available on his site. I bought mine when I was about 12 years old. I still have it and think it was a great idea! You may want to learn more about Popeil's story by reading his book *Salesman of the Century* which just happens to be available at his web site. I found it at my library. See the Appendix for a list of other books on infomercials.

This industry has its share of both reputable and disreputable businesses. Do your homework thoroughly because this is an expensive game and the odds are against you. One industry insider we interviewed claimed that only one out of 15 infomercials makes a profit. You may find help through The Electronic Retailing Association *www.retailing.org/* formerly called the National Infomercial Marketing Association. Another is The Direct Marketing Association. It is well-respected and has been around for a long time. *www.the-dma.org*

If you are serious about the direct response business I believe the best place to start marketing a product is on the web. This is a good place to test products and the costs can be mostly your labor. It may not be easy, but it can be done.

TV TRIVIA

- *Winky Dink and You*, a CBS children's series (1953-1957), might be called the first interactive TV. You sent away for the Winky Dink drawing set, a transparent page that was to be placed over the screen. During the show, if the animated Winky Dink character was chased by a wolf, one could quickly draw a bridge with a crayon to help Winky Dink escape. Today, however, radiation and other dangers from color TV sets make it too dangerous to sit so close to a set, and besides, we have computers.

- According to *The New York Times Encyclopedia of Television*, most stations east of the Mississippi begin their four letter call signs with a W while stations west of the Mississippi begin their signs with a K. This K or W convention for the first letter of U.S. stations was ratified years ago in an international agreement. The remaining letters of a call sign can be chosen more freely. For instance, WPLG was named after Philip L. Graham, and WGN stands for World's Greatest Newspaper, referring to its founder, the *Chicago Tribune*.

- To trace the beginnings of television we need to go back to the 1920's. According to the U.S. Patent Office television was first invented by Philo T. Farnsworth, whom *Time Magazine* later named as one of the 100 greatest scientists and thinkers of the 20th century. For more information visit the Free Library at *www.VideoUniversity.com*

Marketing With Video on the Web

The Internet probably presents as big a change to business today as television did back in the 1950s. Internet business is BIG and is only get bigger. If you are producing a marketing video, TV commercial or infomercial, you should definitely consider putting it on the web. Just don't get carried away with fantasies of great wealth. The number of Internet businesses which have gone belly-up are legion. Some household names in the entertainment business are among the dead and missing in the vast mirage of easy riches on the Internet. So, if you're thinking of starting an entertainment web site where millions of visitors can watch thousands of videos, remember that some very smart people have lost a lot of money betting on such business models. On the other hand, the Internet can be a very valuable business venue if you are careful and take the time to study and learn the business.

There are lots of good examples of marketing videos on the Internet. These videos promote a wide range of products and services. Here's an ideal kind of product to market using a video on the web. This product is a new kind of radio controlled model flight. See *www.rctoys.com*   The short videos on this site are a perfect way to demonstrate and market these cool, expensive toys.

The Blair Witch Project is worth mentioning here, not because it is a great film, but because it made a ton of money by way of some very clever web marketing. The film tells the story of a small group of documentary filmmakers who disappear while making a documentary video about a witch. Some of the video documents what happened before they disappeared. This video is later *discovered* in an attic and a few minutes of the video just *happen* to find their way onto a web site where there's also some information about the missing young people who appeared in the video. Those few minutes managed to convince a great many people, even including some veteran filmmakers, that the video was real and not portrayed by actors. It was so effective a private detective called and offered his services to help find the missing young people!

The web sites put up by the filmmakers and their friends were reported to have generated some 35 million hits *before* the film opened in 1999 and helped to create an instant cult classic. Their technique is somewhat reminiscent of Orson Welles's radio broadcast of *War of the Worlds* in which an unsuspecting nation was fooled into believing aliens had landed and were actually attacking the people of planet Earth. Welles was just having fun and had no idea so many would take him seriously. He was not doing it to make a profit like the *Blair Witch* producers.

Most of *The Blair Witch Project* was shot in Hi-8 video and then transferred to 35mm film although some of it was shot in 16mm film. One reason this did not matter was that this film is presented as a documentary, i.e. that what you see in the film was really happening. Now this may not have that much to do with business marketing, except that according to the Baltimore City Paper Online November 1999, "*The Blair Witch Project* has earned more than $140 million—making it, reportedly, the most profitable film of all time." Other films have certainly grossed more, but *Blair Witch* cost only $22,000 to make and so, in terms of profit, *Blair Witch* is a tough one to beat.

It has been called a "mockumentary" and I'm sure PR and marketing people have told and retold the stories so often that the truth may be lost forever. But the moral of the story is that word travels fast on the Internet. When it does, it can spread like a virus throughout the population, which is why they now call this phenomena *Viral Marketing*. It can quickly create enormous business, but you don't want to be on the wrong side of it. A bad reputation can travel even faster!

If you have a broadband connection, some video web sites you'll want to explore are *www.atomfilms.com* and *www.ifilm.com* These sites specialize in short videos and films. Thanks to the web we're seeing a rebirth of the short form film and video. In the old days these short films were called Selected Short Subjects and they played in movie theaters before the feature was shown. Unfortunately, the short form died when theater owners realized they could make more money by running trailers of upcoming features. So now the web is giving the short film and video a new life.

For producers, the web may well become the ultimate format. Why send someone a DVD when they could click on your video at a web site or receive the video in an email? As broadband web access increases, so will the audience for digital video on the web. CNN's web site *www.CNN.com* is full of video news clips and so, to a lesser extent, is The New York Times *www.nytimes.com* The web site *www.movies.com* has trailers for the 100 most popular current movies. Type in your zip code and you can view the playing times at your local theater!

Want to give your TV show an international audience? You can do it on the web right now. The web is already taking away from the time people spend watching TV. Someday it may well compete directly with cable TV. There have already been some significant Internet-only shows which attract millions of viewers. The Victoria's Secret video, which was advertised on the Super Bowl, was one of the most visible webcasts seen by millions of viewers. The term "webcasting," by the way, is the transmission of live, or prerecorded audio or video over the Internet.

Webcasting can also be done on a small and inexpensive scale. If you look around, you will find many low-budget web sites of young filmmakers who make a few short films available for viewing. There are even Internet-only TV shows. Video on the web changes so quickly that I'll let you find these and other sites on your own.

The technical side of web video is another area that changes quickly. Here are the basics to get you started. You can download video from the web and save it to your hard drive, but you cannot see *any* of that video until the entire file has been saved. A better way is called streaming video. Streaming lets you watch the video as it is processed, so with streaming video you see it much sooner, but you cannot save it. There are three primary types of streaming video files:

1. RealMedia or RM from *www.real.com/*
2. WMV or Windows Media from *www.windowsmedia.com* and

3. Quicktime's MOV from *www.apple.com/quicktime/*
There is also MPEG, which is the same format used for video on
CD ROMs because it can be very compressed. This is not the first
choice for the web, however.

In my opinion, trying to watch a video on the web with a dial-up
connection is simply not worth the trouble. Even with a broadband
connection, the competing formats do not always make it easy for
the viewer. You are nagged continually to download and install their
latest version. Just like the battle of the browsers a few years ago, but
worse.

To put your video on the web you will need to have it in at least
one of the three formats above. It's not an easy choice. Some of the
large sites that specialize in streaming video offer the viewer all
three. Some sites offer video in only one or two formats. Your
choices may depend upon what the host of your web site offers. If
you have a very popular video, you will also need to consider how
much your web hosts will charge you for the bandwidth your visitors
use to watch your video. Some hosts charge for the storage of your
video and give you the bandwidth for free.

If you have a broadband connection and want to explore videos
on the web, you will want to have all three players. Hopefully this
will change in the near future.

Building a Business on the Web

Putting your video on the web is not a big deal. But making a successful business on the web is a very big deal. A lot of it comes down
to getting the right people to visit your web site and become customers. Trillions of dollars have been gambled and lost on this proposition.

Look at www.*Amazon.com* Amazon is an amazing business I
visit often. I must be their model customer— I even bought my telephone system from Amazon! I believe their claim of being the
Earth's largest bookstore. Books and CDs were just the beginning.
They have become much more than a bookstore. Amazon makes it so
easy to buy. When I click on their site and find a book or video I want,
the site says "Welcome Hal Landen, would you like to use One Click
to buy this (book, video, whatever). And yet, despite the fact that

their sales are measured in the BILLIONS of dollars, Amazon is only recently making a profit.

According to the gurus, Amazon invented selling on the Internet. If you're interested in selling, say, a DVD on the web, you can learn quite a lot by doing some serious browsing in Amazon's Video and DVD section. Start by browsing through the genres. In addition to the genres of feature films there are documentaries, Special Interest and other types of non-fiction. Each of these has a list of best sellers. So if you're researching a non-fiction video that you're considering producing, Amazon can help you.

We'll explore that a lot more in the next chapter, but *selling a video* on the web is a little different than *marketing with video* on the web. Let's look at what makes a successful web site.

Content and Community

One great thing about the Internet is that it's easy to see which sites have the traffic and which sites don't. The simple reason is content. On the Internet content is king.

Let's say you're a sailmaker and have a business selling sails—Acme Sails! (Just think of the headlines you could write when you have a sale.) There's a lot of engineering involved in sails because they are just like airplane wings where the exact shape, weight and strength create efficient flight. So your marketing materials—video, brochure and more—would naturally allude to this precision engineering. A web site would also seem natural. You'll talk about all the benefits and features that make your sails superior, you'll show pictures, and give customers a way to place orders and ask you questions.

If you've been marketing already, this should be fairly obvious. Your competitors are going to do the same kind of thing. Hey, they might even try to make their site more beautiful than yours. A beautiful site may well attract a few more visitors than another similar, but less beautiful site. But if you want to really kick butt, then you might want to write or commission an expert article entitled "How Do Sails Work" for your web site. This would not just be a pretty fluff piece. It would go into the physics and engineering that actually make a sail move a boat like a wing lifts an airplane. And it would all be explained for the layman, including diagrams, photos and perhaps even a short flash animation. The goal is to attract more visitors. So this article would need to be carefully checked for factual accuracy. The article would have no marketing hype and not even mention your company. Of course, there would be links below the article to other parts of your web site, especially related product pages.

This might take weeks of hard work, but you'd have a great article to show for your efforts. When it's posted on your web site, it will eventually bring more traffic to your site. If it is an exceptional article that strikes a nerve among your readers, you may find that lots of organizations and individuals in the sailing community make links from their sites to your article. And since the article is a valuable resource for sailors, you'll want to let others know about it. Spend time on the appropriate Usenet groups. Keep an eye out for people who have questions that your article could help answer. Create a signature file for your email account such as

=======================================
John Smith
Author of "How Do Sails Work"
www.mynameisjohnsmith.com/fastsail.html
=======================================

Promote this article because it will help people. Your business will benefit. And that's just the beginning. Follow up with "A History of Sail Makers," "Repairing Your Old Sails," etc. Try to make each one the definitive article on that subject. This is one of the primary reasons people use the Internet. They come to find particular information or content.

When I was starting my first web site, I read everything I could find on how to make a successful web business. I recall seeing two guys on a magazine cover with an unlikely sounding business called The Motley Fool. Brothers David and Tom Gardner had created a web site *www.fool.com* that was attracting hordes of people. When asked what made their site so successful, they summed it up in two words—content and community.

Visiting their site I found rich troves of content including unbiased, expert articles on all kinds of financial issues, free online courses and more. Here's one example:

"What Is the Truth? The stark truth is that the financial world preys on ignorance and fear. But now, gentle reader, you've set your virtual feet on Foolish soil and your days of fear and intimidation are over. We exist to serve you, to teach you, and to have a heck of a lot of fun along the way. The Fool is a highly collaborative forum, and we do have a few rules of the road. What follows is a disclaimer that the lawyers made us write, but one that's aimed to protect you as much as it does our humble enterprise. *So hoist the flags! Cue the fanfare! It's time to read.*"

From there I clicked on the link for "Discussion Boards." I found not just a handful of discussion boards (also called forums) but hundreds, maybe even a thousand different forums on just as many stocks and financial topics. This is a *Community.* And when a web site can provide both content and community to a niche audience, it will probably also discover what that audience wants or needs and find a way to sell it to them.

These two testimonials I found on www.*fool.com* speak for themselves: "I learned more over the past year from being a part of the Fool family than I did while getting my MBA." The second was from Goldman Sachs, the investment banking firm. "The Motley Fool is now one of the most popular communities of any online service in the USA."

If you're taking your business or non-profit agency onto the web, focus on your niche audience. Don't try to be an *Amazon.com* providing everything to everybody. It is a losing battle to try to compete with a company like Amazon or Ebay, which, incidentally, is one of the few profitable Internet companies. What you can do very well on the Internet is to serve a niche market. But I must quickly add a warning. Some niche markets are more active on the Internet than others. Fortunately for me, the net is a natural for video and film producers. And for The Motley Fool, investors are also a natural on the net. Be sure your target audience is on the Internet and that you can find them.

Chapter 12

Training, E-Learning, CD ROMs and More Guerrilla Video Tricks

In this final chapter we will tie up some loose ends—details you'll want to know that just didn't fit anywhere else. You'll learn about E-Learning, CD ROM marketing, duplication, and packaging, You'll see examples of mass-marketing with video, the pros and cons of an in-house studio, and even how to produce a video of your family history. But first, here's something I promised in the beginning—training with video.

VIDEO AS A TRAINING TOOL

Training videos can save valuable management time when, for instance, a business requires repetitive teaching of new employees. A training video insures consistent instruction, month after month. Many training videos are designed with either a printed or computer-based test which the employee must pass to confirm they have learned the material. McDonald's, for example, has long used video to train a continuous stream of new employees in every aspect of their fast food operation.

A much smaller company solved a recurring billing error with a video produced by the employees themselves to train their co-workers in the principles and practices of billing. A year later, as a result of their home-grown video, billing errors had decreased 20%. One reason for their success was that these first-time producers defined the scope and goal of the video in a carefully written outline.

Businesses and agencies in just about every field use training videos. Even the CIA uses training videos. I have personally shot a number of these videos for them. Oh wait, you thought I meant *that* CIA. No, I produced videos for the Culinary Institute of America in Hyde Park, New York! Business training videos can be simple in-house productions like the billing video above. They can be elaborate productions used to train hundreds of employees in a large corporation. Or they can be generic off-the-shelf training videos like those from a British company called Video Arts *www.videoarts.com/*

Video Arts produces and sells very funny, but very effective generic corporate training videos. They call themselves the 'laughter and learning' people. The star of many of the videos is John Cleese, formerly of the BBC television series *Monty Python's Flying Circus.* Cleese is also the author of the famed Dead Parrot sketch, the script of which is available on the Internet. He is credited with making the observation that "Nobody expects the Spanish Inquisition," but I will leave the discussion on Monty Python for another time. These videos from Video Arts cannot be purchased in Blockbuster for $25. Their corporate training videos sell for over $1,000 each, or can be rented for about $250 a week. Most of the titles run between 15 and 30 minutes.

John Cleese brings his brilliant sense of humor to what are normally some pretty boring business topics. In "Meetings, Bloody Meetings," he shows you how NOT to run meetings. Some of the other successful titles include "The Unorganized Manager," "Who Sold You This, Then?" and "How to Lose Customers Without Really Trying Training Video" Executive training has never been more fun. Cleese can be very silly, but many people are surprised to learn that in addition to being a brilliant comedian, he is both an attorney and the founder of Video Arts Inc. This company is also branching out to E-learning which we'll discuss later in this chapter.

On the other end of the business training spectrum is the video taping of business seminars and workshops. This work may appear to be straight forward and simple, but since these are live events, the video production can be more challenging than you might think. The audience is often paying to attend so they must come first and the video second.

The presenter typically moves around as she is talking so a lavaliere mic will usually do the job. It may be hard-wired (if the presenter does not object to the wire) or wireless. You will also want to record any questions or comments from the audience which may be done with a hand mic placed in the audience, or with an assistant pointing a shotgun mic. You'll definitely want to wear headphones so you're sure that every word the speaker says is recorded. If there is an audio problem, you may need to stop the presenter and fix the audio or risk having an unhappy client. As backup you may want to also record audio with a separate minidisk recorder tucked in the presenter's pocket with a separate lavaliere mic. The point is that the audio of a seminar is vital and cannot be fixed in post-production.

Very often you need to light the presenter, but not always. Lighting becomes more complex when the presenter uses an overhead projector. You or your cameraman will need to adjust exposure by pulling the iris as you pan from the presenter over to the very bright LCD projector screen. In many case two or more cameras are necessary to do a really good job. Watch *Oprah* sometime without the sound and count how many different cameras are used. Then turn on the sound and think about how many microphones and sound people are required.

There are a lot of seminars and many of them are videotaped. This can be a good bit of work for a producer. Some producers are able to negotiate a deal where they duplicate and sell copies of the tapes. Hotels, convention centers, and meeting planners often have a list of audio/visual companies that either offer the rental equipment and/or do this kind of work.

Training videos are not just for business. Individuals buy how-to videos to learn every sport, dance, hobby and skill imaginable. To get an idea of the breadth of these videos, look through *www.Amazon.com* in the video/DVD section under special interest, documentary or the non-fiction categories.

Thankfully, training videos are no longer limited to VHS. With CD ROM and DVD ROM, training videos are random-access and can be interactive. These formats can also include written materials as simple text files, or as sophisticated, interactive Portable Document Files (PDF).

E-Learning & Education

In his book *Teaching Online*, William A. Draves says the Internet is the biggest technological change in education and learning since the advent of the printed book some 500 years ago. He believes that E-learning will be responsible for 50% of all learning in the 21st century. Whether he is right about the 50% or not, video will certainly be a natural part of online education. While the use of video in online education is not yet widespread, it will be.

There's lots of video training on the web right now. Adobe, the software company, offers an extensive training section where you can take online courses in nearly any aspect of their products. You can also study online video tutorials for some products, as well as participate in scores of online forums devoted to Adobe products. One of these ten-hour tutorials gives you the option of buying it on CD ROM for $99 or learning online for $25 a month.

These days everyone is getting into online education, not the least of which are universities. CBS's *60 Minutes* reported that E-Education is catering to a new kind of college student. No longer is the typical student between 18–22 years old. Today, the typical college student is older, working full-time and attending school part-time. For this student the advantages of online education are compelling. Some have full-time jobs and young children so they do not have time to commute to a physical brick and mortar classroom. With online education they can attend their classes anytime and anyplace. All it takes is a computer and a phone line, or Wi-Fi which is short for Wireless Fidelity.

One of the leaders in online education is the University of Phoenix *www.phoenix.edu* This fully-accredited university has both degree and certificate programs. It is the largest private university in the U.S. and has more students online than it has on campus. A typical course here lasts five or six weeks. Students download lectures, questions, and assignments from their instructor and read them off-line. Throughout the course, the instructor provides guidance and feedback to each student. To insure that students interact with other students, each student submits a brief bio which is read by classmates. There are chat rooms where they can "virtually" hang out and mingle.

At the moment most university online courses consist of text files. Video is not the preferred medium. Some of the problems are that:

1. Video is not reliable, possibly because there are too many competing standards and viewer software is in a constant state of change.
2. Many courses use video just to show talking heads rather than using more graphic videos to help viewers understand ideas and concepts.
3. Videos are not designed for interactivity and user control. After you press "play" on many video players your options become very limited.

While video is struggling in the E-education area, software solutions are massing. For example, Flash is a drawing and animation tool as well as a video editor. It can easily create interactive user applications which work immediately across all browsers and platforms. Flash animations and Flash programming are becoming more commonplace in online education. Web video in education may eventually find greater use through Flash or a similar language. Macromedia isn't even paying me to say that, but I'm sure they will want to when they read this! See *www.macromedia.com/* to see many real-world education and training examples using Flash.

And just in case Adobe wants to reward me with cash and prizes, I hasten to add that Adobe PDF files can be quite interactive and easily include video clips. May the highest bidder win!

Some people believe that online education may be the next health care industry in terms of financial clout. At the moment, health care is still the largest industry in America. However, entrepreneurs are spending millions creating online universities for profit. The University of Phoenix is perhaps the only college you can both attend and invest in. It is traded on NASDAQ.

How To Produce a Training Video

The first step is to define your audience. You can use the same seven questions we examined in Chapter 3 about audience and intended use—these issues apply equally to the training video. For example, consider the background of your audience. If they are surveyors, you don't need to teach them geometry which they've already mastered.

If, on the other hand, you are producing a video to teach the absolute beginner how to sculpt, assume the viewer knows nothing about sculpting. Start with the basics—the clay, tools and so on.

State right at the beginning of the video (and perhaps even on the label or cover) exactly what assumptions you're making, e.g., "This video assumes the viewer is familiar with "the principles of surveying." You might suggest books or other videos for viewers to study before they can benefit from your video.

A Simple Production Technique

When you've defined your audience and their level of knowledge, define the scope of the video. Give your audience an overview of exactly what you're going to teach them, including specific topics. Explain how this knowledge will help them. By writing an overview for viewers, you are also writing an outline of the script.

Say you want to train viewers to use a scanner, or other desktop equipment. While a marketing video for that equipment might show the steps of operation in an abbreviated manner, leaving out entire steps, your training video needs to show each step clearly and completely.

An easy way to produce such a training video is to film an on-camera expert, who talks the viewer through the subject by demonstrating each step of using the equipment. Using an on-camera expert makes script writing easy. In fact, you may not even need a full-fledged script. An outline may suffice.

Most training videos are at least 15 minutes long (much longer than a marketing video). Writing such a script requires work. It's much easier to write an outline for an on-camera expert since it is not necessary to script every single word and shot. For example, a sculpting teacher and I wrote an outline for *Learn To Sculpt*, a 70-minute video which we filmed in a day. We wrote the outline in just a few hours. First, we divided the material into chapters, each with five or six topics. We assigned approximate running times to each chapter according to how much detail we planned to cover. We filmed the chapters in order, first with a medium-wide shot showing the teacher and her workbench. All the props were in front of her so she could demonstrate as she explained. Since she knew the material thoroughly and knew how much time she had for each section, it was easy for her to speak extemporaneously. She didn't have to memorize or read cue cards. If either of us made a mistake, we could film the chapter again or just pick up from the mistake.

When we completed the medium shot of the entire chapter, we filmed it again, this time in close-up showing her hands working the clay. She didn't speak in the close-ups because we already had her voice from the medium shot. Together, we kept track of continuity so the close-ups and medium shots matched, otherwise, it would have been difficult to edit different position of her hands and the sculpture from medium shot to close-up. To be safe, I filmed shots of her face looking down at the work when she wasn't talking, as well as other cutaways and inserts we could use if continuity problems arose. We filmed all the shots for each scene until we were both happy with her performance, my camera work and the continuity. When we were, we started the next scene.

Editing was fairly straightforward. I created a series of titles without backgrounds. For the backgrounds I shot a number of outdoor scenes of colorful flowers and foliage and purposely threw them out of focus. I waited for the flowers and foliage to move with the wind. Back in the editing room I superimposed the black titles over these moving shots of swirling colors. The result was a series of impressionistic title cards. Each chapter had a title card such as "Sculpting The Basic Head." Then I edited the best takes of the medium shots with her talking. These I cut back-to-back in proper order. Except for a little music at the opening and close, this completed our sound track and many of the visuals. Many of the edits were jump cuts (cutting a medium shot to another similar medium shot), but I had planned on covering these jump cuts with the close-ups or title cards. When completed, the video consisted mostly of close-ups, because the audience needed to see clearly the details of sculpting. With each video we included a short booklet of *Artist's Notes* showing the main steps of sculpting a head.

You can use the same approach to produce your own tabletop training video. Production can be as simple as shooting the entire video twice, once in a medium-wide shot (with your expert talking) and again in close-up showing details of the demonstration. Break the material into short manageable chapters, then film one chapter at a time. This makes it easier for your on-camera expert to give a good delivery of just that one section. Then, after you've filmed the chapter in a medium shot, shoot close-ups to cover any jump cuts (where you stopped and started) and to emphasize important details. Watch continuity to see that your wide shots match the actions of the close-ups, otherwise you'll have needless difficulty in editing.

Be generous in shooting cutaways and inserts for each scene. Shoot every one you can think of. Remember how the clock on the wall saved *High Noon*? Cutaways and inserts have saved many a "hopeless" film. Close-ups will make your video more visually interesting. Use a title card to announce each chapter (and hide a jump cut or other problem). You might even film an audience watching the demonstration. Audience cutaways can be intercut almost anywhere.

If you get employees involved in producing the video, make sure you list everyone in a credit roll at the end. This will boost morale and give employees a sense of ownership. Remember how Tom Sawyer conned Huckleberry Finn into painting his fence? A gentler approach is paraphrased from an old Mickey Rooney/Judy Garland movie, "Hey kids, let's make a movie."

Don't worry if your in-house training video doesn't look like network television. The home movie look, as long it presents a clear step-by-step lesson, is often better than a video that aspires to be a big deal, but isn't. Sometimes, leaving a funny mistake or outtake in your video is an asset. I once ended a video with all the funniest outtakes over which I rolled credits of all the perpetrators. I admit I stole the idea from the Peter Sellers film *Being There*. The same idea was also used in the film *Grumpy Old Men* and has been the premise of several outtake or blooper TV shows.

At the same time, be sensitive to the feelings of your employees. If your oldest employee knows step B of the process better than anyone else in the company, ask him or her to demonstrate that step on camera. I know of one video that caused an unnecessary tempest in a teapot because older workers felt they were being ignored in favor of the younger ones. Don't make this mistake. If you can't include all your employees, at least include representatives from each group. You will avoid hurt feelings and political pitfalls.

Branches

Teaching a computer program on video is a little more complex because computer programs have branches of interaction between the user and the program. When you make one of these choices, you're presented with the next branch of choices. There can be hundreds of branches the user could choose. Instructions for navigating each branch would be too complex a task for most videos. You certainly would not attempt this back in the old days when video was only available on linear VHS tape. But now you can easily provide interactive training video content for hundreds of different branches on DVD, CD, or video on the web.

Even so, you would want to simplify the process by demonstrating the most common branches, rather than every possible branch. You might want to explain briefly what the other choices were and why you chose this one. To give the audience an overall view of the choices, you could show a decision tree on the screen and indicate which path you are following. Another option is to produce a collection of different videos on different areas of the program. And remember, if it has anything to do with software, you'll probably need to redo it every six to twelve months.

The Orientation Video

Another in-house video to consider is the orientation video for new employees. This could be primarily "talking heads" with the boss welcoming employees to what he or she hopes will be a great new career; testimonials from older employees about why they like working here; and customers talking about what they like about the people who work here. Keep the tone light and friendly rather than formal or didactic. An orientation video would be ideal on a company-wide intranet.

A Video to Train Customers

Customers will judge your company by each contact you make with them, so think of each contact as a marketing opportunity. Therefore, a training video for customers, as opposed to one for employees, requires the same high production values and care as a marketing video. You'll need professional camera work and editing. Instead of using an on-camera expert, you may want a professional actor to do the demonstration (guided by your off-camera expert). The actor will probably not be able to work from a script outline and fill in the blanks in her own words as the on-camera expert would, so you'll need to write a complete script. If the script runs 15 minutes or less, the actor may be able to memorize it, but if it's longer or very technical, you'll need a teleprompter. See Chapter 6 "Preproduction Planning."

The script of a training video intended for customers must be thoroughly tested before you film. To test it, read the script aloud to another person, as if that person were watching the video. You'll see whether he or she can learn the material without any additional explanations. If your test audience needs additional help, your script needs more work.

Unlike a written manual where one can insert additional pages of errata after the manual is printed, correcting a completed training video for customers can be expensive. Even if you can afford to reshoot and replace just one incorrect sentence or shot, it may be impossible to exactly match the look and sound of this shot with those filmed earlier. Make sure your script is clear and accurate before you shoot.

Consider what additional learning materials might help your viewer. Many instructional videos are intended to augment rather than replace a written manual. An electronics company hired me to produce such a training video for their customers. Even though the company had already published a clear and thorough instruction manual for using their new widget, many customers did not read it. Instead, they called the company for help. This diverted valuable manpower to answering basic questions which had been covered in the manual. This phenomenon is probably the result of too much television. As much as I like video and more business, I do not wish to see video replace the written word.

In any case, the training video we produced was designed as an introduction to the equipment. It briefly discussed and listed some of its more advanced capabilities, but asked the viewer to refer to the manual for more information. Apparently the video worked, because my client reported a dramatic reduction in the number of calls with elementary questions. When the product was significantly upgraded, we produced a new video for customers and distributors.

In-House Video Studio

After you've produced your first business video, keep all your original camera footage, logs and edit masters organized and in a safe place. These materials are the beginnings of a video library from which you can produce different videos for different purposes.

If you find yourself doing more video work, it might seem sensible to buy equipment and establish an in-house editing studio. Until you are doing a consistent volume of work, it's more cost-effective to use freelancers who own their own gear rather than buy equipment. Then the payments are on a per job basis.

When you hire freelancers who bring their own gear to the job, you are essentially renting their equipment. Renting has several advantages over buying. For one, renting is cheaper and does not require that you insure or maintain the equipment. Unless you can pay for it in a couple of years, it may become obsolete before it's amortized. Let someone else deal with this problem. Renting gives you the latest gear without the headaches. When you own, there's always something else to buy and the new gear is usually better and cheaper than the equipment you bought just last month.

Buying used gear is an option you may want to explore. It can be a smart way to go if you are willing to research and study. To buy used equipment, you'll first want to study the manufacturers' literature and see how others like it. An Internet search for the model number may reveal a good bit about what others think of this equipment.

The Internet is also a great place to search for specific models for sale, but exercise caution in sending money to strangers you've found on the Internet. Buying and selling on the Internet can be done safely if you use some common sense. Pay by credit card, but first check with the card company to be sure of your liability.You should also know that a debit card, even though it may look and act like a regular Visa or MasterCard, does not have the $50 or $100 liability of a true credit card. You could also use an online escrow service which protects both the buyer and seller by acting as a middleman in the transaction. Sales fraud on the web is a major problem for a site like Ebay, but they also host thousands of legitimate auctions without incident.

Since editing takes a lot more time than shooting, it would be smart to purchase an editing system first, but most people do it the other way around and first buy the camera. A used camera can be a good deal. See Doug Graham's article "How to Buy A Used Camcorder And Not Get Taken to The Cleaners" at

www.videouniversity.com/buycam.htm

A used editing system is probably best found through a dealer you trust.

As you gather the equipment necessary to produce a compelling business video, one thought is bound to occur—you could make money doing this! Yes, you could, and if you're serious, I can help you. Start by studying video businesses that interest you. There are actually a number of different video businesses and you should treat them as separate propositions. Even though there may be some crossover of skills and equipment, marketing and other important aspects will be quite different.

In the Appendix of this book you will find descriptions of three video business home-study courses:

Professional Video Producer is about the business of producing videos for corporations, small businesses and non-profit agencies. The book you are now reading is the first part of that course.

The next course is about the wedding and event video business. It is a called *Wedding Video For Profit.*

The third course is about Legal Deposition Videos and that, too, is a specialty business. Feel free to contact me about these video business courses.

These courses are all available through *www.VideoUniversity.co*m our web site which is dedicated to helping you succeed in video production. The free library at the web site has a growing collection of in-depth, expert articles. The VideoUniversity forums are a lively community of expert video producers, technicians and artists, as well as neophytes. New technology, equipment, techniques and business practices are just a few of the topics which are discussed every day in the forums.

Marketing by CD ROM

Did you know there's a web site called "No More AOL CDs" at *www.nomoreaolcds.com*? It was created by people who are sick and tired of those AOL CDs. They want AOL to stop. Their efforts finally appear to be working. But why did AOL send millions of CDs to everyone on the planet? Simple. They make money everytime they mail those ubiquitous CDs which both include AOL software and a free introductory subscription to America Online. These marketing CDs could easily include video, but my guess is that video might distract from the intended goal of your installing their software and logging onto America Online. Whether they include video or not, CDs by mail are a potent marketing tool.

An example is from Avid Technology, the professional editing system company. Avid mails a marketing CD ROM to video producers and other interested individuals. Their CD ROM gives a very impressive product tour of Avid Express DV edit software. And there are lots of powerful video clips in this CD. Not surprising, since the intended audience is video editors who would not be easily moved by mediocre marketing. As Avid says "From documentaries to drag racing, Avid systems can edit anything you can dream of. Click on the thumbnails to see how real people are expressing themselves."

One significant advantage of this kind of marketing on CD or DVD is that web links embedded in the CD can help keep the message fresh and up to date. For instance, the Avid CD above has been on my shelf for quite a while now. They love guys like me who hold onto these things! The product details and price have undoubtedly changed by now, but the embedded web links in the CD go to *www.avid.com* where you see all the latest product details and prices. Their web site is of course very easy to update. The embedded web links allow the company to continually update the offer without even contacting me again. The "Buy Now" link in the CD took me straight to a current order page on their web site. This up-to-date capability of web links in a CD is a great advantage for marketers. Of course, the CD will eventually become obsolete, but this feature definitely extends the useful life of this marketing CD. For some products like a video editing system, a CD ROM is vastly superior to a printed brochure or even a VHS tape.

One company that has been in the video duplication business for a quite a while is the Duplication Factory. They are large enough to have teamed with the U.S. Postal Service to jointly sponsor a direct mail campaign in which they sent tens of thousands of videos to market their own video duplication services as well as U.S. Post Office services. That was back in the mid-nineties. Today while they still offer VHS duplication, DVDs and CD ROMs are taking the lead as the preferred marketing media.

One of their recent direct mail CDs arrived here in what looked like a small plastic Frisbee. The enclosed CD from the Duplication Factory was 86 MBs and, like the Avid CD above, it was programmed in Flash. This one extolled the virtues of marketing with video and CD. It included interactive menus, animation, music, video and narration. It also included links to web pages where you can request more information. Web links from CDs and DVDs can be designed so they can be visited only by those who view the CD or DVD. This provides an easy way to measure accurately the results of the CD marketing campaign allowing you to count the visitors who click that link. A common way to get people to click on the link is to offer more information. An even stronger incentive would be a discount coupon.

For example, one of the case studies in this CD was of a store's direct mail campaign using a CD. The CD invited a target audience of shoppers to attend the store's grand opening. One of the hooks was a discount certificate, which could be enabled by clicking on a link to what was actually a dedicated web page. With that click two things happened: the shopper got a discount coupon and the store knew how many sales were made as a result of mass mailing the CD. Precise, measurable results!

In addition to conventional CD ROMs, you can also have CD business cards in the so called "hockey rink" shape or other custom shapes, even a maple-leaf-shaped CD ROM which iss used by the Toronto Maple Leafs hockey team. There are many options for CD packaging, including a variety of sleeves and jewel cases, applied labels or thermal printing on-disc, as well as tray cards and booklets. More important is your mailing list and offer.This is the work of ad agencies, direct marketing companies, and list brokers. Most direct mail campaigns cost a good chunk of change so it is worth consulting experts and reading everything you can find on the subject.

Duplication and Replication

If you're not ready to market on the scale of tens of thousands at a time, here are some tips to help you start small. Look for duplicators in the trade magazines, the Internet and your local yellow pages. The costs of duplicating an eight minute video on CD ROM in quantities of 100 or less can be as low as $2 each if you shop around.

For CDs and DVDs, the length does not affect price in the same way it did linear VHS tapes. In the world of discs there are two ways to make copies.

Replication enables discs (CD ROM or DVD ROM) to be mass produced at very low cost. The catch is that you must first make a glass master which can cost up to $500. If you're making 500 or more DVD copies the total cost is typically a couple of dollars each, including printing on the disc and a case. CD ROMs might cost $1.25 each.

Duplication is a different process. Copies are made by lasers in the CD burner rather than stamped. This is how you make one CD at a time on your home computer, or on a dedicated duplication system. You can probably find local CD duplicators in your area, and for making less than 500 copies, this is the quickest way to go. It costs more per unit than replicating, but there's no need for an expensive glass master. A typical price for 100 CDs of any length is about $2.50 each. *Before sending a master out for duplication be sure to make a backup that is an identical digital copy!*

Audio CDs will be around for a long time to com because there so many CD music players. However, CD ROMs which are intended for data are an endangered species and are slowly being replaced by DVD ROMs.

FAMILY HISTORY ON VIDEO

The family history video has nothing to do with marketing. (Unless, of course, your family name is Acme.) Nevertheless, it is one of the nicest things you can do for your family. Family history videos are a documentary form which has evolved from the tradition of oral history. They often consist of filmed interviews with family members who relate the family's history. Throughout the interviews you can insert photographs, home movies transferred to video, and other memorabilia like wedding announcements, art work or trophies. You can use titles with names and dates to help tell your story, and add music with special significance or to reflect historical periods.

Show your video at a family reunion and I guarantee there won't be a dry eye in the house.

STAY TUNED

Digital video permeates our society like radio waves. Just as computers and the Internet have permanently changed our society, digital video is doing the same thing—video on cell phones and palm pilots, for instance. Feature films are now being shot and edited entirely in High Definition video pioneered by George Lucas with his *Star Wars: Episode II*. Mike Blanchard, the film's technical supervisor said "Digital production today is the worst it will ever be," He went on to say "One day we'll remember how *Star Wars* helped drag the film industry kicking and screaming into the digital age."

Digital video is here to stay. We're seeing just the beginning of what this wonderful technology can do, but remember, it is only as worthwhile as *you* make it. I hope this book and our web site help you do just that. I look forward to hearing from you.

Sincerely,

Hal Landen
www.VideoUniversity.com

RESOURCES & PRODUCTS MENTIONED

The following products and resources were mentioned in the book and are available from *VideoUniversity.com* unless otherwise indicated. Prices and availability are subject to change. Please check *VideoUniversity.com* or call (401) 253-2800 for current information. Ask for our free catalog!

Chapter 2

The Marketing Video Magazine - Item #102 Video shows examples of successful marketing videos. $24.95 plus $4.50 shipping.

Chapter 3 & Chapter 4

Script Werx - Item #SWW Script formatting program for Microsoft Word. $129.00 plus $4.50 shipping.

A list of countries and their video standards can be found at *www.VideoUniversity.com/standard.htm*

Chapter 4

The Best of NASA Video - Public domain stock footage library available on MinDV in NTSC or PAL. $97.77 Postage Paid.

General Stock Footage Libraries. See *www.VideoUniversity.com*

Guide to Public Domain Footage - Cross Platform CD ROM. Remarkable guide to thousands of public domain videos produced by the U.S. Government with complete contact information. $29.95 Postage Paid.

Chapter 6

Releases for Personnel, Talent, Location, Minor, Materials available in the Appendix and at *www.VideoUniversity.com*

Chapter 7

The Rembrandt Card with Complete DV Shooters Guide to Advanced Videography on CD ROM. $49.00 plus $4.50 shipping.

Chapter 10

Buy Out Music Libraries

The Music Bakery *www.musicbakery.com/*

Gene Michael Productions *www.gmpmusic.com/*

Pro Background Theme Music *www.PBTM.com*

Blacksmith VHS video $14.95.

Fourteen-minute documentary film by Hal Landen. Portrait of a seventh-generation, modern blacksmith who recounts the history of his trade and shows his work at horse farms and in forging wrought-iron tools. Accompanied by bluegrass music. American Film Festival Finalist. CINE Golden Eagle.

Storyboard Artist is a sophisticated storyboarding program capable of producing animatics. Available at *www.filmmakerstore.com/stbdart.htm*

Chapter 11

For information about Public Access shows in your area, see Video Links page at VideoUniversity

videouniversity.com/resource.htm

Also see *www.alliancecm.org/* The Alliance for Community Media 666 11th Street NW, Suite 740 Washington DC, 20001 (202) 393-2650

The Salesman of the Century by Ron Popeil 1995 Delacorte Press, and available from Ron's web site *www.popeilfamilystore.com*

STARTING YOUR OWN VIDEO PRODUCTION BUSINESS

The following home study courses and resources are available from VideoUniversity.com

Professional Video Producer, Item #77, is about the business of producing videos for corporations, small businesses and non-profit agencies. The book you are now reading is the first part of that course. The course includes a sophisticated direct-mail marketing plan with all documents. In addition the course includes a highly effective Proposal Template, Letters of Agreement, Guide to Public Domain Footage and much more! $147.77 Postage Paid

Wedding Video For Profit, Item #112. This book and CD ROM is guaranteed to start or expand your wedding video business on the road to profit. Includes the best contracts, marketing letters, brochures and everything you need to build a thriving business. $64.00 Postage Paid.

The Video Guide to Professional Wedding Videography, Item #114A This companion DVD shows you step-by-step how to shoot and edit a professional wedding video. Discover the secrets of planning, shooting and editing a wedding video that will thrill your clients. $69.96 Postage Paid.

Legal Video Specialist Business Kit, Item #140. Learn how to record Video Depositions and more. $97.77 Postage Paid.

Video Basics by Herbert Zettl, 2005: Thompson Learning. Called the "Bible" by hundreds of college professors. This book has launched thousands of video careers. Available from *www.VideoUniversity.com*.

How To Produce, Market and Sell A Successful Non-Fiction Video (and build your own video publishing business) by Hal Landen. 2005. Soon to be available from Oak Tree Press at *www.VideoUniversity.com*

Feel free to contact us about these and other video resources.

VIDEO BOOKS

Many of the following books may be found in your local library. If not, ask your reference librarian about borrowing them through inter-library loan. However, some of these titles may be too specialized for public libraries. Ask your reference librarian for non-profit video or marketing organizations in your area. Many of these organizations have extensive libraries that can be used by the public. You can also order books through your bookstore.

Video Production Handbook by Gerald Millerson. 2001: Focal Press Boston, MA.

Film and Video Editing by Roger Crittenden. 1996: Routledge. ISBN: 1857130111; 2nd edition. Based on the highly acclaimed first edition, this updated version is an excellent in-depth examination of the aesthetics and techniques of editing. These techniques are illustrated with numerous examples from past and present films and individual editors' work. Highly recommended.

When The Shooting Stops...the Cutting Begins by Ralph Rosenblum and Robert Karen. 1979: Viking Press, NY. Rosenblum edited many of Woody Allen's films. Even though many of the examples are from the 60s and 70s, Rosenblum is a master of the film editing craft. He also writes with insight and emotion. As you read, you'll learn how a film is "cut", how a film evolves, and what makes a film "work."

Clearance & Copyright by Michael C. Donaldson. 1996 Silman-James Press. A Los Angeles-based entertainment attorney explains what you need to know about copyright and entertainment issues that apply to video and film.

The AIVF Guide to International Film and Video Festivals by Michelle Coe. How and where to enter your video to win cash and prizes.2003: Available from: Association for Independent Video & Film, 304 Hudson Street, 6th floor, New York, NY 10013 (212)807-1400 x303 *www.aivf.org*

CABLE TV RESOURCES

Federal Communications Commission
www.fcc.gov/

The Alliance for Community Media
666 11ᵗʰ St NW Ste 740
Washington DC 20001
202-393-2650
www.alliancecm.org
Association for Public, Educational and Governmental (PEG) access television channels on cable television systems

Extensive list of PEG Access Centers including Public Access Community TV Stations
www.world.std.com/~rghm/alpha.htm

PERIODICALS

Write for a sample copy and current subscription rates.

Videomaker, P.O. Box 469026, Encino, CA 92046, (619) 745-2809. The "prosumer" approach to video.

DV Magazine P.O. Box 1212, Skokie, IL, 60076, Toll Free: (888) 776-7002.

Videography, CMP Information, Inc, 460 Park Avenue South, 9th Floor, New York, NY 10016.

Video Systems, 9800 Metcalf Ave. Overland Park, KS 66212. (913) 341-1300.

AV Video, PO Box 3034, Northbrook, IL 60035. (847) 559-7314.

MUSIC CLEARANCES

Harry Fox Agency. HFA is the first place to look for answers on using music in video productions, including mechanical licensing, collections, and distribution for U.S. music publishers. *www.harryfox.com*

ASCAP (American Society of Composers, Authors and Publishers) 11 Lincoln Plaza, New York, NY 10023. (212) 621-6000. *www.ascap.com/index.htm*

BMI (Broadcast Music Inc.) 320 W. 57th St., New York, NY 10019. (212) 586-2000.

VIDEO EQUIPMENT MANUFACTURERS

Sony Business & Professional Products (800)635-SONY. *www.SonyStyle.com*

Panasonic Broadcast & Television Systems, One Panasonic Way, Secaucus, NJ 07094 (800) 528-8601. *www.panasonic.com*

JVC Professional Products, Slater Drive, Elmwood, NJ 07407 (800) JVC-5825. *www.pro.jvc.com*

Lowell-Lighting 140 58th St., Brooklyn, NY 11220 800-334-3426 (718) 921-0600. *www.lowel.com* Excellent lighting equipment and tutorials

Markertek Video Supply, 4 High St., Box 397, Saugerties, NY 12477. (800) 522-2025. *www.markertek.com/* Extensive catalog of hard-to-find video equipment and supplies.

ASSOCIATIONS

Media Communications Association-International, 7600 Terrace Avenue, Suite 203, Middleton, WI 53562. (608) 827-5034, Fax: (608) 831-5122 *www.mca-i.org*

Formerly called ITVA this is the largest association of video producers with over 100 chapters throughout the U.S. and abroad. Look for a chapter near you so you can attend their meetings. This can be a great way to meet producers, technicians and artists. The national and local chapters also offer courses and newsletters.

Association for Independent Video & Film, 304 Hudson Street, 6th floor, New York, NY 10013. (212) 807-1400 *www.aivf.org* A wealth of resources for low-budget independent film and video producers. They publish *The Independent Film & Video Monthly* and offer trade discounts, workshops, and seminars as well as an extensive series of books.

LOW COST SOURCES OF FOOTAGE

Encyclopedia of Associations Gale Research Co., Detroit, MI 48277-0748. This printed book can be found in most libraries and is a good starting point for finding free or inexpensive footage from 22,000 groups dedicated to specific industries and causes.

There is also an online version, but you will need to visit your library for this version also.

To find footage of the manufacturing of widgets, for instance, see if there's a widget association. Call them and ask if they have produced videos for their industry. Describe the footage you want. If they have it, ask for permission to use it in your video.

National Aeronautics and Space Administration Videos

NASA footage is free of copyright and can make your video look like a million dollars. *The Best of NASA Video* is a collection of stunning shots which can be purchased from *www.VideoUniversity.com* This video is in Mini DV. If you have the equipment to do transfers from Beta SP tapes you can purchase Beta SP tapes directly from

NASA on the web at *www.sti.nasa.gov*. NASA does not offer digital video or DV so if that's the format you want, see *The Best of NASA* above.

US Government Films and Videos

The US Government has produced thousands of films and videos and the vast majority are in the public domain. See our *Guide to Public Domain Footage, Item #103* above for up-to-date detailed instructions for finding and using this wealth of footage and for other amazing, low- cost sources of public domain video.

Media Research Associates

This is a private company that specializes in locating public domain footage. They know their way around the government film libraries. Joy Conley, the research director, is quite helpful. If you are having trouble finding just the right government footage, she can find it for you. Their charges are reasonable.

Media Research Associates Inc., 502 Greenbriar Drive, Silver Springs, MD 20910. (301) 585-2400.

GLOSSARY

B ROLL - Cutaway shots which are used to cover the visual part of an interview or narration.

BETACAM SP - formerly the most common broadcast quality video format.

BETAMAX - the obsolete home video format that lost to VHS even though it was slightly superior.

BOOM - An overhead pole device used to position a microphone close to the actors, but out of the shot. A FISHPOLE is the portable version.

BURN IN - See Window Dub

BUY OUT - Music or music libraries for which a one-time fee enables the buyer to legally use the music in many productions without paying additional licensing or "needle drop" fees.

COLOR BARS - A standard video test pattern which includes samples of primary and secondary colors. Used to adjust the colors in video monitors and other equipment.

C.C.D. - Charged Coupled Device. An integrated circuit which captures video images. It has largely replaced tubes in modern video cameras.

CD-R - Compact Disc-Recordable. Describes the technology, software and media used to make recordable discs. The format is being replaced by DVD Roms.

CU - Close-up.

CG - Character Generator. This is an electronic typewriter that creates titles for video.

CONFORMING - Online editing to create the final edit master. The offline edit master is used as a guide.

CONTINUITY - Controlling the elements in a shot to ensure that edits will flow smoothly and produce a coherent motion picture story without jarring the viewer.

CRAWL - Text that moves horizontally across the screen.

CUE CARD - A card with the actor's lines written on it so it appears that the actor is speaking spontaneously.

CUTAWAY - A shot of something outside the frame which can hide an edit, e.g. during a testimonial.

CYCLORAMA - A background where all corners and intersections are rounded.

DP - Director of Photography.

DVD - Digital Versatile Disc or Digital *Video* Disc depending on who you believe. Includes several formats such as **DVD Video** the format used to distribute movies, **DVD-ROM** similar to DVD Video, but it also includes computer-friendly file formats. It is used to store data. DVD-ROM is quickly replacing the CD-ROMs found in nearly all computers. CD-ROMS will become obsolete like floppy disk drives. **DVD-R** and **DVD+R** are simlar to the CD-R format in that users can write to this disk just once. Originally designed for professional authoring, consumers are using these formats successfully. This format has a capacity of 4.7 gigabytes.

DV FORMATS Four similar digital video formats **DV, DVCAM, DVCPro,** and **Digital8** which revolutionized the video production business by eliminating the problems of generation loss. All of these formats are 720 x 480 pixels.

DVE - Digital Video Effects. A shot can bend, twist and fold into various shapes. Before the advent of the Video Toaster, this was an expensive post-production special effect.

DISSOLVE - A transition where one shot gradually fades out while a second shot fades in.

DOLLY - A camera platform on wheels. "To dolly" is to smoothly bring the camera closer or farther from the subject.

DROPOUT - A defect on the videotape which can cause the image to display large blocks of color instead of the image. Commonly found at the beginning and end of tapes.

DUB - Copy of a videotape.

ECU. - Extreme close-up.

ESTABLISHING SHOT - A wide shot showing much of the location.

F.C.C. - Federal Communications Commission. The agency which governs radio and television broadcasting.

FADE - A video picture that gradually increases or decreases in brightness, usually to or from black. Sound can also fade to or from silence.

FILL LIGHT - After the key light (primary light) is set, a fill light softens the shadows created by the key light.

FOCAL LENGTH - A measurement of the magnification of a lens indicated in millimeters. A zoom lens has a variable focal length which allows the camera to film closer or farther from the subject without moving the camera or subject. A 9mm - 100mm lens makes its widest shot at 9mm, its closest at 100mm.

FOLEY - Personal sound effects, like footsteps, used to heighten realism.

FORMAT - describes the video equipment and tape used. Popular formats listed in ascending order of cost and quality include VHS, SVHS, Betacam, and DV.

GAFFER - The technician responsible for placing, rigging and adjusting lights.

GAFFER'S TAPE - Similar to duct tape, but vastly superior. Used extensively in film and video production.

GENERATION LOSS - Created when editing or copying one videotape to another videotape. Most apparent in less expensive analog video formats. No longer an issue in DV editing.

GENLOCK/ENCODER - Device which allows computer text and graphics to be recorded or superimposed on videotape. Also includes a fader to fade video or computer graphics.

GRIP - Crew member who carries, sets up and strikes equipment.

GOFER - Film or video production assistant often sent to "go for" coffee or other essentials.

GUERRILLA PRODUCER - One who quickly produces an effective video on a shoestring budget.

HARD LIGHT - Type of light that creates brilliant highlights and sharp shadows.

Hi-8 - A small cassette video format technically similar to SVHS. Hi-8 has now been replaced by the DV Formats.

INSERT - A close-up shot used to hide an edit, or emphasize a detail.

INTERLACE - The manner in which a television picture is composed, scanning alternate lines to produce one field, approximately every 1/60 of a second in NTSC. Two fields comprise one television frame resulting in the NTSC television frame rate of approximately 30 fps.

JUMP CUT - An edit which visually jars. The jump cut is caused by the choice of shots rather than a technical imperfection.

KEY LIGHT - The primary light used to illuminate a subject.

KICKER - Also called a "hair light." Placed behind the subject to create a glamorous halo effect on the hair, or a rugged-looking highlight on the cheek. Helps separate the subject from the background.

KINESCOPE - Also called "Kine." A method of making a film copy of a television program in the days before the existence of video recorders. A movie camera was aimed at a specially designed television monitor. Before video recorders were invented this was the only means of recording TV programs. Many kinescopes are now over 40 years old and have the potential to outlast videotapes that were created much later.

LAVALIERE - A small microphone that is clipped to a person's clothing.

LOCATION - Any place filming occurs except a studio.

LOG - A paper listing of the time code addresses of shots, scenes and takes. The log is an efficient way to find shots during editing.

MOS. - "Mit Out Sound" a slang term for silent shooting.

MONITOR - A video display similar to a TV, but having superior visual quality and without a tuner. An audio monitor is a speaker.

NTSC. - National Television Standards Committee created this first international television system for use in the U.S. and other countries. It produces pictures by creating 525 alternating lines across the TV screen for each frame of video. Since PAL and SECAM, the other two world systems, were developed later, they took advantage of better technology. Insiders joke that NTSC means "Never The Same Color Twice."

OFFLINE - A nearly obsolete creative editing process which uses copies of the camera tapes on a typically "cuts only" inexpensive editing system. All creative decisions and approvals are made during this process.

ONLINE - A nearly obsolete final technical editing process which uses the original camera tapes to repeat all decisions made in the offline editing process. Online editing uses a more sophisticated and expensive editing system capable of transitions like dissolves and wipes.

OXIDE - The magnetic coating on video and audio tapes that stores picture and sound information. Iron oxide is created by combining iron and oxygen. The more primitive form is called rust.

PAL - Phase Alternation by Line. An international television standard. (see NTSC)

POV - Point Of View. A subjective shot from the actor's point of view. The 1946 film *The Lady In The Lake* holds the dubious distinction of being the only feature film in which every shot is a point of view shot. The hero is seen only once in a mirror.

PAN - Movement of the camera on a horizontal axis. Also an unfavorable review.

PAPER EDIT - A list of edits made entirely on paper by viewing Window Dub copies of the original camera tapes.

POST-PRODUCTION - The complete editing process.

PREPRODUCTION - The vital phase of production in which the script, budget, locations, actors and props are planned.

PREROLL - 5 to 7 seconds of camera running before a shot can be used. In editing, this refers to a similar amount of automatic backspacing the edit decks perform to ensure a stable edit.

PRODUCTION - The actual filming and creation of the raw elements described in the script.

PROTECTION MASTER - A high quality copy of the master tape. Inexpensive insurance in the event the master is lost or damaged.

REACTION SHOT - A shot of a person reacting to dialogue or action.

ROLL - Video text moving vertically up or down the screen. Credit rolls usually move from bottom to top.

RUN AND GUN - A documentary style of shooting video that is fast, lean, and productive. Derived from news cameramen and before that from guerrilla soldiers.

SAFE TITLE AREA - The area on a monitor defined as 80% of the screen area measured from the center. Keeping the title within this area insures that the complete title will be visible on ALL TV sets.

SAMPLE REEL - also called a demo reel or tape. Contains samples of a person's or company's best video work.

SECAM. - SYSTEME ELECTRONIQUE POUR COULEUR AVEC MEMORIE. An international television standard. (see NTSC) developed in France. Used in most of the former communist countries. Many SECAM countries have changed to PAL.

SHOTGUN MICROPHONE - A highly directional microphone that may be hand-held or mounted on a boom.

SLATE - A board on which script information, such as scene and shot numbers, is written. The slate is then filmed at the beginning of a shot to make the editor's job easier.

SOFT LIGHT - Light which is diffused and creates only soft shadows.

STORYBOARDS - A series of drawings to indicate different shots to be filmed. Used extensively in big budget commercials and feature films.

SVHS - Super VHS. Now a nearly obsolete video format developed by JVC which has now been replaced by the DV Formats.

TAKE - An individual shot. When budgets permit, many takes may be filmed of the same shot.

TARGET AUDIENCE - The intended viewers. Successful business videos must define and address this audience.

TILT - Movement of the camera on its vertical axis.

TRUCKING SHOT - A camera move which films the subject from side to side.

TBC (TIME BASE CORRECTOR) - A device to correct timing errors in videotape. These errors are caused by the slight mechanical defects inherent in the playback of video tape machines

TIME CODE - A system of numbering each frame of video with a unique address divided into hours, minutes, seconds and frames. There are 30 video still frames per second.

U-MATIC - Trade name for the 3/4 inch video format developed by Sony. The enhanced version is 3/4 SP. Formerly the standard for broadcast-quality videotape.

VCR. - VIDEO CASSETTE RECORDER.

VHS. - VIDEO HOME SYSTEM. Formerly the most popular consumer video format used in the majority of home VCRs.

VTR. - VIDEO TAPE RECORDER.

VIDEO TOASTER - Software/hardware developed by NewTek for the Amiga Computer. Made special effects affordable for the low budget producer.

VIDEOGRAPHER - A video photographer who specializes in weddings and other events.

WHITE BALANCE - A color camera function which determines how much red, green and blue is required to produce a normal-looking white. Shots made with improper white balance will have an abnormal color tint.

WILD SOUND - Sound recorded after the visuals in order to improve the editing of sound and enhance realism.

WINDOW DUB - Also called a "burn in." A copy of the original camera tape with time code numbers visually displayed. A window dub that is made in the VHS format can be viewed, logged and edited on paper with a home VCR to save editing expenses.

WIPE - A visual transition between shots in which the first shot is replaced with the next via a moving pattern.

ZOOM - To vary the focal length from one size to another. Professionals most often use the zoom to set rather to make a shot.

ZOOM HAPPY - One who indulges in the gratification of zooming in and out to torment viewers. Common in home movies.

Footage Release
(Consult Your Attorney Before Using)

Date:_____

To: (Your Company Name and Address Here. You are the USER)

Gentlemen,

For $1.00 and other considerations, receipt of which is hereby acknowledged,

I,_____(OWNER) hereby release and give_____, (USER) permission to incorporate in a video to be produced by USER all or portions of OWNER'S video or film described as follows:

_____

_____

_____

This agreement does not prohibit USER from applying for copyright of USER'S video as a compilation or other form. By this agreement, USER does not claim rights in OWNER'S video save for the release granted herein.

Very truly yours,

_____ (Name)
_____ (Title)
_____ (Company)
_____ (Address)
_____ (City, State, Zip)

Personnel Release
(Consult Your Attorney Before Using)

Date:_____

To: (Your Company Name and Address Here)

Gentlemen,

I hereby grant to you permission and consent to photograph, (by video photography or still photography and with or without sound track) my image, voice and name for use in a promotional video described as follows:

_____

_____

and to use such images and recorded sounds in the exhibition, advertising, editorial use and publicizing thereof as you, your assigns, successors, and licensees may elect. I affirm that I am more than_____ years of age.

    (The age of consent in your state)

Very truly yours,

_____ (Name)

_____ (Address)

_____ (City, State, Zip)

GUARDIAN'S CONSENT: I am the parent or guardian of the above named minor and hereby approve the foregoing use, subject to the foregoing terms and conditions.

Very truly yours,

_____ (Name)

_____ (Address)

_____ (City, State, Zip)

Location Release
(Consult Your Attorney Before Using)

Date:_____

To: (Your Company Name and Address Here)

Gentlemen,

I hereby grant to you permission and consent to photograph (by video photography or still photography and with or without sound track) all or any portion of the following property (herein called "the property").

_____

_____

and such episodes, scenes and activities as may occur therein, and to simulate all or any of the same and, if you elect to do so, to use the name of the property; all in and in connection with such motion picture photoplays and in the exhibition, advertising and publicizing thereof, as you, your assigns, successors, and licensees may elect.

In the exercise of your rights hereunder, you may enter upon the property with your necessary photographic, sound and other equipment and with such personnel as you may require to use and enjoy the rights herein granted to you.

Very truly yours,

_____ (Name)

_____ (Title)

_____ (Company)

_____ (Address)

_____ (City, State, Zip)

Index

Order Form

Three easy ways to order:

1. On the web Visit www.VideoUniversity.com
2. Telephone Credit Card Orders:
   Call (401) 253-2800 We accept Visa, MasterCard and Discover.
3. Postal Orders:
   Photocopy this page and mail with check or money order to: Oak Tree Press, 9 King Philip Ave, Bristol, RI 02809

Name:_____

Company Name:_____

Address:_____

City:_____State:_____Zip:_____

Email:_____

_____ Put my name on your mailing list. I'd like to know more about the business of video.

Please send the following via Priority Mail:

_____

_____

Sales Tax: Postal Orders please add 7.25% for shipments to Rhode Island addresses.

Shipping & Handling: $4.50 for the first item includes Priority Mail and $.75 for each additional item unless a prices is indicated as including FREE SHIPPING

Satisfaction Guaranteed

What Others Say

"An excellent guide to how an economical video can be achieved. I wish I had this book when I first began founding production companies many years ago." –**William Johnston, Ph.D., columnist "Video Systems" Magazine**
"I wish some of our clients had read this book before producing their first video. It would have saved them $1000's and a lot of heartache." –**Bill Hahn, VU Video, Duplication Division**
"An especially effective reference guide for those in the field of marketing, advertising or public relations. *Marketing With Video* offers the right information for those who are ready to use the power of video to sell." –**Videomaker Magazine**
"It will revolutionize your business and help accomplish what old-fashioned marketing never could." –**Jay Conrad Levinson, author of Guerrilla Marketing**
"This information could save you thousands of dollars." –**Library Research Associates**
"I give it to my new sales reps to learn the basics of what we do...This book is definitely in a class by itself." –**Jim Perkins**
"Your book is a MUST for anyone in video or just getting into video." –**Bob Perl, Atlanta Videographers Association**
"I'm sending you a copy of the video I just completed using your book. My client is thrilled with the video. Your book is a Must-Read, IMHO. I'm saying this stuff publicly because I know someone out there will find it helpful and useful. It was so helpful to me!" –**Clay Mikolasy**
"Designed for small organizations on a limited budget. The tips and techniques it contains will prove valuable to anyone involved in video production whatever their level of experience."–**Library PR News**
"A most thorough book on a subject the author knows well"–**Bernard Kamoroff, author of *Small Time Operator***
"The best book on the subject." – **Joey Wall, producer of the TV show *Conversations***